# A Theory of Race

Social commentators have long asked whether racial categories should be conserved or eliminated from our practices, discourse, institutions, and perhaps even private thoughts. In *A Theory of Race*, Joshua Glasgow argues that this set of choices unnecessarily presents us with too few options.

Using both traditional philosophical tools and recent psychological research to investigate folk understandings of race, Glasgow argues that, as ordinarily conceived, race is an illusion. However, our pressing need to speak to and make sense of social life requires that we employ something like racial discourse. These competing pressures, Glasgow maintains, ultimately require us to stop conceptualizing race as something biological, and instead understand it as an entirely social phenomenon.

**Joshua Glasgow** is Senior Lecturer in Philosophy at Victoria University of Wellington.

# A Theory of Race

Joshua Glasgow

Routledge
Taylor & Francis Group

NEW YORK AND LONDON

First published 2009
by Routledge
270 Madison Ave, New York, NY 10016

Simultaneously published in the UK
by Routledge
2 Park Square, Milton Park, Abingdon, Oxon OX14 4RN

*Routledge is an imprint of the Taylor & Francis Group, an informa business*

© 2009 Taylor & Francis

Typeset in Sabon by Wearset Ltd, Boldon, Tyne and Wear
Printed and bound in the United States of America on acid-free
paper by Edwards Brothers, Inc.

*Library of Congress Cataloging in Publication Data*
Glasgow, Joshua.
A theory of race / Joshua Glasgow.
p. cm.
Includes bibliographical references.
1. Race–Philosophy. I. Title.
GN269.G52 2009
305.8001–dc22                                    2008026894

ISBN 10: 0-415-99072-6 (hbk)
ISBN 10: 0-415-99073-4 (pbk)
ISBN 10: 0-203-88095-1 (ebk)

ISBN 13: 978-0-415-99072-1 (hbk)
ISBN 13: 978-0-415-99073-8 (pbk)
ISBN 13: 978-0-203-88095-1 (ebk)

To my parents
Renée Glasgow and William Glasgow

# Contents

# Preface

This is a book on race, in race theory. More specifically, it is a contribution to the philosophy of race. When I went to graduate school—not *that* long ago—there were relatively few people with whom a student might hope to study the philosophy of race, but among my many excellent teachers I was very fortunate to be taught by Robert Bernasconi, Jackie Scott, Ron Sundstrom, and Paul Taylor. Of course, the philosophy of race does not reside in a vacuum. I bring to this book a commitment not only to interdisciplinary research construed broadly, but also to using instruments and ideas from other domains within the discipline of philosophy. And I wouldn't have found my grip on many of those instruments and ideas were it not for the mentorship of Mark Timmons. To these and my other teachers, I am deeply grateful.

Heartfelt thanks also go to my many colleagues and collaborators, including especially those who have taken the time and care to thoughtfully challenge me. They are too numerous to name all of them, but in bringing this book to life, Stuart Brock has been my utility player—as he would say in his cricket-speak, my all-rounder—with whom I have had background conversations that influenced much of this work. Those who have helped in the foreground, providing feedback on ancestors of at least some of what appears below, also include Sondra Bacharach, Robert Bernasconi, Dan Boisvert, Jan Dowell, David Eng, Jorge J. E. Gracia, Philip Kitcher, Joshua Knobe, Ron Mallon, Donna Marcano, Julie Shulman, David Shoemaker, David Sobel, Quayshawn Spencer, Steve Wall, and Ryan Wasserman, as well as my Philosophy 409 Honors students at Victoria University of Wellington, and audiences at California State University—Northridge and the University of San Diego. Referees for the previously published material, one of whom I later learned to be Sally Haslanger, supplied very useful comments on that material. I am also very grateful to several referees for Routledge, two of whom I learned to be Ron Sundstrom and Naomi Zack, for lengthy and very helpful comments on my manuscript. (Those who have been on the referee's side of the manuscript know that the referee stands to gain little by shedding anonymity, but by graciously offering to do just that, Naomi, Ron, and Sally enabled some very useful discussions.) While the material that follows this preface is no doubt riddled with many imperfections that follow from my own, it would contain many more if I hadn't been able to interact with all of these people.

This work came to fruition in part via sage advice from Bill Lycan, Michael Lynch, and Kim Sterelny. Joanna Baber provided extremely valuable research assistance. And Kate Ahl, editor at Routledge, as well as Routledge's Mike Andrews, both supplied much-needed help in turning a book proposal into a book. Kate's guidance was in demand at several points in this process, and I am certain that this would have been a lesser product had I not had access to her editorial chops.

Chapter 3 is a slightly modified version of my "On the Methodology of the Race Debate: Conceptual Analysis and Racial Discourse," *Philosophy and Phenomenological Research*, vol. 76 (2008), 333–358. Chapters 6 and 7 contain material from my "A Third Way in the Race Debate," *Journal of Political Philosophy*, vol. 14 (2006), 163–185. Permission to reprint here has been granted by both journals and by Blackwell publishing. I also want to fondly acknowledge Victoria University of Wellington, for providing me with Research and Study Leave that allowed me to complete the manuscript for this book, and the University of California, Berkeley, and its Philosophy Department, for providing me with research support during that leave.

Special thanks go to two people. First, to my brother, Andrew, who has been a steady and wonderful presence in my life no matter where it has been headed. Second, to Julie Shulman, whose companionship, and whose encouragement and thoughtful criticism, have helped shape my thinking in more ways than I can count.

Before proceeding, a final note of gratitude is due. The people working in the philosophy of race who I read in graduate school, in addition to my teachers, people like Linda Martín Alcoff, Kwame Anthony Appiah, Robert Gooding-Williams, Jorge Gracia, Charles Mills, Lucius Outlaw, Michael Root, and Naomi Zack, and others, breathed life into this discussion. Without them, this now-thriving field may very well have failed to blossom, this book would never have come about, and I would not have learned what I have in fact learned. Now it will not surprise many that in what follows I will disagree with each of them on at least some of the things they have said. Our endeavor is such that we emphasize the critical. Nevertheless, the critical arguments that are, we hope, worthy of writing up are supported by the 90 percent of consensus submerged below the surface. Knowledge is a beautiful thing, and I am grateful for having learned from a generation of pioneers.

Josh

# 1 The Race Debate

This book is an attempt to grapple with a problem: the concept of race seems irredeemably corrupted but in some ways too valuable to do without. Now of course this isn't the only race-related problem worthy of our attention. There are the venerable and important questions of racism, and of affirmative action and reparation. And questions of identity, and of the phenomenology and existential significance of race, have been resurgent topics for a couple of decades now. But the questions that motivate this volume excite different curiosities.

In 1897, W.E.B. Du Bois, faced with the question of whether people of African descent should assimilate or carve out a distinct community in the United States, and indeed on the world stage, gave his seminal lecture, "The Conservation of Races." He argued, with characteristic power, not only that this population constituted a race, but also that it had something of a unique mission in the history of humankind, and thus he concluded that the elimination of racial differentiation would be a grave mistake. In the decades that followed, the soundness of racial thinking mostly became a topic to be studied by social and natural scientists, not philosophers. Indeed, with a few notable exceptions, race-thinking was a largely dormant topic in philosophy until the 1980s. At that point, in a now-classic article, Kwame Anthony Appiah (1985; 1992) reexamined Du Bois' conservationism. Dispatching Du Bois' claims like so many badly outdated fashions, Appiah began a series of arguments in defense of the position that race is an illusion unworthy of our credence.

The desire to leave race behind is, of course, a dominant theme of the modern United States. In its least contestable form, it is the sentiment expressed in Martin Luther King, Jr.'s hope that his children be judged not "by the color of their skin but by the content of their character." But *racial eliminativism* makes a stronger claim than that. According to one political version of eliminativism, we should eliminate racial categories from all or most state policies, proceedings, documents, and institutions. Californians rejected such a proposal when in 2003 they voted to defeat the "Racial Privacy Initiative" (Proposition 54), which would have prevented most government agencies from collecting most types of racial data. Not one to be found in lock-step with Californians, George Will (2003), the prominent conservative columnist, has called for removing racial categories from the census. Sometimes, as with Will, political eliminativism is motivated not only by the claim that the way we think about race might be incoherent, but also by the rationale that eliminating racial categories will undermine other policies, such as affirmative action, which presuppose race. Indeed, in case there was any question, the brouhaha over eliminativism was that same year declared "a national debate" by the front page of the *New York Times* (Nov. 9).

A second, more sweeping form of eliminativism is the public version. Public eliminativism advises that we get rid of race-thinking not only in the political sphere, but in the entirety of our public lives, so that we neither assert nor recognize one another's races. Finally, there is global racial eliminativism. The goal of this view is for us to eventually get rid of race-thinking not only in the political or even public world, but altogether. That is, even in our most private inner moments, race-thinking should go the way of belief in witchcraft and phlogiston: a perhaps understandable but hopelessly flawed, antiquated way of making sense of our world, a way of making sense that has no place in our most sophisticated story about The Way Things Are.

Now, in the wake of eliminativism's rise, several respondents have tried to update and defend Du Bois' basic position that race-thinking is worthy of conservation. These *conservationists* argue that, for various reasons to be examined within these pages, eliminating race-thinking would be a serious error. Thus, to take them out of order, the first of four main questions to be asked here, the question that will set much of our agenda in crucial respects discussed below, is

**The Normative Question:** Should we eliminate or conserve racial discourse and thought, as well as practices that rely on racial categories?

Those, anyway, are the conventional options. But, as is often the case with convention, this set of choices unnecessarily presents us with too few options. Or so I will argue. To turn over my first card, the normative position I will advocate is neither that we should out-and-out eliminate race-thinking, nor that we should wholeheartedly conserve it, but that we should *replace* racial discourse with a nearby discourse. The basic idea to this position—what I will label *racial reconstructionism*—will be that we should stop using terms like 'race,' 'black,' 'white,' and so on to purport to refer to biological categories—

as we currently use them. Instead we should use them to refer to wholly social categories.[1]

It is worth pausing for a moment to emphasize who 'we' are here. We are neither philosophers in particular nor academics in general. The Normative Question is whether *all of us*—everyone in our linguistic community—should keep or abandon racial discourse. Racial reconstructionism says that all of us should reconstruct our racial discourse. (Arguably racial discourse operates differently in different communities, so I will focus particularly on my linguistic community, which comprises competent English speakers in the United States. That said, I suspect that the arguments found below are relevant in many other communities as well.)

Whether we should be eliminativists, conservationists, or reconstructionists depends on two main considerations. First, a clutch of particularly salient evaluative considerations bear on this question: is racial discourse morally, politically, or prudentially valuable? For instance, if someone wants to be identified in a certain way, we arguably have a moral obligation—one that in some contexts can be overridden, to be sure—to identify them in this way. Obviously, racial identities are key components of some people's self-conceptions, so moral value will have to be addressed here. A political question relevant to our discussion is whether race-thinking enables important policies for redressing racial injustices, or whether, as the biologist Joseph L. Graves (2001, 11) maintains, "the survival of the United States as a democracy depends on the dismantling of the race concept." Less bold, but equally pressing and more common, is the political *and* moral claim that getting rid of race-thinking is part of a program of getting rid of racism (Appiah 1996, 32; Graves 2001, 200). Finally, abandoning race-thinking might be prudentially bad because doing so would disintegrate one's individual identity; or it might be prudentially good because it allows us to pursue relationships that are difficult to pursue in a race-conscious world. And, of course, sometimes all of these values are thrown together into one mess. For instance, Graves (2001, 199) proposes an item that potentially impacts the putative political, prudential, and moral value of eliminating race-thinking: doing so will foster economic growth.

Before we get to those kinds of concerns, though, note a second relevant issue. If race is not real, then that generates one reason to get rid of racial discourse; if it is real, then that provides at least one reason to retain it. This presupposes a principle of epistemic value: if our beliefs should be sensitive to available evidence, then it is bad both to believe

---

1   Following convention, I use single quotation marks when mentioning words and phrases, and small caps to name concepts.

in something that evidently doesn't exist, and to pretend that something that evidently does exist doesn't. Other things being equal, you shouldn't believe that an invisible goblin is typing these words for me so that I can relax and enjoy a beer. And other things being equal, you shouldn't pretend that the moon doesn't exist. If you're with me on this—if you agree that, other things being equal, we shouldn't believe in things that evidently aren't real and that we should believe in things that evidently are real—then you're with me in attributing importance to the second main issue to be discussed in this book, namely

### The Ontological Question: Is race real?

When I first mention to civilian friends and students that many academics think that race is nothing but an apparition, one common reaction is incredulity. To such a way of thinking, the fact that each of us has a race, or multiple or mixed races, is unassailable. Any departure from conventional wisdom here might make academics appear to be unglued from the real world by sheer force of theoretical peculiarity. Whether or not the glue still holds will be an overarching theme in this book, as one of my main concerns—a concern that, I will argue, has been problematically ignored by many (myself included, at times)—is to account for, or at the very least confront in a richly informed way, commonsense thinking about race.

Though we will see below that commonsense thinking about race is in fact strikingly complex, one fairly predominant element of the folk theory of race is that races are biological entities. Now there is more than one way that race might be biologically real. According to one understandable line of thought, we have skin colors and hair textures and facial features—we have, as biologists like to say, *phenotypes* (roughly, the macro-level expressions of our *genotypes*, our genetic makeup). If we can classify these phenotypes in a biologically kosher manner, then this is one way in which race might be biologically real. As it features something that can be superficially read off of the way we look, I'll call this view the *superficial theory*. Another way in which race might be biologically real is not in terms of what we look like, but in terms of the genetic material that significantly determines what we look like—a theory we can call *genetic racial realism*. And then there is the source of our genetic material, namely our ancestry. So a currently popular wave of biological racial realism—*populationism*—holds that races are breeding populations or clusters of breeding populations, populations whose intra-group reproductive rate is sufficiently higher than their rate of reproduction with other populations, thereby ensuring genetic distance (and, usually, phenotypic difference) from each other over multiple generations.

As we will see, all three biological accounts of race have problems; but there is another branch of racial realism. Many contemporary realists, taking inspiration from Du Bois, maintain that race is not ultimately about biology at all. Instead of being a biological kind of thing, race is, on this alternative theory, socially constructed but real nonetheless. That is, race is real as a *social* kind of thing. This view, which I'll call constructivism, holds that just as journalists or doctors are real but socially constructed kinds of people, so racial kinds of people are real but socially constructed—racial groups are real groups that have been created by our social practices, rather than by some biological process. Thus there are several different types of realism one might adopt (see Figure 1.1).[2]

Anti-realists generally think that race is not real because race purports, but fails, to be a biological kind. (Strictly speaking, though, this specific route to anti-realism is not required to be an anti-realist.) Obviously, each kind of realism is inconsistent with this anti-realist thought in its own way. Biological racial realists argue that anti-realism is wrong, because there is (they say) a biological reality to race. Alternatively, constructivists argue that race doesn't need to be a biological kind of thing to be real; instead, it's a socially constructed kind of thing. Thus on my way of defining the various theoretical positions, 'constructionism' names the view that the *idea* of race has been socially

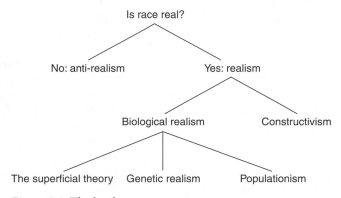

*Figure 1.1* The landscape.

2  What I am here calling 'racial realism' others sometimes call 'racialism.' Racialism, however, is often taken to be a more robust view of race (such that, say, phenotypic features are correlated with intellectual capacities). 'Racial realism,' which just holds that there really are races, is meant to be neutral between these more robust and other, more austere, accounts of race. I should also note that, in this way, I am also using 'real' in what is sometimes called its *minimalist* sense, according to which something is real just in case it exists. The use of the minimalist sense, which creates conceptual room for constructed or response-dependent entities, is required if we are to take constructivism seriously.

constructed, and to that extent it is neutral between anti-realism and the view that there are socially constructed races. This latter view is what I call 'constructivism,' and given the theoretical space it occupies, in order to know whether race is real we now have to answer the more basic question of what race is *supposed* to be. Is it supposed to be a biological kind (and if so, of what sort), or a social kind? Put somewhat differently, what are we purporting to talk about when we use words like 'race'? This is the third main issue of contention that will be examined here:

**The Conceptual Question:** What is the ordinary meaning of 'race,' and what is the folk theory of race?

Rather than asking whether there is something in the world that matches up with our race-talk, this question just targets our race-talk itself: what kinds of things are we purporting to talk about when we talk about race? Are we trying to talk about real scientific kinds, as we do when we talk about, say, water or gold? Or are we purporting to talk about illusory kinds, as we did with, say, witches or phlogiston? Or, finally, could we be talking about some element of the socially constructed world, as when we talk about money or journalists or universities, which have no place, in and of themselves, in the world studied by natural scientists? Although, as we will see, what is in the world can sometimes help determine the meanings of our terms, the Conceptual Question is in the first instance a question about our racial discourse: What kinds of things are we *purporting* to refer to when we talk about race? At its core, this is simply a question about the *meaning* of 'race' and cognate terms. So the core part of the Conceptual Question is semantic. At its periphery, this question asks not about the ordinary meaning of 'race,' but about the folk *theory* of race; so the other part is folk-theoretical.[3]

It's hard to overstate the importance of this question. If racial discourse does not purport to refer to a biological kind, then it will be a non-starter to argue that races are not biologically real. For, assuming that some things, such as universities or newspapers, are real not as biological things but instead as social things, race might be non-biologically real, too. If, however, racial discourse *does* purport to pick out biological categories, then when constructivists tell us that race is a

---

3   I should note, then, that I am using 'conceptual' in an exceptionally broad way. Concepts are just the meanings of terms, but as used here, 'conceptual' covers not only concepts, but also folk theory and belief, or conceptions. This distinction doesn't matter now; it will matter below, though, starting in Chapter 2.

social kind, they will be the ones who are talking about something else besides race, and their position would be the one that is irrelevant. It would be comparable to a debate about whether there were any real witches in colonial Salem, in which I insisted that there were, because some of Salem's residents practiced Wicca. Aside from it being factually false that they practiced Wicca, you'd legitimately have a more basic conceptual complaint: those 'witches' are not the witches you're talking about when you deny that there were any witches in Salem. In that context, by 'witch' one means the kind of person who casts spells and cavorts with the devil, so it is irrelevant whether anybody in Salem was practicing Wicca.[4] In a parallel kind of way, once we know what race is *supposed* to be, we can figure out whether there is, in fact, any such thing.

That's all by way of saying that the Conceptual Question is dialectically important: if we want to figure out an answer to the Normative Question, it seems as though we're going to have to try to answer the Ontological Question, which means having to answer the Conceptual Question. Without minimizing this dialectical importance, we also should not forget that the conceptual truth about race has a substantial impact on the real world. Lucius Outlaw makes the point powerfully in the course of examining the nature and function of our racial categories:

> this is more than an issue of philosophical semantics in racially hierarchic societies which continue to engage in efforts to promote and sustain forms of racial supremacy. In this context, racial categories take on the various valorizations of the hierarchy and affect the formation and appropriation of identities as well as affect, in significant ways, a person's life-chances.
>
> (Outlaw 1996a, 33)

And lurking behind the crucial Conceptual Question is one final issue. The Conceptual Question asks what racial discourse purports to talk about: anti-realists, such as Appiah (1996) and Naomi Zack (1993, 1995, 1997, 2002, 2007), think that ordinary racial terms (erroneously) purport to refer to some sort of interesting biological reality, while

---

4  Here I depart from Appiah (2007, 38–39), who holds that, while the identity *witch* has different criteria of ascription in the two contexts, there is a live question as to whether we should "give up the concept" or preserve the *term* 'witch' for picking out practitioners of Wicca. I think this way of framing things obscures a more natural reading of the linguistic and conceptual terrain: we can simply say that the term 'witch' is ambiguous, such that on one meaning it purports to refer to a supernaturally gifted friend of the devil and on the other to practitioners of Wicca. Indeed, we should say this *because* of the two contexts' radically different criteria of ascription. In this way, you don't have to make a hard call about giving up *the* concept; you simply give up one concept and keep the other, while the term remains the same.

many of their opponents think that they purport to refer to some sort of social reality. But, then, if we're going to try to figure out what racial terms purport to refer to, we need to know *how* to figure that out. That is, we must also answer

**The Methodological Question:** How should we identify the folk concept and theory of race?

As we shall see, one answer to this question is that in order to identify the folk concept of race, we should look at how experts have historically used racial terms. To turn my second card face up, I will argue that this methodology is, by and large, misguided. Instead, I will maintain that, for the most part, we should focus our attention squarely on how racial terms are used in contemporary mainstream discourse. Some people agree with that approach, and then proceed to engage in personal reflection—they reflect from the armchair, as we say—about the nature of contemporary folk racial discourse. I will also argue that the armchair-based approach is, while useful to an extent, insufficient. As an alternative, I adopt what I call the 'experimental approach,' which holds not only that the meanings of racial terms are, for our purposes, at least partially fixed by commonsense, but also that we should inform our analysis of folk racial discourse with data gathered from actual empirical research conducted in a manner consistent with the practices of the social sciences. To be sure, I, like many, accept that we can also identify some of the content of our racial concepts while comfortably ensconced in the armchair. But even the data gathered from such armchair expeditions must be consistent with the empirical data. So that's how I answer the Methodological Question.

Let me reveal the rest of my hand at this point. After setting out, in Chapter 2, some conceptual limits from the armchair and defending my methodological approach in Chapter 3, I turn in Chapter 4 to completing my answer to the Conceptual Question by looking at recent provocative empirical research. Once that conceptual groundwork is laid, we will be in a position to address the Ontological Question of whether race, as defined in that relevant sense, is real. In Chapters 5 and 6, I will argue that it is not. Thus Chapters 2 to 6 constitute an extended argument for the claim that race is not real. But when we consider the Normative Question in light of that claim, we're left with something of a puzzle; for, as I suggest in Chapter 7, we'd be poorly advised to simply get rid of racial discourse. My attempt at a solution is, again, to argue that instead of merely conserving or eliminating racial discourse, we need to replace it with a nearby discourse. Now there are various nearby discourses that are candidates for replacement.

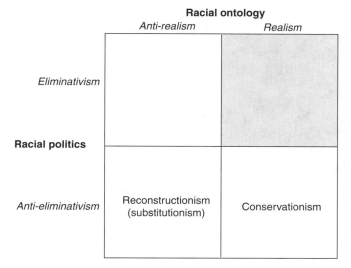

*Figure 1.2* The theoretical options.

To mark the general theoretical genus of which this reconstructionism is a species, I generally call replacement theories *substitutionism*. So reconstructionism is one particular kind of substitutionism (see Figure 1.2).

Those, then, are the issues engaged in this volume. In brief, the question of whether we should eliminate or conserve race is tangled up in the thorny question of whether race is real or illusory. Whether or not it is real, in turn, depends on what race is supposed to be—on how we use racial discourse—which requires us to do some analysis of ordinary racial concepts; this analysis, in turn, requires us to answer a methodological question about how to analyze our folk concepts and theories. Taken together, I am calling the ongoing disputes over how to best answer these four questions *the race debate*. Should my answers carry the day, the ultimate payoff is the normative proposal of racial reconstructionism. At this point, then, we can preview the three arguments that jointly comprise the overall master argument of this book. Philosophers have found that readers tend to find books that present arguments in lists of displayed premises and conclusions 'page-turners,' so without further ado:

## The Conceptual Argument (Chapters 2–4)

1   The discourse relevant for the race debate is folk racial discourse, and analysis of folk racial concepts (and conceptions) should be informed by empirical study.

2   According to the most plausible, empirically informed analysis, folk racial concepts (and conceptions) are composed of biological elements and sometimes also social elements.

Thus,

3   The relevant racial concepts (and conceptions) are composed of biological, and sometimes social, elements.

## The Ontological Argument (Chapters 5–6)

3   The relevant racial concepts (and conceptions) are composed of biological, and sometimes social, elements.
4   There are no biological races; and purely social 'races' aren't races in the relevant sense.

Thus,

5   Race, in the relevant sense, is not real.

## The Normative Argument (Chapter 7)

6   What we should do with our racial discourse is ultimately a matter of which of the various proposals—eliminativism, conservationism, and substitutionism—best satisfies various normative (moral, political, prudential, and epistemic) constraints.
7   Given that (5) race is not real, adopting racial reconstructionism is the best way to satisfy all of the normative constraints.

Thus,

8   We should adopt the policy of racial reconstructionism.

That's the set-up. But before moving on to defend these arguments, I want to address one last preliminary issue. Some—the *exclusionists*, as I will call them—think that the only business philosophers have in the race debate is to tackle normative or evaluative problems: we do ethics and politics, but we should leave the biology to the biologists, the anthropology to the anthropologists, and so on. Now I of course agree that I have no business doing biology, but I think it's too quick to say that the race debate doesn't involve *non*-normative philosophical questions, in particular ontological and conceptual questions. I favor the non-exclusionary thesis that addressing the ontological and conceptual questions is both a philosophical job and a job worth doing. So I want to finish this chapter by driving home why, and in what respects, the questions taken up in this book are both philosophical and well motivated. I don't hope to *answer* the conceptual or ontological questions just yet. Rather, the current goal is to ascend to the meta and determine, on the assumption that we want to answer the Normative Question, which other questions must be answered, and in particular which must be answered by doing some philosophy.

The exclusionists are surely right to insist that the Normative Question is of independent importance and that any answer to the Ontological Question does not by itself settle the issue of what policy we should adopt.[5] For even if race is real, racial discourse could be harmful; and even if race is an illusion, racial discourse might serve some important interests. But the exclusionists go beyond merely advocating that we give special attention to distinctively normative concerns. Ron Mallon (2006, 551) adds that the Normative Question is *the* important question, and that the ontological and conceptual questions should be "left behind." Anna Stubblefield (2005, 73) similarly considers attention given to the Ontological Question not only "unhelpful," but actually also a hindrance to answering the Normative Question.[6] And, whether or not the Ontological Question is helpfully relevant to the Normative Question, Bernard Boxill (2004) maintains that it properly falls under biologists' area of expertise and so is not a philosophical question at all.

To begin to see why one might go exclusionist, briefly recall the dialectic discussed above: it is sometimes held that (in part) because race is not real, we should eliminate racial discourse; and race is not real, some say, because races are supposed to be certain biologically grounded collections of people, which as it happens turn out not to exist. Their opponents, the conservationists, often defend keeping racial discourse partly on the grounds that race is real. So the broader dialectic is such that the normative dispute over whether to eliminate racial discourse often—though not always—boils down in part to an

---

5   Non-exclusionists often seem to tacitly agree with this; for some who have explicitly agreed, see Glasgow (2006); Kitcher (1999, 90; 2007); Sundstrom (2002a); Taylor (2000, 2004).

6   What Mallon and I call 'the normative question' Stubblefield in many places calls 'the moral question.' 'Normative' seems like a more apt term, since diverse realms of normativity besides just the moral bear on the issue, including the political, the prudential, and the epistemic. Or perhaps Stubblefield intends us to focus, even more exclusively, on *just* moral issues, and to not attend to political, prudential, and epistemic issues at all. My reasons against making our focus so very narrow are presented below.

ontological dispute: if race is an illusion, we should abandon racial discourse, while if race is real, we may keep it (barring overriding evaluative concerns). And, again, the ontological debate itself partly reduces to a further dispute over the meaning of ordinary racial terms. Thus the broad orientation of the race debate is that the normative is held to depend on the ontological, which in turn is held to depend on the conceptual. Mallon calls this dialectical move, of defending a normative position partly on the basis of ontological and at bottom semantic (and, I would add, folk-theoretical) theses, "the semantic strategy."[7]

Part of Mallon's resistance to this strategy stems from the fact that amidst the din of disagreement there is an important and robust set of claims that everyone agrees on, which he rightly calls the "Ontological Consensus." It includes such propositions as that "[t]here are no biobehavioral racial essences," that people use such factors as skin color and ancestry as criteria for racial identification, and that racial classification has had oppressive effects (Mallon 2006, 545). The list is longer, but what is remarkable about it is how widespread the agreement is. I certainly don't wish to dispute that point: we should agree with Mallon that this common ground should not be neglected. Nevertheless, I do want to defend the value of tackling the ontological and conceptual questions against the exclusionist arguments to the contrary. So let us take those arguments one at a time.

One exclusionist argument is based on a sensitivity to disciplinary boundaries and a healthy respect for expertise. Here is how Boxill makes his case:

> philosophers are probably not in the best position to prove that there are no races. Full-time biologists seem to be in a better position, given that by 'race' we mean here *biological* race, namely a group of individuals defined biologically, like a breed or a subspecies.

Appended to this claim is a footnote: "Recently, 'race' has sometimes come to have a different meaning, as referring to a social construct. The existence of race as a social construct is not controversial" (Boxill 2004, 209).

---

7  Mallon and others, including my past self (Glasgow 2006), treat it as *just* a semantic dispute, but sometimes the contentious matter is not about the *meaning* of folk racial terms, but about the folk *theory* of what race is. To wit, two parties can use a shared concept, such as RACE, but disagree about the substantive nature of race, e.g., as to whether it is a natural or social kind. Hardimon (2003) has shed light on this distinction by noting that what is often claimed to be the *concept* of race is actually an account of the ordinary *conception* of race. Again, this distinction will receive fuller treatment in Chapter 2.

Boxill is surely correct that if the reality of race were just about the biological facts, then (most) philosophers should step aside. Still, it would overstate the implications of this claim to infer from it that philosophers aren't the ones to argue that there are no races. For while biologists certainly give us the biological facts, there are reasons—at least four reasons—why the answer to the question of whether race is real is underdetermined by facts supplied by other disciplines, including biology.

First, we need to justify what Boxill takes as given, namely that "by 'race' we mean *biological* race." (Since he takes this as given, perhaps Boxill could agree on this.) According to anti-realists like Appiah and Zack, we do mean this, but according to constructivists we do not. So there is an important disagreement over what we mean by 'race' that has to be sorted out before we can hand the discussion over to biologists, and, of course, conceptual analysis is a philosophical task.

This point is not just idle disciplinary defensiveness; it allows us to identify errors that show a strong tendency to afflict all parties to the race debate. For example, as part of his attack on the view that races are real, Graves (2001, 5) writes that "[t]he term 'race' implies the existence of some nontrivial underlying hereditary features shared by a group of people and not present in other groups." While Boxill is right that most philosophers have no business questioning the science behind Graves' attack, it is our business to question the definition of race that Graves presumes. He gives no argument for his definition, although he does reassert it several times, such as when, considering *The American Heritage Dictionary*'s six-part definition of race, Graves insists that only the fifth part, on heredity, is "a correct scientific definition of race" (Graves 2001, 6) (which ends up having no real-world referent, he argues). But this approach assumes what it needs to prove, namely that 'race' is defined in the scientific way he thinks it is, for, if those who see races as social kinds are right, then Graves' semantic presumption in favor of a biological analysis is wrong. And if that analysis is wrong, then, no matter how compelling his argument that there is no biological reality to race, this won't establish that race isn't real, because race is (if the constructivists are right) some *other* kind of thing, some *social* kind of thing. In this way, the semantics of race can, at least in principle, render biology irrelevant.

In contrast to Graves, Vincent Sarich and Frank Miele (2004, 14–15) defend racial realism, but in so doing they make a mistake that runs exactly parallel to the one committed by Graves: they also assume that the dictionary definition of 'race' (which they take from the OED: " 'a group of persons connected by common descent' or 'a tribe, nation, or people, regarded as of common stock' ") reflects the "commonsense" definition, and that this commonsense definition is self-evident. But simple fiat cannot be a substitute for thorough analysis. So whether one makes Graves' faulty presumption in favor of racial anti-realism or Sarich and Miele's faulty presumption in favor of realism, either way there is a faulty presumption, namely that one can simply assert the ordinary definition of 'race.' Indeed, if it were as obvious as they suppose, then Graves and Sarich and Miele should converge on the same definition. Tellingly, they don't.

The more general point is that any argument that utilizes biological facts for or against the reality of race requires that 'race' be defined in a way that makes those facts relevant. And so long as we are trying to characterize the *folk* concept of race, rather than simply stipulating a definition that as a consequence of being stipulated may not engage the race debate at all, any such definition itself needs defending. Giving, and arguing for, those definitions is where philosophical work is animated. That is to say, to analyze the ordinary concept of race, which may or may not pick out something real, we need to bring philosophical tools to bear—counterexamples, thought experiments, fine-tuned analysis, and so on. These tools will then shape the analysis of both the core concept of race and the broader folk theory of race that realists will seek to vindicate and anti-realists will seek to eviscerate. Note: to say that it is a philosophical task is not to say that the best analysis will not be informed by empirical psychological data regarding how we think about race. Indeed, if Chapter 3 is correct, the reverse is true. Furthermore, it of course need not be *philosophers* who do the work of conceptual analysis (although philosophers presumably have the kind of training which facilitates that work, just as biologists have training that facilitates doing biology); but it is *philosophical* work, no matter who does it.

A second uniquely philosophical issue is whether breeds or subspecies are real. Even if biologists could come up with a sensible division of the human species that includes human races as subspecies, it is an open philosophical question whether subspecies count as real. So in this way, even when the biological facts are centrally relevant, the door is not altogether shut on philosophy. Third, it is not uncontroversial that race exists as a social construct, contra Boxill. While it might be uncontroversial that racial *discourse* exists as a social construct, the claim that *race* is a real social construct is the kind of premise that folks like Appiah, Zack, and myself would reject on semantic grounds: for us, whatever might exist as a pure social construct is not, we argue, what ordinary people call 'race.' So those who want to defend the social reality of race must show how it is semantically kosher to fold race into a wholly social reality—how, that is, they are not talking about something else other than race when they talk about social constructs. The general point here is parallel to the general point made about biological realism and anti-realism: if social facts are going to be marshaled in support of the reality of race (as ordinarily talked about, that is, as the potential target of elimination or conservation in *public* racial discourse), 'race' will need to be defined in such a way that social facts are not irrelevant, such as would be the case if RACE turns out to be a purely biological concept. Fourth and finally, some might deny that non-scientific, social kinds are real at all.

I hasten to emphasize that I do not mean to suggest that any of these questions cannot be decisively answered. All I mean to argue currently is that they are not closed and that obtaining answers to them will come from doing philosophy. The second and fourth of these areas of dispute fall in the domain of the philosophy of biology and metaphysics, while the first and third open up conceptual questions about race. So it appears that some important questions pertaining to the reality of race are, in fact, philosophical. With that, we can now turn to a different kind of exclusionist argument, which holds not that questions about the reality of race fall outside of philosophy's domain, but that focusing on the reality of race in relation to the Normative Question is a bad idea. Instead, the critics say, the question of conserving or eliminating ordinary racial discourse and race-based practices should be decided independently of the ontological and conceptual questions.

We would have one reason to avoid pursuing the ontological and conceptual questions if the semantic strategy were "obfuscating," and, according to Mallon (2006, 548), it is obfuscating, because "it makes a philosophical debate over the reference of racial terms and concepts appear as a genuine metaphysical disagreement about what is in the world." However, the semantic strategy need not be seen as concealing a semantic dispute within a superficial, merely apparent ontological one. Rather, it may be understood such that it presents a *genuine* ontological issue as coexisting alongside of, and in significant part because of, a semantic issue. Indeed, far from obfuscating, some anti-realists are transparent that they aim to answer the Ontological Question by showing that the world doesn't match up with our discourse (e.g., Appiah 1996; Glasgow 2006; Zack 2002). Furthermore, this kind of argumentative gambit is nearly ubiquitous in philosophy. Debates over the existence of free will, for instance, sometimes trace to deeper disputes concerning the meaning of 'free will.' Or, for a further example, Walter Sinnott-Armstrong (2006, 7) observes that in meta-ethics, "[o]ntological conclusions are often drawn from semantic premises." In this way, just because an ontological issue partly reduces to a semantic issue, we should not conclude that there *is no* ontological issue.

A second objection to the semantic strategy is not that it obfuscates, but rather that with respect to the independently important Normative Question—*Should* we conserve or eliminate racial discourse?—the correct metaphysics and semantics of race might just be *beside the point*. Now it is certainly true that the Normative Question does not *fully* reduce to the Ontological Question. This creates theoretical space for people like me to endorse anti-realism but avoid eliminativism and for others to hold that race-thinking is dangerous, even if race is real (Boxill 2004). On these grounds, Boxill (2004, 224) concludes that what is important to the Normative Question seems to be whether racial discourse is valuable, not whether race is real. In a similarly exclusionist vein, Stubblefield (2005, 80) thinks that we should challenge "the assumption that the morality of taking race into account is dependent upon whether or not race is somehow real."

Now as Mallon (2006, 549–550) recognizes, when asking whether race-talk is valuable, we have to consider not only its moral, prudential, and political value, but also its epistemic value. And if we can agree that it is epistemically bad to believe in something that evidently doesn't exist, and if our ordinary race-talk encourages us to believe in something that evidently doesn't exist, then the epistemic consequence of anti-realism is that we should get rid of race-talk. But, of course, whether our racial discourse concerns something that doesn't exist is the Ontological Question, which depends, as we have seen, on the Conceptual Question. Similarly, if on the correct semantics (whatever they may be) races do exist, then, if we can also agree that we should not pretend that what is real is *not* real, we have that much epistemic reason to keep race-talk around. In this way, part of the project of answering the Normative Question is determining the epistemic value of racial discourse, and determining the epistemic value of racial discourse depends on determining whether race exists (the Ontological Question), which depends on determining what race is supposed to be (the Conceptual Question).

Of course, epistemic value might ultimately be outweighed by some moral, political, or prudential value that is assessable independently of the reality of race. But, first, I will argue that we have the ability to avoid trading away *any* of these values, and, second, even if we needed to determine such a weighting, we'd not only have some fairly complicated moral, prudential, and political issues to sort out, we'd also have to identify the relevant epistemic harms and benefits. That is, rather than simply sidelining some of the relevant values, we need to have all of them before us. So while Stubblefield (2005, 11) holds that we "end up going around and around on the question of what race is and whether it is real and never get to the heart of the matter, which is the moral question," we should instead recognize that the morality is not the only relevant axis of value.

But even if the Conceptual and Ontological questions are neither obfuscating nor beside the point, Mallon (2006, 548) presents a third objection: the semantic strategy is "ineffective," insofar as it holds the normative debate "hostage to issues in the philosophy of language and metaphysics" that are themselves contentious and possibly incapable of being settled (cf. Stubblefield 2005, 73). Presumably the biggest of such issues are the ongoing disputes in philosophy between causal and non-causal theories of reference and between descriptivist and non-descriptivist theories of meaning. Now I think that Mallon is on to something here that we had better respect: we don't want to get bogged down in questions in the philosophy of language when we're trying to sort out answers to questions about race. Call that piece of wisdom *Mallon's caution*. Given Mallon's caution, I want to grant for the sake of argument that the disputes over reference and meaning are intractable (although I am not confident that this is so) and suggest that, even given that premise, two ways of pursuing the semantic strategy bypass this potential hazard.

One strategy for finding meanings for racial terms is to *separately* utilize rival theories of meaning, in order to show that no matter which side of the linguistic fence one is on, each independently requires us to adopt a certain ontological position with respect to race. Appiah (1996, 32–74) follows this path in arguing that whether we adopt an "ideational" view of meaning, according to which a term's meaning is determined by what people think about the term, or a "referential" view, according to which a term's meaning is determined by the nature of that to which it applies when we use it, we will end up with a set of biologically oriented meanings for racial terms that have no biologically interesting referent in the world. Realists could in principle adopt an analogous strategy.

Mallon's (2006, 549) concern about this first strategy is that "there is no reason to believe that all the plausible [theories of meaning][8] converge on a single answer regarding whether or how race exists," as evidenced by the fact that so many different semantic premises have been marshaled to support different ontological conclusions. However, there is another way of evaluating this evidence: rather than it providing a reason to stop the semantic and therefore ontological parts of the race debate, we should take it as a reason to do more philosophy. That is, the appropriate response to semantic puzzlement is not to give up on conceptual analysis, but rather to do more analytic work to resolve the puzzlement. As such, whether different theories of meaning can independently converge on a univocal semantics of race that supports a single ontological conclusion is what the arguments are for on this first viable, cautious way of pursuing the semantic strategy: Appiah presents arguments concluding that this is exactly the case, and Paul Taylor's (2000) response is based in part on demonstrating that Appiah's analysis is faulty. For current purposes, the point is not to crown a champ in this dispute. Rather, it is to make

---

8  Mallon here actually talks about theories of reference, rather than theories of meaning, but as Appiah (Mallon's foil) is concerned with different theories of meaning, the latter seems to be the more relevant domain. In any case, the point should hold whether we are focused on reference or on meaning.

plain that the conversation is an important one to have, and that there is no reason to expect that some arguments cannot be given to help us come up with some answers.

The second way of identifying the meaning of racial terms without being held hostage to developments in the theory of meaning and reference is to analyze racial concepts in a manner that is, from the get-go, independent of debates among the rival theories of meaning and reference. A given term's referent (to focus on the theory of reference) is normally underdetermined by contentious theories of reference. Theories of reference are designed to account for various pre-theoretical semantic intuitions, such as that 'water' refers to $H_2O$, and if we can identify those intuitions independently of a theory of reference, as it seems we often can—after all, it is because of those intuitions' pre-theoretical appeal that the rival theories of reference can use them as evidence for their views—then we don't need a theory of reference to determine those terms' referents. For instance, Bill Clinton knows who the name 'Al Gore' refers to without, presumably, being able to spell out the correct theory of reference. And, of course, most of us can similarly know the referents of many of our terms. (This is not to deny, though, that there may be some hard cases where it is difficult to choose a referent without a settled theory of reference, nor even that there are some indeterminate cases, where a term has no stable referent.)

So, if we have an independently plausible definition of terms like 'race,' we can heed Mallon's caution by making sure that the proposed definition is consistent with plausible theories of reference and meaning, perhaps by stopping the search for a definition at a theoretically superficial level—or even at the level of analyticity—so that it hovers above debates over reference and meaning. And we see such attempts in the literature. For instance, Michael O. Hardimon (2003) provides an intuitively plausible analysis of the ordinary concept of race (which will receive extended treatment in the next chapter) that does not rely on any controversial theory of reference or meaning.[9] Now, this argument makes an inductive leap: just because we have been able to analyze racial terms without appealing to a deeper theory of meaning and reference, this doesn't decisively prove that, in the case of racial concepts in particular, we will *never* get stuck in a referential jam that requires some more controversial tools. However, the evidence for the inductive leap is potent, so before entering the semantic debate we should be confident, if not entirely certain, that we can analyze

---

9  Slightly more technically, I think that Hardimon's analysis could be worded in the language of either descriptivism or direct reference theory, to either present a description of racial groups or to provide a way of talking about the racial groups directly referred to.

racial concepts without being held hostage to disagreements in the theory of reference or meaning.[10]

For these reasons, then, we should not endorse Mallon's (2006, 550) claim that "[i]f the only source of disagreement about 'race' talk were semantic, we could simply pack up and go home." It seems to me that if this were the only source of disagreement, the work would fall directly into the lap of those whose job it is to do conceptual analysis. For that matter, even if conceptual analysis turns out to be a fool's errand, that meta-philosophical question is itself something to be settled by doing philosophy. (Again, though, we should allow that some non-philosophers, including psychologists and cognitive scientists, also have some important contributions to make to conceptual questions about race, among other domains of inquiry.)

In the end, the exclusionists urge philosophers to focus exclusively on normative issues and forsake the ontological and conceptual discussions, and Mallon (2006, 551) in particular asks us to follow Sally Haslanger's (2000) recommendation to attend to what racial discourse *should* be like. I want to close the case for inclusionism by recalling another lesson from Haslanger: we need not choose between these two enterprises. The ontological and conceptual debates need not take place at the expense of tackling the undeniably paramount normative questions that many in the race debate are concerned to address. Indeed, the projects are complementary, for we'd be better informed as to both what our racial discourse *should* look like and how best to effect any necessary changes if we knew the truth about what it actually *does* look like. It is to this question that I now turn.

10  Note that Hardimon's theory-of-reference neutrality is but one instance of another philosophically ubiquitous method: to note a couple of conspicuous examples, Gettier cases are supposed to inform our analysis of knowledge, and Frankfurt-style cases are supposed to inform our analysis of blame- and praiseworthiness, but neither presupposes any particular theory of reference or meaning.

# 2 Dispatches from the Armchair
## Thinning Out the Concept of Race

In recent years, a lot of ink has been spilled trying to define 'race.' One notable point of contention between the different proposals concerns the thickness of folk racial concepts. At one end of the spectrum, Hardimon (2003, 442–447) has proposed the following "logical core" of the concept of race, understood as a kind of group (such as the Asian race) rather than a property of an individual (such as a person's being Asian). The concept of a race is, according to Hardimon, the concept of a group of human beings (H1) "distinguished from other human beings by visible physical features of the relevant kind," (H2) "whose members are linked by a common ancestry," and (H3) "who originate from a distinctive geographic location." Because this, like other similar analyses, ascribes comparatively few commitments to ordinary racial concepts, I will call it a *thin* analysis of the concept of race. As we proceed across the spectrum, others add to the thin account more robust contents:

> **The Robust Genetic Kind analysis:** "[t]he term 'race' implies the existence of some nontrivial underlying hereditary features shared by a group of people and not present in other groups" (Graves 2001, 5).

> **The Biobehavioral analysis:** The twentieth-century "popular conception" of race that "fused together both physical features and behavior … was and still is the original meaning of *race* that scholars in many fields turned their attention to in the latter part of the 20th century and the early 21st century" (Smedley & Smedley 2005, 19). Or, "According to contemporary European and American belief, racial groups are phenotypically distinct by definition. However … the expectation that races differ in less physical qualities (including customary forms of conduct, culture, morality, and psychology) is equally part of the meaning of the race concept" (Hirschfeld 1996, 53).[1]

**The Purist analysis:** "the term 'race' always connotes purity" (Zack 1995, 300). Or, "the concept of race ... requires that the majority of humans be and always have been racially pure" (Zack 1993, 17).

**The Sociobiological analysis:** "I shall use 'race' to refer to a group of persons who share, more or less, biologically transmitted physical characteristics that, under the influence of endogenous cultural and geographical factors as well as exogenous social and political factors, contribute to the characterization of the group as a distinct, self-reproducing, encultured population" (Outlaw 1996b, 136).[2] Or, "In addition [to having a biological component], the definition of 'race' is partly political, partly cultural" (Outlaw 2001, 70).

It hardly needs mentioning that some of those people cited above do not endorse the ontological claim that 'race,' understood in their thick senses, refers to anything real (although Outlaw, for one, is a realist). Indeed, the purpose of many thick analyses is to be used as premises in arguments against the reality of race. So in and of themselves, these accounts are only meant to be ontologically uncommitted analyses of the ordinary concept of race. This chapter's question is similarly limited: Which analysis of the folk concept of race is correct, or, at least, which is closest to the correct analysis? To show another card early, I mostly agree with Hardimon's thin account, although I will suggest a friendly adjustment that even *it* be thinned out and modified a little.

But while I broadly agree with the thinnish spirit of Hardimon's account, I believe it needs supplementing, for the bulk of his article contains little in the way of an *argument* for the thin analysis of RACE. Rather, he spends most of his time *articulating* the ordinary concept of race, and *clarifying* what it does and does not say. Now this contrast between articulation and argumentation is not meant as some sort of underhanded criticism. On the contrary, I think Hardimon's articulation of the thin concept of race has done us a great service, for (unlike those who simply assert their analyses and move on) he has given us an extended analysis that carries significant intuitive force. And he is quite up front that this is exactly what he hopes to accomplish, namely to

---

1   Here Smedley and Smedley and Hirschfeld collapse the *meaning* of 'race' with ordinary *conceptions* of, and *beliefs* about, race. Below, much will hang on differentiating concepts and conceptions, and if Smedley and Smedley and Hirschfeld (as with anybody) meant to only talk about the *conception* of race, then my argument in this chapter does not target their views. But if they should be read literally, as analyzing *meaning*, then the argument below does, indeed, call their analyses into question.

2   While it might appear as though Outlaw is simply stipulating his own definition rather than trying to capture the ordinary definition, he is clear that he intends for his account to reflect ordinary racial thinking (Outlaw 1996b, 137).

present an analysis of the folk concept RACE that has considerable *intuitive* appeal (Hardimon 2003, 441). So Hardimon's article should be seen as a step forward in our understanding of race. But while *I* find it intuitive, others apparently do not, as they come up with other, and, what is common to them all, *thicker*, analyses of the concept of race.[3] And that pushes defenders of thin accounts to do one more thing: to offer an argument for the thin analysis, as a codicil to its intuitive strength. To be sure, such an argument can be based on various semantic intuitions; it just cannot rely solely on the at-a-glance intuitive appeal of the analysis itself.

Thankfully, we need not look far for such an argument. Indeed, the argument I will make shamelessly borrows from a discussion that has been going on for some time now in meta-ethics, namely Terrence Horgan and Mark Timmons' Moral Twin Earth argument against new-wave moral naturalism, which itself utilizes a modified version of Hilary Putnam's original Twin Earth thought experiment. So really I'm borrowing twice over. (Shameless indeed.) The plan is as follows. In the next section I will say a little bit more about the project of conceptual analysis. What I say here is not new, and leans heavily on Hardimon's paper (2003, 439–440); the goal is simply to be clear about the rules of engagement. In section 2.2 I briefly present the Twin Earth and Moral Twin Earth thought experiments, and in section 2.3 I mobilize an analogous thought experiment, Racial Twin Earth, in defense of a thin account of the concept RACE. I close in section 2.4 by tying up some loose ends.

## 2.1 Concepts and Conceptions, Meanings and Theories

To get a handle on the concept of race, it might be ideal if we had a fleshed-out theory of what a concept is. But conveniently, as it turns out, we won't need a robust theory of concepts. What we need, in order to decide whether thinner or thicker definitions of 'race' are the right ones, is something more modest: a distinction between concepts and conceptions, or, somewhat differently, between meanings and theories.

Consider the concept HORSE. It is part of our concept HORSE that horses are animals. If someone said, 'Horses are plants!' we would think one of two things: he is conceptually confused, or he is using the word 'horse' to mean something different than what we mean by 'horse' (let's stipulate that he and we have come to a shared understanding of what a plant is, so there's no confusion there). That we, linguistically

---

3   This should not be taken to suggest, however, that Hardimon is alone in defining race thinly. It appears, for instance, that in 1988, the U.S. Congress defined 'racial group' in a manner that includes something like H1 and H2, though not H3 (see Haney López 1995, 195).

competent users of the word 'horse,' have this intuition is evidence that it is part of the folk concept HORSE that horses are animals. Now, by way of contrast, imagine a young girl whose parents refuse to allow horses on the farm, and they refuse to let her venture off of their property. (They also disallow pictures of horses. They hate horses. They have even banned television, just because they fear that a horse might appear in some show.) To acquaint herself with these curious creatures, the most she can do is look longingly, two farms over, where the neighbors keep horses. From this distance, she forms the incorrect belief that horses have no teeth. Unlike the person who believes that horses are plants, in harboring her incorrect belief this farm girl is neither conceptually confused nor using the term 'horse' idiosyncratically. Rather, while she shares with us a *concept* of horse, she has a different *conception* of horses.

Illustrated thus, a change in concept is tantamount to a change in *subject*: the person who holds that horses are plants has stopped using 'horse' in the sense we ordinarily mean by 'horse.' By contrast, a change in conception doesn't change the subject. The farm girl is still talking about horses in the sense we ordinarily mean by 'horse.' Instead, she has a different *conception* of what a horse is. Put slightly differently, for the first person the word 'horse' has a unique *meaning*, while the farm girl, staying within the ordinary meaning of 'horse,' has a unique *belief* or *theory* about horses. Understood in this way, we can say that some concept (e.g., of an animal) is part of some other concept (e.g., of a horse) just in case it is deeply embedded—if, and only if, we cannot eliminate the first without also abandoning the second. By contrast, if a concept (e.g., of having teeth) can be abandoned without abandoning a second concept (e.g., of a horse), the first is at most part of a conception that falls under that second concept.

The concept/conception distinction has at times played a significant role in philosophy. Perhaps most famously, John Rawls (1999, 5) called upon it to emphasize that he wasn't simply using a different *concept* of justice than utilitarians were using. Rather, they shared a concept of justice, such that he could say that both utilitarianism and his own Justice as Fairness were alternative ways of making sense of justice: each offers its own conception of justice, both of which fall under a common concept of justice. The concept/conception distinction, then, is important not least because it makes sense of *disagreement*. If Rawls was using a different concept of justice, he wouldn't have been disagreeing with the utilitarians. He would have been talking right past them, using the same word, 'justice,' to theorize about something other than justice. Had he done this, he might have signified his intentions by using not the word 'justice,' but some other word, such as 'shmustice.' But he was, in point of fact, disagreeing with utilitarians. He was not simply talking past them. The way to make sense of this is to say that, first, they shared a concept of justice, but, second, they had different conceptions, or theories, of justice.

The agenda here, again, is to find the content of the *concept* RACE: we want to know not (just) when people have different understandings or conceptions of race, but rather when we have stopped talking about race and started talking about shmace. In analyzing the ordinary concept of race thinly, Hardimon (2003, 440) is charging that the thicker analyses can only be appropriately understood, not as analyses of the ordinary *concept* of race, but as analyses of the ordinary *conception* of race. Our task, accordingly, is to find some argument to justify this charge.

Before we get to such an argument, note that I will mainly be using three key, conventional ideas to determine whether some proposition follows from the concept of race. The first is, again, *disagreement*. If two parties disagree over whether someone is a member of race *R* (and if they agree on everything else about that person), then they must not simply be talking past each other. Instead, they must share a concept of race but have different conceptions of race. Saying that Rawls and Mill disagree about whether some practice is just presupposes that, while they have different theories of justice, they share a common concept of justice. Similarly, if one person holds that Jewish people constitute a race, while another disagrees, then the propositions that Jewish people constitute a race or that Jewish people do not constitute a race cannot be conceptually embedded in the concept RACE. Otherwise, these two 'disputants' would not really be disagreeing; they would simply be talking past one another, using the same word, 'race,' to refer to two different things.

The second is *inter-translatability*. If we were considering translating some non-English word into the American English 'race' (and our 'race' into the non-English word), but linguistically competent American English speakers resist the proposed translation because it would (say) commit us to the proposition that people with 'inny' and 'outty' belly buttons each constitute a race, then our resistance is very good (though defeasible) evidence that the non-English word expresses a different concept than our concept of race.[4]

Finally, throughout this book I will be relying on the idea of a *non-negotiable* proposition (Joyce 2001). A lot has been said about the nature of concepts, and most of it outstrips our concern. But there are certain elements of conceptual analysis that should be non-controver-

---

4   I should emphasize that the required linguistic competence can be domain specific. So rather than limiting ourselves to considering the use of language by those who are competent with respect to the entire language (surely not the weakest criterion), we might more openly focus simply on those who are *relevantly* linguistically competent. For our concerns, the obvious scope of relevancy would be those who successfully employ racial language.

sial. One of those elements is that when it comes to just about every concept, there is *some* proposition that is strongly non-negotiable.[5] You might be able to convince me, with enough good evidence, that the earth turns out to be flat, despite what we've been told for so long. You might also be able to convince me that I'm a brain in a vat and that all the world is an illusion. In either case, I'd be resistant to modifying my beliefs to accept those propositions, but I wouldn't think that we were simply talking past one another—that you didn't understand the term 'earth' or 'brain' or something. But if you tried to tell me that horses are plants, I'd start thinking you were using 'horse' in an idiosyncratic manner. For me, it is non-negotiable that horses are animals; being an animal is simply part of the concept HORSE.

Now care should be taken in making this point. Putnam (1962) taught us that we might come to make radical discoveries about our world, such that cats (or horses) turn out to have the innards of robots, or for that matter live off of photosynthesis, and my stubbornness about horses being animals is not inconsistent with such discoveries. Rather the point is simply that given the way the world is and the knowledge of it that we have accumulated, you've stopped talking about horses if you say that horses are plants. In addition, Mallon's caution advises us to stay away from most debates over the nature of reference and meaning, and it might seem that by saying that the proposition *that horses are animals* is conceptually non-negotiable, I've committed myself to descriptivism. I haven't; I've just used what I take to be a pretty uncontroversial example of a non-negotiable proposition, but the point could just as easily be made in less descriptive language. For instance, if someone pointed at what you and I ordinarily identify as a lily and said, 'That thing over there is a horse,' you and I would rightly think that this person doesn't understand what a horse is, or else is using the term in an idiosyncratic way. The proposition, *that thing over there is not a horse*, is non-negotiable for us.[6]

Now there is, so far as I know, no algorithm for deciding when some proposition is non-negotiable or how we should translate it or which

---

5    I am assuming, here and throughout, that negotiability comes in degrees.

6    I am not as hostile to analyticity as some, but hopefully it is also clear, then, that a non-negotiable proposition is not (necessarily) an analytic one. Even though I want to say that the statement that *that thing isn't a horse* is not analytic, I do think it is conceptually non-negotiable if you're pointing at a lily when you say it. With respect to race, I will suggest below that the proposition *that each race by and large has a distinctive set of visible traits* is conceptually non-negotiable. Among those who accept my suggestion, fans of analyticity will think that this proposition is not only true, but also analytically true. If you're no fan of analyticity, think of such propositions as central in our web of meanings (as among the least revisable of our race-related claims), or as linguistically obligatory, or some such. However you chop the theoretical salad here, you'll get to the idea of non-negotiability.

ways we can disagree with it.[7] We can only make fallible decisions about these things, and to do that we have to appeal to various forms of evidence, both about the way the world is and about the way our concepts, language, and thought operate. Regarding the latter, one tried-and-true device, set up for just this purpose in other domains of philosophical inquiry, namely natural kind terms and moral terms, is ready and waiting for our use here. I now turn to that device, the Twin Earth thought experiment.

## 2.2  Conceptual Border-Drawing: A Tale of Two Sets of Twins

Putnam's (1975b) Twin Earth scenario contains a world that is exactly like good old earth, but with one key difference. Like Earth, Twin Earth has a twin America, where a twin Wynton Marsalis runs the twin Lincoln Center jazz program, where a twin George W. Bush took his country to war against twin Iraq, and where the prevailing language is twin English. In particular, twin-English speakers have a word, 'water,' that is orthographically and phonologically just like the English word 'water,' and, importantly, that is used in much the same way as English 'water': it names the mostly clear, liquidy stuff in the twin Tasman Sea, the stuff that falls from and composes the twin clouds, and the stuff that twin Earthlings can drink to hydrate themselves. The only difference is that while Earth's water is, of course, composed of $H_2O$, twin water is chemically composed of XYZ.

Now Putnam thinks—and very many readers have agreed—that when we consider such a world, our intuitions about what 'water' refers to run strongly in one direction. According to this interpretation, the English word 'water' and the twin-English word 'water' refer to different things ($H_2O$ and XYZ, respectively). So when an English speaker and a twin-English speaker meet, and the former insists, 'Water is $H_2O$' while the latter insists 'Water is XYZ,' they are not actually disagreeing. Instead, they are talking past one another. For, despite the orthographic, phonological, and functional similarities in their two 'waters,' each has a different referent and, arguably, a different meaning.

Many interesting conclusions are supposed to follow from this story: that 'water' and like terms are rigid designators, that meaning (to some

7   I should reiterate here that these ways of distinguishing concepts from conceptions do not presuppose anything about the reality of our subject matter: an adequate articulation of the concept of race should be able to have no ontological commitments. (Just as it is non-negotiable that horses are not plants, so it is non-negotiable that unicorns have horns.) I will also use terms like 'black,' 'white,' 'racial groups,' and so on, but in so doing I do not mean to use them in ontologically weighty ways.

extent) "ain't in the head," that at least many natural kind terms' refer-ents are at least partly fixed by a causal chain, and so on. We need not pause here to chew over these interesting results, for the lesson I want to take from the Twin Earth thought experiment will not have much to do with any particular theory of reference or meaning. Instead, I simply want to focus on Putnam's particularly vivid way of establishing when we've honed in on the meaning and reference of a term. In this case, the referent is $H_2O$: this chemical composition is essential to our concept WATER, such that if something that otherwise is a lot like water isn't $H_2O$, then it isn't water. And this kind of result interestingly contrasts with our next set of worlds.

Starting in the early 1990s, Horgan and Timmons (1991, 1992a, 1992b, 1996a, 1996b, 2000, n-d) penned a series of articles that run a moral version of the Twin Earth thought experiment. Originally, they deployed Moral Twin Earth against those realist theories, such as Richard Boyd's (1988), which tried to recruit causal theories of refer-ence to get a naturalistically kosher realist moral semantics. This kind of theory posits that the semantics of moral discourse aren't guaranteed a priori, but are instead regulated by the natural world, much as the meaning of 'water' is regulated by its chemical composition, $H_2O$. And Horgan and Timmons have since made clear that they believe the Moral Twin Earth thought experiment generates an argument not just against Boyd-style realism, but against *any* naturalist moral realism; in its most general form, Moral Twin Earth provides a "recipe" for criticizing any naturalist pretenders to the realist throne.

According to their version of the thought experiment, there is again a Twin Earth—a Moral Twin Earth—that is just like Earth, with one modification. Moral Twin Earthlings have twin moral judgments that regulate their behavior, that they take to present weighty reasons for acting, and that employ moral terms orthographically and phonologi-cally just like ours—'right,' 'wrong,' 'good,' 'bad,' and so on—to evalu-ate actions, policies, character traits, and the like. Indeed, the vast majority of the actions we call 'wrong' ('right,' etc.) they also call 'wrong' ('right,' etc.). Now plug in Boyd's theory, or at least a highly simplified version of it—again, we need not pause for details that are tangential to our purposes. According to this view, our use of the term 'wrong' is regulated by the natural world. Stipulate that the way the natural world regulates our use of 'wrong' is captured in a consequen-tialist theory, $T^c$. Twin-English moral discourse, though, has this wrinkle: the twin-English use of 'wrong' is regulated by Moral Twin Earth in a way that is captured in some rival, deontological theory, $T^d$ (perhaps because Twin Earthlings more readily feel guilt, in contrast to Earthlings, who more readily feel sympathy).

The question Horgan and Timmons ask us to consider is the same that Putnam has us consider: is our 'wrong' inter-translatable with twin-English 'wrong'? The powerful intuition that they have (and that is arguably presupposed by moral naturalism, which is generally committed to avoiding relativism) is that, in contrast to the case of 'water,' the two 'wrongs' *are* inter-translatable. When the Earthling and the Twin Earthling meet, and they eventually come to some moral debate—say, about whether the Iraq War is morally wrong or about whether uttering a lie to prevent two more lies of the exact same type is wrong—they are not talking past one another, as they would be if they got into a debate about whether 'water' is XYZ or $H_2O$. Instead, they share a concept of wrong, and differ in, as Horgan and Timmons regularly put it, "belief and theory." Or as it was put in the previous section, while they share a concept of wrong, they have different conceptions of what is wrong (Horgan & Timmons 1996a, 16). By contrast, the argument continues, Boyd's theory, according to which meaning is regulated by the natural world, would commit us to the diagnosis that Earthlings and Twin Earthlings *refer to* different things by 'wrong,' in which case they are talking past one another rather than having a substantive disagreement; but that is a counter-intuitive diagnosis.

As with Putnam's Twin Earth scenario, several interesting conclusions are supposed to follow from the Moral Twin Earth thought experiment, but, again, I want to bypass these meta-ethical lessons and proceed directly to what's relevant for our purposes. What is relevant for our purposes is the inter-translatability, the way the conceptual border of WRONG is *not* exposed in this thought experiment. In contrast to Putnam's original Twin Earth scenario, it is intuitive to say that when Twin Earthlings and Earthlings discuss whether the war in Iraq is wrong, they really disagree rather than merely talk past one another. This intuition compels us to say that the English word 'wrong' should be translated into the twin-English word 'wrong,' and to diagnose the difference between users of English moral discourse and twin-English moral discourse not as one of *concept* or *meaning* or *reference*, but as one of conception, or theory and belief. This contrast between the two sets of twin worlds, in turn, illuminates a path to a sound analysis of RACE.

## 2.3  Racial Twin Earth: An Argument for a Thin Account

Given what we have so far seen, for any analysis of the concept RACE, we should be able to construct a Racial Twin Earth scenario, and if our reaction to that scenario runs in the direction of Putnam's story about 'water,' where we say that our 'race' and Twin-English 'race' are not inter-translatable, we will have pinned down at least one boundary of the concept of race. If, by contrast, we are inclined to say something similar to what Horgan and Timmons say in response to the Moral Twin Earth scenario, that Earthlings and twin Earthlings share a concept of race, then we'll have shown not that that analysis has given us an analysis of the Earthling, or more accurately yet, American (or any linguistic community's) *concept* of race, but that it has given us some particular *conception* of race that falls under some thinner concept—a concept that must be thin enough to accommodate the twin Americans' alternative conception.[8] What we will find, I will suggest, is a vindication of a concept of race with thin content, indeed one that is even thinner than the analysis proposed by Hardimon. Let us start with the thick analysis that 'race' means, at least in part, a biobehavioral grouping.

Racial Twin Earth is, as you've by now no doubt deduced, very much like Earth. Twin United States is in the twin northern hemisphere, while there is a place called 'New Zealand' in the twin southern hemisphere. The twin Yankees have won more twin World Series than the twin Red Sox, a fact that irritates twin Bostonians no end. And so on. And in twin America, they use words like 'race,' 'Asian,' 'black,' and 'white,' and they apply those terms to people in ways that exactly parallel the ways that Americans apply them to their American counterparts. Further suppose, for the sake of testing the proposed biobehavioral analysis of our concept RACE, that Smedley and Smedley and Hirschfeld are right that Americans are semantically committed to the proposition that Asians, black people, and white people each have their own biobehavioral nature. Twin Americans, by contrast, deny this. Like Americans, they affirm that the people they call 'Asians,' 'black people,' and 'white people' each, as a group, have distinctive physical features. But twin Americans differ from Americans on, and only on, a further claim, namely that each race has a unique behavioral profile.

There are two candidate interpretations of this scenario. On the first, we interpret it as we interpreted 'water' in Putnam's Twin Earth thought experiment: Americans and twin Americans have different *concepts* of race, and the American word 'race' is not translatable into the twin American term 'race.' Furthermore, if the American and the twin American met, and the American said 'Each race has a biobehavioral nature,' while the twin American denied this, they would not be *disagreeing*. Instead, they would be talking past one another without realizing it: the American would mean that each *race* has a distinctive biobehavioral nature, while the twin American would mean that each *shmace* does not have a distinctive biobehavioral nature. On the second interpretation, Racial Twin America stands to America as Moral Twin Earth stands to Earth: we can indeed translate the American English-

---

8    As noted in the previous chapter, it is commonly held that criteria for racial groupings differ from community to community, so we'll play it safe and just stick with American racial concepts, though again I suspect that what follows might be open to extrapolation to other communities.

language word 'race' into the twin American English word 'race,' and, in fact, the two parties do disagree about whether races have distinct sets of biobehavioral traits.

I submit that the second interpretation is decisively more intuitive than the first: on reflection, we'll want to say that Americans and twin Americans disagree about whether races have distinctive biobehavioral natures. Of course, it would be problematic for me to assume that everyone shares this intuition. In the next chapter, I will argue that such an intuition carries its strongest evidential force when we have reliably found that it wins widespread endorsement. Unfortunately, however, no such study has (to my knowledge) been undertaken. So the most I can do is to offer a burden-shifting argument, by pointing to some implausible implications of the biobehavioral analysis. In the end, advocates of that analysis can bite these bullets; the point is simply to establish a case that bullets must be bit.

So notice what follows if you deny that, in this Racial Twin Earth scenario, Americans and Twin Americans share a concept of race. You not only must deny the intertranslatability of 'race' and twin-English 'race' and the appearance that the two parties *disagree* about whether races have biobehavioral natures. Indeed, you not only have to say that Americans and twin Americans are simply talking past each other. You must also say that folks of yesteryear, who commonly believed that each race had a biobehavioral essence, and folks of today, who clearly sometimes deny that races have biobehavioral essences—as we *will* see in the discussion in Chapter 4 of the empirical data on this question— do not, despite appearances, have different ideas about the nature of race. For they would simply be talking past one another, using the same conjunction of letters, 'race,' to represent different concepts, RACE and SHMACE. So, according to this view, when we think we disagree with our ancestors about whether each race has a behavioral essence, we are simply confused.[9]

I find that bullet tough to chew. Instead, I think the intuitive thing to say is that we really *do* disagree with our ancestors about the nature of race, and that Americans and twin Americans really *do* disagree about whether each race has its own biobehavioral nature. And, as we have seen, the way to say this is to also say that the different parties share a concept of race, one that is thin enough to be consistent with *both*

---

9   As with Moral Twin Earth and the debate between deontologists and consequentialists, so with Racial Twin Earth: we need not travel to such an exotic location to appreciate the point of the thought experiment. We can simply observe our own racial thinking. Twin earth thought experiments are, of course, normally used to see whether something like the causal theory of reference holds in some domain of linguistic items (e.g., moral terms, natural kind terms), but they are, in the end, just vivid representations designed to tug on our linguistic intuitions.

divergent views. They do not simply talk past one another; rather, they disagree in theory and belief, or as we're saying here, they subscribe to different *conceptions* of race.

The conclusion that follows from this set of intuitions about the Racial Twin Earth thought experiment is that, since twin Americans and Americans can intelligibly disagree about whether races have biobehavioral natures, the proposition that each race has a biobehavioral nature is not part of our folk concept of race. That is to say, twin Americans neither *contradict* themselves, nor *mean* something extraordinary by 'race,' when they say, 'Races have no biobehavioral natures.' Instead, they have a non-biobehavioral *conception* of race, which falls under a thinner *concept* of race that they share with those who are committed to the thought that races have biobehavioral natures.

I strongly suspect that the Racial Twin Earth thought experiment can be mobilized against any of the thicker analyses of race that have been proposed. It would be tiresome to go through all of them, but let me briefly present one more just to shore up my case. Instead of believing that races have biobehavioral essences, let us now suppose that Americans hold that races are pure groups. Twin Americans, while again sharing with Americans a vast amount of beliefs and practices related to race, deny this, because they hold that each racial group has interbred, to a considerable degree, with most or all other racial groups. Here again, we have two choices. We can say that twin Americans and Americans mean different things by 'race' and as such are simply talking past each other when they use terms like 'race,' or we can say that they share a concept of race, and disagree, in conception, about whether races are pure. Again, I submit that the second interpretation is much more intuitive.

I believe these two results are generalizable: for any of the thicker proposed analyses of RACE catalogued at the start of this chapter, and for any other similarly thick analysis of RACE, each will require us to render an interpretation of a suitably tailored Racial Twin Earth case in which we would have to say, implausibly, that twin Americans (who deny the thicker part of the proposal) and Americans (who endorse it) are simply talking past each other rather than disagreeing. It is, as Horgan and Timmons would say, a recipe for an argument that can be applied to any thick analysis of RACE.

Suppose I am right to make such a generalization. It still wouldn't vindicate the thin concept of race proposed by Hardimon. To see whether his proposed analysis of RACE can be vindicated, we should also run *it* through the thought experiment. What we need, in order to test Hardimon's thin analysis, is a world where twin Americans say either that (~H1) races are not distinguishable by "visible physical features of the relevant kind," or that (~H2) a race's members are not "linked by a common ancestry," or that (~H3) races need not "originate from a distinctive geographic location." We would then need to ask whether, upon making one of those claims, twin American 'race' would not translate into American 'race,' and we can fix our intuitions on the translation question by deciding whether, in denying H1, H2, or H3, twin Americans are *disagreeing* with Americans, or are instead simply talking past them, talking about something else.

I said above that while I think the thinness of Hardimon's analysis is broadly on target, I also think that even it needs to be thinned out and modified a little. I can now explain why: the Racial Twin Earth thought experiment suggests that H1 is part of the ordinary concept but in need of modification (or at least explicit precisification), and that H2 and H3 are not actually part of the concept of race. If Racial Twin Americans were to say (~H2) that members of a given race are not linked by common ancestry, and are instead linked *only* by physical appearance, my intuition, at any rate, is that we should still translate our 'race' into their race. Imagine, for instance, that tomorrow God creates a world exactly like ours, such that the only difference is that the people in it— our *doppelgangers*—and everything else, were created from scratch. Should we say that those people—the people who look *exactly* like us in twin Africa, Asia, Europe, and so on—constitute races any less than we do, just because the members of each apparently racial population have no distinctive ancestries? That seems excessive (cf. Root 2000, S632, n. 4). Similarly, if twin Americans were to deny (H3) that races have different geographical origins, this would not be sufficient to say that they have a different concept of race. Instead, they must have some different theory about the origin of the races. Perhaps, like Voltaire (2000), they think that the races originated in separate spontaneous creations of "providence," but, unlike Voltaire, they think that providence immediately put all of the races in one and the same location. This would indicate not that they have a different concept of race, but only that they have a distinctive theory about the origin of races. So I propose that we jettison H2 and H3.

Element H1, however, is trickier. On the one hand, if Racial Twin Americans' use of 'race' (and cognate terms) is not responsive to the relevant physical traits, as H1 says Americans' use of 'race' is, then at that point they seem to be talking about something other than race. Their 'race' and our 'race' are not inter-translatable. When we say, 'Races have different physical features of such-and-such a kind,' and they say, 'While there are races, they are not physically distinguishable in that way,' we appear not to be disagreeing, but to be talking about different things. Put otherwise, if we eliminate the relevant physical features from our concept of race, we no longer seem to be talking about race in the ordinary sense. Indeed, while there are families and tribes and clans, and so on, what seems to set races off from non-racial ancestrally related populations is, at a minimum, physical appearance of a certain kind (Hardimon 2003). So physical appearance seems conceptually embedded in RACE.

On the other hand, it has been repeatedly observed that we cannot coherently list a set of the relevant visible traits for any given race such that all members of that race, and only members of that race, have those traits (Hardimon 2003, 449; Zack 1995, 303). Even the U.S. Supreme Court has apparently recognized that we seem to allow that people ordinarily classified as black can have any of the visible traits commonly attributed to people classified as white (Haney López 1995, 195); and some white people have darker skin than some black people (Gracia 2005, 86). But if it is true that there are no traits shared by all and only members of a given race, then it seems that we cannot include H1, for H1 posits that physical traits of such-and-such a kind are what individuate the races. Indeed, this kind of phenomenon—that an individual of race *R* need not have the visible traits typical of *R*—might seem to be a reason to reintroduce H2 into the equation: if that individual is a member of *R* not because of her visible traits, perhaps it is because of her ancestry (Blum 2002, 100–101).

How can we resolve this dilemma? We might appeal to cluster concepts (Outlaw 1996a, 1996b), or we might say that the ordinary concept of race is incoherent, but I think another solution is available: we can modify H1 to say that members of racial groups *by and large* have the relevant, distinctive racial traits. Put more precisely, the concept of a race is, at least in part, the concept of a group of human beings that is (H1*) distinguished from other human beings by visible physical features, of the relevant kind, that the group has *to some significantly disproportionate extent* (cf. Outlaw 1996b, 11).

Now that alone doesn't solve the dilemma, for we're still stuck with the question of how H1* provides a criterion that details the properties by virtue of which any given individual is a member of her race. The answer is that it *doesn't*. Not every property of a racial group is had by every individual in that group (as when the pile of bricks weighs one ton but not every brick in the pile weighs one ton). And this can be neatly explained: the group has some properties that are the products of the properties of its members considered collectively (namely that as a group they tend, to a significantly disproportionate extent, to have such-and-such visible traits), and the members obviously won't individually have any property that attaches to the group only at the group level. So the point of emphasis here should be that the concept of race being analyzed is the concept of race understood as a *group*, rather than as a property of an individual. (The assignment of individuals to racial groups will receive more attention in Chapter 4.)

Other ways of navigating the dilemma are possible. One might insist that the racial group is just a collection of its individual members. Since it is not the case that any particular visible trait is shared by all and only members of any given race, such a view must do one of three things: again, it can avert to a cluster concept, which seems less satisfying than an account that supplies necessary and sufficient conditions for being a race; or it can simply conclude that the concept of race is incoherent, which seems like a step that is not only uncharitable to realism but is unnecessarily drastic, given that there is an analysis that doesn't sacrifice coherence; or, finally, it can give up the concept of visible features altogether and consequently be impaled on the horn of the dilemma that it classifies many non-racial populations as races. I prefer H1*, as it doesn't incur any of these costs.

Alternatively, one might modify H1 to say that the concept of a race is the concept of a group of human beings (H1**) *whose ancestors* are distinguished from other human beings by uniformly having visible features of the relevant kind. But H1** seems insufficient, for ancestral phenotypic difference alone is not enough to justify calling two current populations different races. Consider what our reaction would be if current racial populations lost their visible differences and converged phenotypically. Imagine, for instance, that a group of radical egalitarians infused the global water supply with a newly invented agent whose only effect was to spontaneously make everyone on the planet look like the members of one race; in fact, imagine that we all look roughly like the Dalai Lama. Again, given the paucity of empirical data on this question, I can only appeal to my own intuitions on the matter, but my strong inclination here is to say that specifically racial difference no longer exists in such a world of uniform physical appearance. So what it seems we need, to adequately capture the ordinary concept of race, is the relevant kind of visible differentiation between racial groups.[10]

Thus H1* seems like the most viable candidate, of those I've considered, to replace H1. If the intuitions that lead to dispatching with H2 and H3 and replacing H1 with H1* are widely shared, then that widespread convergence will constitute very strong, though defeasible, evidence (more on this in the next section) for an analysis of RACE: the concept of race is simply the concept of a group of human beings distinguished from other human beings by visible physical features of the relevant kind that the group has to some significantly disproportionate extent. It is *not* the concept of a population with its own geographical origin and with a certain ancestral trajectory, or of a pure group, or of a group with a unique biobehavioral nature.

If my generalization is correct, it also follows that none of the other thick analyses of the concept of race work. Instead of capturing the

---

10  Obviously, "the relevant kind" is crucial here in ruling out non-racial groups that are also distinctive by virtue of their (racially irrelevant) visible traits. I will proceed as if the realist can tell a plausible story about which visible traits are the relevant ones.

content of the *concept* of race, all of these thicker claims can be, at most, accounts of the ordinary *conception* or *theory* of race. (Whether they succeed as accounts of the ordinary *conception* of race is also one of the questions tackled in Chapter 4.) However, that is just a generalization. I have not shown decisively that the concept RACE is analyzable *only* into H1\*. So it remains possible that this analysis should be thickened by adding other elements. Below I will require that we add more specificity to H1\*, but my suspicion is that not much more can be added to an analysis of RACE besides H1\*. Of course, the only way to confirm such a suspicion would be to run every proposed element through the Racial Twin Earth thought experiment (or some similar mechanism), and I couldn't hope to mount any comprehensive search and test of such elements. So I leave it as a challenge: advocates of thicker analyses should use this (or some similar) mechanism to test any elements they may think deserve to be added to the most adequate analysis of the ordinary concept of race. If it turns out that there is a widespread intuition that when twin Americans deny the proposed element they are simply talking about something else, we should say that it is part of our ordinary concept of race and therefore that RACE is thicker than I have argued for here; but if our intuition is that when they deny the proposed element they are disagreeing with us about race, and that we should therefore translate their twin 'race' into our 'race,' then we should say that that element is not part of the concept of race, and the thin analysis will stand to fight another day.

## 2.4 Loose Ends

While intuitions about Racial Twin Earth thought experiments are compelling, they do not constitute a knock-down argument. As Horgan and Timmons note repeatedly, such intuitions are empirical, and therefore defeasible, evidence for drawing inferences about the contents of our concepts (1992a, 163, 169–170; 1992b, 257, n. 37; 1996a, 15, n. 8). That defeasibility notwithstanding, they are distinctly powerful, assuming our Twin Earth intuitions are widespread among competent language users.[11] Thus our conclusion should be only that those who continue to insist on thicker analyses of racial concepts have some work to do. They must either deny what appear to be compelling intuitions

---

11 Again, it is worth restating what will be the main thesis of the next chapter, namely that it might help to test this assumption and empirically study how people actually respond to the various thought experiments considered in this chapter. If it turns out that my intuitions are idiosyncratic, I should give them up (otherwise I might be like the guy who says, 'Horses are plants'). As I argue in Chapter 3, we should consider all kinds of data about how we think about race, and in Chapter 4 I will be sure to explain how the judgments rendered in this chapter are at least consistent with the existing research.

about the Racial Twin Earth thought experiment, or provide some wholly independent argument for their thick analysis to counter the evidence provided by those semantic intuitions. The dialectical upshot is that the argumentative burden has been shifted onto those who seek to defend a thicker analysis of RACE.

Another loose end needs to be tied up with a point about how thin the thin concept of race is. First, note that the thin concept allows that races might ultimately be genetic kinds, that races could have unique biobehavioral essences, that races could be pure groups, that races could be socio-biological kinds, and so on. In this regard, contrast the thin account with this analysis: " 'Race' means a ... set of physical categories that can be used consistently and informatively to describe, explain, and make predictions about groups of human beings and individual members of those groups" (Zack 2002, 1). By now you will have anticipated that I think that, as a statement of *meaning*, this definition is too thick: it would incorrectly require us to deny that those who think race has no explanatory or predictive power are *disagreeing* with those who think it does. Racial Twin Earth thought experiments work in this way to provide evidence of a very thin concept of race, thin enough to accommodate varied, though not all, theories of race. Second, however, the thin concept's ability to accommodate various thicker conceptions of race does not necessarily guarantee that it will vindicate any of those thicker conceptions as pointing towards anything *real* or, for that matter, anything illusory. That is a task for ontology, of which conceptual analysis is only one part.[12]

Finally, accepting the thin concept of race allows us to make sense of several debates about race. A cursory glance at the thick analyses listed above tells us that if we take them at their word and treat them as analyses of the *concept* RACE, then the different parties would simply have different *semantics* of 'race' (Mallon 2006). But if that were so, then they would be talking past one another when they offer their analyses, and that would make for an unfortunately unproductive dialectical landscape (Haslanger 2005, 2006). If we have a thin account, by contrast, we can say that while those analyses have sometimes overstated their cases by trying to thickly fix the concept of race, we should make the friendly adjustment to each that it is an account not of the ordinary concept of race, but of the ordinary conception of race. That is, we can say that race is by definition something thinner than pure groups, or biobehavioral groups, or whatever, something along the lines of H1*, and that those thicker accounts are attempts to provide the folk

---

12  While we are on the subject of accommodation, I should also stress that this analysis is meant to be consistent with any (mainstream) general theory of meaning. It should be no more controversial than ordinary analyses, such as analyzing the concept of bachelor into the concept of an unmarried male.

*theory* of race. In that case, the different accounts would disagree, and they wouldn't be talking past one another.

Now we still have more conceptual work to do. I haven't given much consideration to the various criteria by which we assign individuals to the several races, or to what the several races are, which can supply useful data about the content of the concept, and conception, of race. But before getting to those questions, before revisiting the thinned-out analysis delivered from the armchair in this chapter, a metaphilosophical interlude is in order. While armchair-based reflections like those I have presented here are useful, I argue next that the most complete picture of the ordinary concept and conception of race would be one that is informed by empirical studies that examine how ordinary people think about race and employ racial discourse. Once that methodological claim is established, we can not only return to examine the extent to which the analysis of racial groups provided thus far is consistent or convergent with such studies, but we can also see what that research tells us about how we ordinarily attribute race to individuals. That conceptual groundwork should put us in a secure enough position to subsequently attempt to answer the questions of whether or not race is real, and if not, what we should do about it.

# 3 Methodology
## How Should We Figure Out the Shape of Racial Discourse?

This chapter's thesis is a straightforward methodological maxim: if we want to analyze the ordinary concept and conception of race, we ought to consider as many and as reliable data as possible about how ordinary people actually deploy racial terms. If this is right, then the last chapter's armchair analysis at least must be consistent with, and ideally would substantively dovetail with, such data. I'll return to examining how my armchair analysis comports with ordinary folk intuitions about race in the next chapter. The current task, however, is to argue that armchair-generated data, while useful, are most compelling when fortified by systematically gathered empirical data on ordinary racial discourse. If you already find this kind of claim agreeable, you could jump to Chapter 4 without missing a beat. If you stick around, however, we'll see here that many *don't* already accept it and that there are some reasons for those detractors to reconsider.

## 3.1 Three Methodologies

One theory of racial conceptual analysis[1] has been particularly influential. It has been presupposed by non-philosophers, and it has been explicitly defended by philosophers, such that it often appears to be *de rigueur* in the race debate. As we will see in more detail shortly, it holds, roughly, that the meanings of racial terms are determined by how those terms have been used by historical experts. Accordingly, I'll call it the *historical-expert* approach. One aim of this chapter is to argue that the historical-expert approach is misguided. Its main rival directly

---

1   By 'racial conceptual analysis,' I do not mean to imply that there are particularly racial ways of analyzing concepts. Rather, I mean by that phrase an analysis of racial concepts. That is, I am using 'racial conceptual analysis' in the way that we conventionally talk of 'moral theory,' which is not to say that the theory itself has the property of being moral, but that it is a theory about morality. Recall also that my use of 'conceptual analysis' is broader than standard usage, since I use it to refer to the analysis of both concepts *and* conceptions, as I explain shortly.

attends to contemporary ordinary uses of racial discourse, and it does so from the armchair (as I did in the previous chapter). While I will argue that this approach, the *armchair* approach, is right that contemporary folk racial discourse should be privileged over historical expert racial discourse, I will also argue that it would be a mistake to conclusively determine commonsense meanings of racial terms from the armchair.

Instead, I think we ought to adopt a third approach, which I'll call the *experimental* approach to racial conceptual analysis. The experimental approach joins the growing experimental philosophy movement in insisting that we accommodate empirical data when doing conceptual analysis. It agrees with armchair enthusiasts, first, that the meanings of racial terms are at least partially determined by commonsense usage of those terms. Call this first component the *folk* approach to racial conceptual analysis. The folk approach is different from the folk theory of race itself. The folk theory of race is whatever common sense thinks about race; by contrast, the folk approach to racial conceptual analysis holds that the contents of the relevant racial concepts and conceptions are at least partially determined by folk racial discourse. Second, and this is where I get up from the armchair, the experimental approach holds that analyses of ordinary racial concepts should be informed by systematic empirical study of ordinary racial thinking and discourse.

The point of this chapter is to argue that this approach to analyzing racial concepts and conceptions should be favored in the race debate. This claim has two implications. The first is that much work on race will need to be reevaluated. The eliminativist or conservationist proposals and the realist and anti-realist arguments that rely on historical-expert or armchair approaches will have a false premise, namely that the conceptual premises that support their normative and ontological positions rest on the strongest possible methodological foundation. Which will mean that we need to start over. We need to independently perform the preferred analysis—that is, we need to make empirically informed analyses of the folk concept and conception of race—in order to provide more compelling support for, or opposition to, the various ontological and normative positions in the race debate. Second, rather than defending semantic proclamations about race, such as ' "Race" refers to a biobehavioral essence,' wholly by armchair reflection or excavation of historical thinking, these statements will actually be empirically testable semantic *theories*. Whether or not the theories are true will be decided in part by how participants actually respond in empirical studies designed to test these theories.

One preliminary point is important here: I am here concerned with both concepts and conceptions. What I want to argue is not merely that the experimental approach will better reveal the conception of race we are after, nor merely that it will more accurately reveal the nature of the concept RACE, but that it will better reveal both. That said, I will, simply for convenience, mostly talk of analyzing concepts and just note for the record now that I think that the arguments presented below also justify identifying the folk conception of race in an empirically informed manner.

## 3.2  The Historical-Expert Approach

The historical-expert approach combines two theses. The first holds that when we want to know what racial terms mean, we ought to look at what the *experts* have to say about race. Appiah (1996, 41) has said that this "semantic deference" is the methodological output of what Putnam (1975b, 227) characterized as the "division of linguistic labor." Below I will explain how what I have to say is consistent with the intuitions that many share with Putnam, and we'll see that Appiah's theory differs in important ways from the standard causal-historical theory of reference, but for now note that the historical-expert approach includes the thesis that the judgments of the experts set the meanings of racial terms. I'll more specifically call this kind of semantic deference 'expert deference.' The second thesis of the historical-expert approach is that when we want to know what racial terms mean, we ought to look at how they have been used *historically*. That is, the meanings of racial terms are primarily determined by how they have been used throughout history. Call this 'historical deference.' In a distinctive step, the historical-expert approach then *combines* the two deference theses into one novel historical-expert thesis:

> **HET:** The meanings of racial terms are set by how they are used by the historical experts (no matter what non-experts say about them).

To pause for a moment, the implication of HET for the race debate is that, roughly speaking, if the historical experts conceived of race as a biological kind, then there actually need to be biological referents of racial terms in order for race to be real; if, by contrast, the historical experts conceived of race as a social kind, then there actually need to be social referents of racial terms in order for race to be real. So, to follow out the terms of the overall race debate as set in Chapter 1, we need to know how the experts have historically conceived of race if we are to determine whether we should conserve or eliminate racial discourse, since that depends in part on whether or not race is real.

The basic problem with HET is that it is too deferent. There are at least four reasons why this is so. All stem from what I'll call the 'mismatch' phenomenon, the possibility that if we only look at what the experts or history has thought about race, their concepts might not match the racial concepts that *we* use. (Where 'we' here is shorthand for those who employ contemporary common sense, rather than a uniquely historical and/or expert 'sense.')

First, if the mismatch phenomenon occurs, HET's racial concepts will simply miss the point of the race debate. The point, recall, is to determine whether racial concepts should be conserved in or eliminated from contemporary, public, mainstream discourse and practice. But, of course, if the historically and expertly deferent racial concepts do not match *our* racial concepts, then were we to follow HET, we would end up talking about conserving or eliminating something else—a concept of race that simply isn't the contemporary public concept of race.

Second, if the mismatch phenomenon occurs, we'd be changing the subject (cf. Jackson 1998a, 38). Words can have all sorts of meanings—folk, expert, stipulative—but the race debate is about certain specific meanings. In that context, the concepts that are the subject of debate are, again, the public ones. So if in our arguments we purport to draw conclusions about the public concept of race based on premises about a mismatched concept of race, we'll have changed the subject midstream.

From these first two problems stemming from the mismatch phenomenon, a third follows: as Frank Jackson (1998a, 31) points out, in many cases where we give up the ordinary concept, we give up the interesting concept. The general point holds in this specific context, for mismatched racial concepts aren't very interesting from the perspective of the race debate. Recall that the range of the race debate includes, say, California's recently defeated Racial Privacy Initiative, which would have prohibited publicly funded agencies from collecting racial data. Such issues are, of course, particularly interesting, and if (say) eliminativists miss those interesting issues, they will invite shrugs from their opponents in the public sphere: 'Well, that's fine if you want to get rid of racial data in *your* sense of "racial," but that's simply not what we're trying to keep.'

Finally, the mismatch phenomenon threatens to blind us to and maintain an ethically and politically problematic status quo. If we use a concept of race in our theories that doesn't match the folk concept of race, we might end up with a theory of race that cannot address particular unjust or immoral race-conscious practices. For instance, if we privileged a concept of race that was mismatched insofar as it posited no Asian race (see Chapter 5), we might not have the conceptual resources to confront anti-Asian racism, and thus our political and moral attention to social racial issues might be problematically misdirected. If we're going to address our political and moral problems having to do with what is ordinarily considered race, we must make sure we have the conceptual resources to think about *our* racial concepts.[2]

In sum, we should give up HET. For the purposes of the race debate, we want to know what *we* mean by 'race,' not what Darwin or Du Bois meant by it. If so, then when we analyze racial terms, we ought to examine what we mean when we use racial terms—that is, folk discourse determines the (relevant) meanings of racial terms. This, again, is the folk approach to racial conceptual analysis. Before examining its merits, however, it will pay to more clearly state this argument against HET and examine how HET's defenders might respond. So, in brief, here is an anti-HET argument:

1   Whether the historical/expert concept of race matches the folk concept must be determined by independently analyzing folk usage of racial terms and seeing if it defers to (or otherwise matches) the historical/expert concept.
2   Rather than independently demonstrating that folk usage defers to the historical/expert concept, HET makes the historical/expert concept of race the folk concept of race by theoretical fiat.

Thus,

3   HET cannot adequately determine that the historical/expert concept matches the folk concept of race.
4   For the purposes of the race debate, the relevant concept of race is the folk concept of race.

Thus,

5   For the purposes of the race debate, HET generates an irrelevant concept of race.

Premise 4 is biased towards the concerns laid out in Chapter 1: as I'm stipulating it, the race debate is about whether to eliminate or conserve contemporary, public, folk racial discourse. Just to cover my bases, then, below I will note some other lines of inquiry for which the investigation of non-folk discourse is appropriate. Premise 2 is simply a characterization of HET, which holds that regardless of what common sense says about race, what ordinary folk *really* mean is what the historical experts meant by 'race.' For HET, there is no way to

2   On these points, see also Glasgow 2003.

independently identify the contents of the folk concept of race, because for it the folk concept of race is automatically deferent. Premise 1, then, is the more controversial claim. But note its modesty. It does not suppose that contemporary public users of racial terms *do not* defer, only that they *might* not. If they do, that would no doubt be an important result. But HET should still be rejected because such a result must be the substantive outcome of independently establishing that public discourse does in fact defer, rather than such deference being entailed prior to analysis by methodological proclamation.

It might be objected against this that since advocates of HET think that the folk concept of race *just is* the deferential concept, suggesting that the folk concept must be identified independently begs the question against HET. The problem with such an objection is that it simply stipulates that there is no way that HET could be false. No matter how opponents of HET might try to show that there could be a mismatch between the historical expert and the ordinary concept of race, this defense of HET just claims that there *can be* no mismatch, because the ordinary concept of race is simply whatever the historical expert concept says it is. That is, this defense makes HET true by theoretical fiat. But that kind of bootstrapping cannot help solve a substantive debate, where it's not a *given* that ordinary users are deferent to historical experts. So only independent arguments can establish the purported deference, which, if it exists, can then be taken on as a premise in further arguments.

There seem to be two likely ways in which such an independent argument might be advanced. On the one hand, the level of deference in ordinary racial thinking might be determined by independently establishing what the ordinary concept of race is and then seeing whether it is deferent. This is the folk approach, advocated here: we first figure out what the ordinary concept of race is, and then see if, among other things, it contains semantically deferential elements. Of course, this route departs from HET: if the extent to which ordinary usage defers is decided partly by first figuring out the contours of its concepts, then we are not saying that it defers as a methodological starting point. On the other hand, the level of deference might be inferred from other, non-racial concepts or from global theories of meaning. This approach might not be impossible, but it doesn't seem very promising, given the potentially unique nature of racial semantics and the limited scope of broader theories of meaning. For example, the causal theory of reference, the scope of which is traditionally limited to most names and natural kind terms, has at best controversial application to race, whose potential status as a (purported) natural kind is far from settled and in part requires a prior, non-question-begging conceptual analysis. Thus the burden on proponents of HET is to discharge this difficult task.

Some proponents of HET have taken up this challenge, so we should examine existing defenses of HET. To do this, a bit of dialectical context is in order. The first thing to note here is that HET seems to have been presupposed by some without any explicit argument for, or even statement of, the premise. For just one example, in their watershed book, *Racial Formation in the United States*, sociologists Michael Omi and Howard Winant (1994) try to expose the nature of race-talk in a way that privileges expert and historical views on race (though, importantly, they also take note of popular movements, such that their methodology actually seems to be a hybrid of HET and a highly attenuated version of the experimental approach).

Second, within philosophy we have come to analyzing ordinary racial discourse only very recently. It wasn't really until 1996, when Appiah published his more developed view on race, that it was claimed in publication that in order to argue that race is not real because it purports to be a biological kind, one first had to argue that race purports to be a biological kind. That is, one needed to do some conceptual analysis, where, if Appiah is right, we will discover that racial terms (erroneously) purport to refer to something interesting about the biological world. It was this work, accordingly, that prompted the ensuing debate about racial semantics. As I track the literature, Taylor stands out as the most thorough critic of Appiah on the semantic front (though others find fault with Appiah's arguments on other fronts). But Taylor's *semantic* critique plays out within the confines of Appiah's *methodological* approach, according to which HET is the main rule of engagement: Taylor's response is that while Appiah can point to historical experts such as Jefferson, Herder, and Darwin as evidence that racial terms purport to have biological connotations, Taylor can call on other sources, such as Du Bois and Alain Locke, who use racial terms to refer to social kinds. In addition to this HET-presupposing discussion, Appiah's claims have also been put to use by others engaged in various projects in the philosophy of race, such as Robert Bernasconi (2001, 30) and Zack (2002).[3] In short, HET seems to have become *de rigueur* in large part because others either grant it to Appiah for the sake of argument or actually countenance Appiah's defense of it. So if we want to know why HET has been influential, at the very least we will have to look at Appiah's argument on its behalf.

After briefly surveying various ways to go about racial conceptual analysis, Appiah (1996, 32–42) settles on the view that, depending on your favorite theory of meaning, following HET is either required or strongly advised. As a first step, he holds that since "current ways of talking about race are the residue, the detritus, so to speak, of earlier ways of thinking about race," we ought to find the meanings of our racial terms by investigating how they have been used historically

(Appiah 1996, 38). Now the sociolinguistic observation here is no doubt true, but it is unclear why we should take the residual nature of our racial terms to motivate the thesis of historical deference. That fact that we've inherited our words doesn't entail that the definitions of, and uses for, those words have not changed, which is a point that Appiah himself seems to wield at times. Given that platitude, it seems that if we want to know what we mean by 'race,' we ought not put too much stock in potentially outdated historical thinking about race.

Appiah's second justification for historical deference is that he thinks it is required by the causal theory of reference, according to which, on his gloss,

> for $X$ to be the best candidate for the job of $Y$'s referent ... is for $X$ to be the thing that best causally explains [the community's] talk about $Y$s. So what we need to do, on this view, is explore the history of the way the word 'race' has been used and see if we can identify ... some objective phenomenon that people were responding to when they said what they said about 'races'.
>
> (Appiah 1996, 40)

Now we learned from Kripke and Putnam that, for many names and natural kind terms, if we want to identify the referent of term $T$, we ought to find out which superficial objects were 'baptized' as $T$s when the term was first used, and then the referent will be whatever the "underlying nature" of those original superficial objects ends up being.[4] Similarly, Appiah's reasoning seems to be that if we want to apply the causal-historical theory of reference to racial terms, we have to look for referents to those terms as historically used.

---

3   While Zack often focuses on the ordinary concept of race, she also holds that the ordinary concept of race is whatever the experts say race is. (See especially Zack (2002, 2–3; 2007, 117), where she appears to hold this because of certain armchair intuitions she has about the ordinary conception of race.) For Taylor's critique of Appiah on the semantic front that grants Appiah's methodology, see especially Taylor (2000, 122–125). See also Taylor (2004, 87–89), where while he still marshals non-biologically oriented historical experts such as Du Bois to criticize Appiah (and elsewhere (e.g., p. 55) suggests that the government can be a "codifier" of common sense), he also explicitly notes that he is primarily interested in ordinary thinking about race. I should note, then, that in various places throughout (Taylor 2004), he seems to recognize some of the limitations of HET to which I am calling attention. Finally, Sundstrom (2002b, 198) also critiques Appiah's semantic theory, but on the grounds that Appiah is wrongly using a theory of reference designed for natural kind terms to draw conclusions about race, which (for Sundstrom) should not be thought of as a natural kind.

4   The phrase "underlying nature" is Putnam's (1975b).

I don't want to argue against the causal-historical theory of reference. Instead, I want to make three points that suggest we should not go back to the first time racial terms were used. To be clear, what I say below is meant to at least be consistent with the idea that we might identify the referents of racial terms by finding the underlying natures of the superficial objects that we identify racially, if any such underlying natures exist. What my view is inconsistent with is the claim that the referents of racial terms are the underlying natures of the objects that were identified racially back when racial terms first got a foothold in public discourse, rather than the objects that are currently identified racially.

It is worth observing first that even Appiah doesn't really privilege the original uses of racial terms. On his analysis of racial concepts, he is quite willing to trace the *evolution* of racial terms' meanings (Appiah 1996, 42–67), which means that on his own historical analysis he's not sticking to the meanings of racial terms as they were first used. Furthermore, he uses a double-dose of expert deference that is alien to the standard causal-historical theory of reference. That is, Appiah does follow Kripke and Putnam in holding that for many terms we should use today's experts to tell us about the underlying nature of the things whose names were set in an historical 'naming ceremony.' But he goes beyond this in also claiming that the naming rights are held not by those who first used racial terms, but by the historical experts (such as Jefferson or Herder) and that the ceremonies where they claimed these rights were, in essence, the publications where they discuss race.

A second, and related, point is that if we were to adopt the originalist element of HET, we would need to know which superficial objects were originally baptized with which racial terms in order to let (today's) scientists determine what, if anything, are the underlying natures of those superficial objects. Of course, we simply don't have a good list of which racial terms were originally given to which human bodies in the initial 'naming ceremony.' Perhaps the closest we can get is the first recorded *theory* of race. In one respect, this might appear to provide a rationale for expert deference, but Appiah himself doesn't suggest it, and in any case there are mismatch problems with this approach. According to Bernasconi's (2001) plausible line of argument, the first true "concept of race"—where this roughly means the first time we got a tightly used, consistent, and coherent (if ultimately bankrupt) theory of race—comes from Kant. But Kant's work on race is so implausible to contemporary eyes that one response to reading it—a response that is both reasonable and common (at least as measured by reactions I have heard from colleagues and students)—is, 'Well, surely that's not what *we* mean by "race."' This semantic alienation from Kant's understanding of race means that if the causal theory of reference is right, then somewhere along the way we must have had new, revising naming ceremonies for racial terms, such that they now refer to different things than they used to. In which case, the originalist component of HET is inappropriate with respect to racial terms.[5]

One might dig in one's heels on this count and claim that since we inherited our racial terms from Kant's linguistic community, then while perhaps our *theory* (or *conception*, rather than *concept*) of race is obviously different from Kant's, our racial terms still pick out the same paradigmatic, superficial objects that Kant's were meant to pick out. But whether our racial terms still pick out the same paradigmatic, superficial objects that Kant's terms picked out is, to opponents of HET, the question at issue. According to opponents of HET, we need to know what *we* mean by 'race,' and of particular relevance at the moment is that we need to know what our ostensive definition of race is, and we cannot satisfy that desideratum by simply assuming that our definition matches Kant's definition. As it happens, there are actually some good reasons to think that there might be a mismatch here. To choose just one example, if contemporary folk racial discourse purports to pick out Latino/as as a race, this would not match Kant's set of races, as he did not classify Latino/as as a race. Of course, it might be the case that contemporary folk discourse does not actually recognize Latino/as as a race ... *but this is the whole question*, and an answer to it cannot be determined until we independently identify the contemporary folk concept of race. And, to bring it all home, the very *possibility* of this mismatch presupposes that our concept of race cannot be *simply* identified with Kant's concept of race. That is, positing the transhistorical identity of racial terms' references as a presumptive methodological *starting* point, rather than as the substantive outcome of analyzing contemporary folk racial concepts and conceptions, is unwarranted.

The point, again, is that we want to know what our racial terms mean, and if this is the goal, then given that the term 'race' might be directed at a different kind of thing today than it was centuries ago, we ought to look at how we use our racial terms. Kant's or Du Bois' understandings of race are interesting moments in the history of ideas, but the race debate isn't about that history. It's about what we should do with *our* racial terms.

5   Sort of. To be more precise, the historical component might still be right; it's just that we would have to start with a more recent moment in history, namely that moment at which *newer, revising* naming ceremonies took place, rather than the moment of the original naming ceremonies, perhaps like Kripke's (1972, 163) "Madagascar" example (attributed to Gareth Evans). Presumably the best evidence for which objects are baptized with *our* terms is *our* referential intentions. For a similar criticism of Appiah, and other points similar to some of those made here, see Don Loeb's review of the Tanner Lectures from which Appiah (1996) was spawned (Loeb 2001, 174).

So much for historical deference; what about expert deference? Here Appiah (1996, 41) explicitly states that he doesn't want to "look at the words of more ordinary people." His justification for this anti-folk approach is that during the nineteenth century, racial terms came to be thought of as scientific terms, and given Putnam's division of linguistic labor, ordinary people would have taken the definitions to be something to be worked out by scientists, rather than by ordinary people themselves.

I have three concerns about this. First, Appiah's evidence that 'race' came to be thought of as a scientific term of art, rather than a popular term, in the nineteenth century is that this is how the *experts* saw it. But we wanted to know how ordinary people conceive of race, and in particular whether they defer to the experts, and the fact that the experts anointed their own scientific expertise authoritative doesn't answer that question. Second, as argued above, the race debate is not about how folks (ordinary or not) in the nineteenth century used racial discourse; it is about how we publicly use racial discourse today. So the crucial question would be whether *we* think that racial terms are scientific, and any deferential attitudes from the nineteenth century cannot without further argument ratify an analysis of what we mean by 'race.' Third, even if ordinary folk in the nineteenth century thought that the inner workings of race were something to be studied by scientists, surely they thought that they had a good superficial idea of what races were, such that the scientists' task was to identify the underlying natures of the different superficial objects that ordinary folk assigned different racial terms to. Consider an analogy. Scientists tell us that the referent of 'water' is $H_2O$, but only on the condition that $H_2O$ is the chemical composition of the superficial stuff that ordinary people identify as 'water.' If $H_2O$ were instead the chemical composition of the superficial stuff that we call 'salt,' and if scientists nevertheless insisted 'Water is $H_2O$,' we simply would not assent to this scientific definition of 'water.' We'd say that the scientists missed their target, because they have been analyzing the stuff we call 'salt,' not the stuff we call 'water.'

The general point here is that while scientists have authority to determine the referents of scientifically relevant terms (and it is plausible to think that they have this semantic authority only because the broader linguistic community confers it upon them), we accept their analysis of term $T$ only on the condition that the superficial stuff they analyze under the label '$T$' matches the superficial stuff we call '$T$.' This is a standard part of the causal theory of reference: for folk terms, it is the *folk's* referential intentions that determine the superficial referent, and only then do experts tell us its micro-level nature.

One exception to this rule is, then, the term of art. In the case just given, we might say that $H_2O$ was the referent for the scientists' *specialist* word, 'water,' in the way that they have a specialist sense of 'force field' that does not match the sense of 'force field' as it is understood by the casual *Star Trek* fan, as some sort of invisible shield. So I am not denying that terms of art are under the exclusive domain of science; but I am suggesting that 'race,' as a term for superficial objects that is the topic of the race debate, is a popular term, not a term of art. So in order to know whether there is any scientific referent for race, in the relevant sense of 'race,' we still have to first know which superficial properties ordinary folk identify as racial. This, it should be noted, is consistent with the causal theory of reference.

Appiah (1996, 42) offers one final argument for expert deference: if you want to use folk theory, "you should probably offer some criteria—vague or strict—for applying the term ['race']. This is because ... the arguments against the use of 'race' as a scientific term suggest that most ordinary ways of thinking about races are incoherent." I should confess that I'm not sure whether this is truly meant to be an *argument* against the folk approach. If the challenge is to offer some criteria for applying racial terms, then such criteria, if they exist, will be teased out of the contours of folk discourse. Perhaps, alternatively, Appiah means to emphasize that since the scientific concept of race fails for the same reasons that the folk concept will fail, it won't matter whether we use HET or the folk approach. Maybe that failure will be realized, but this cannot work as an argument against the folk approach: even if the folk concept of race is incoherent, this doesn't mean that ordinary usage shouldn't guide our analyses of racial concepts. It just means that folk racial discourse is incoherent. Again, consider an analogy: just because ordinary thought about witchcraft proved to be inconsistent with various pieces of knowledge, this doesn't mean that 'witch' was somehow a scientific term of art rather than a folk term. So it seems that we ought to identify the folk theory of race, and only then should we decide whether or not it is incoherent.[6]

In short, it seems that we've not been given a satisfactory argument for the historical-expert approach. Now I should stress what I said above, namely that there are questions, other than the ones we're asking, for which a close examination of historical and expert racial discourse is entirely appropriate. In addition to terms of art, one obvious case is when we want to analyze a particular thinker's or movement's conception of race. Many people, quite independently of the race debate, are curious to know what Du Bois thought about race, or what Kant thought about race, or what the Republican Party of the 1980s thought about race. Others want to see how these lines of thought have

---

6   Moreover, it is unclear whether if the folk concept of race turns out to be incoherent, it will be incoherent in the same way as Appiah's HET-derived concept of race. Given his attachment to HET, Appiah himself doesn't say much about what kind of analysis the folk approach would generate, so it's hard to know why it is supposed to be as incoherent as the HET-generated concept of race.

evolved and to sketch a broader narrative about racial thinking that spans different eras and perhaps different concepts of race. For such questions, it is obviously necessary to go to the source.[7] Another, related exception is when we must use experts to analyze the way in which race was historically conceived of by a particular lay community. For the most part, we don't have the resources to investigate past folk theories of race, since we cannot talk to past users of racial terms and there simply isn't much folk data, and so the best we can do is to investigate the expert conception of race at that time. (One case where this might not be true is if we have a public, recorded forum where race is discussed, such as in letters to the editors of various newspapers. But even then there may be reasons to avoid drawing very conclusive lessons about past folk theories of race, given the need for a sufficiently large and representative sample.) Yet another exception is when we want to know what the *best expert theory* says about dividing human populations. For example, if scientists have replaced talk about race with talk about populations, this might inform our understanding of race. But, again, the best expert concept(ion) is not *necessarily* the same as the folk concept(ion).

So there are some purposes for which the investigation of historical and expert race-thinking makes sense. But the historical-expert approach has been used not only to analyze a figure's conception of race or the conception of race at a particular historical moment, but also to tell us what *we* mean by 'race,' in arguments about the ontological and normative status of race as discussed in the contemporary public sphere. Now even here, there may be some use to considering history. One of the little ironies of this chapter is that Appiah (2008a, 2008b) has very recently expressed some sympathy for the idea that philosophers should adopt something in the neighborhood of the experimental approach I am defending. These sympathies have not, so far as I know, led him to revisit his earlier enthusiasm for HET in the race debate, but in any event he is surely correct to observe that by seeing how discourse has evolved, we might gain some insights into how we ordinarily deploy our terms today. Our contemporary racial discourse is, as he put it, the detritus of past usage, and, furthermore, certain social facts about the groups we identify as races, such as facts about disparities in access to housing, income, and health care, are in large part the legacy of a history of racism. It is important to emphasize, then, that the folk approach does not imply that we should ignore the history of racial discourse and practice. However, even then we

---

7    In this way, Bernasconi's (2001) "Who invented the concept of race?" may be an example of how one might focus on historical usage in a kosher manner, as he is looking for the historically first robust theory of race, i.e., the first expert conception of race, rather than a contemporary or lay conception.

can only be justified in recognizing historical racial discourse as the predecessor to our racial discourse because we have an independent grip on our racial discourse. And when the nature of that latter discourse and the firmness of that grip are in question, I've argued, the historical-expert approach is not going to be very helpful. Since that is the question—since what we mean by 'race' is the relevant conceptual question for a debate about whether we should be eliminating or conserving our racial discourse—we ought to adopt the folk approach in the current context.

## 3.3 Some Potential Objections to the Folk Approach

The folk approach (whether pursued in the field or the armchair) holds that contemporary folk discourse fixes the meanings of racial terms for the race debate. One might think that this kind of methodology is flawed in at least four respects. First, one might worry about the anti-expert nature of the folk approach. After all, we should listen to what biologists, physical anthropologists, and others who have dedicated their work to questions about race have to say about the topic. Surely biologists can inform us about whether race is real, for instance.

At the same time, however, in listening to the experts we need to be sure that we are still talking about race. If we end up talking about non-racial populations, we will actually be *mis*informed about whether races have biological referents, because we'll think that we are talking about race, when we are in fact talking about something else. Thus, before we apply, say, biologists' theories about human groupings to discussions about race, we ought to bring to the table a solid understanding of what we're asking about when we wonder whether races have any biological referents. And this means that we need to protect our discussions by independently analyzing what *we* mean when using our racial terms.

Of course, what we mean can often be informed by what science tells us, but a point made above is relevant here: we accept the scientifically identified underlying referent of ordinary language term $T$ only if the gross physical stuff that scientists call '$T$' overlaps with what we call '$T$.' Scientists sometimes find the underlying referent, but the folk determine what they're finding the referent of. That is, aside from terms of art, scientists do not normally tell us to revise which medium-sized objects we pick out with which ordinary language terms. Instead, they tell us to think differently about the *underlying* properties that are associated with medium-sized objects (which differences do occasionally require us to reclassify borderline cases). And as Putnam (1975b, 240–241) points out, natural kind terms do not have to have an underlying structure to have a reference; for some words, such as diseases that only name a cluster of symptoms, there are *only* superficial characteristics. In addition, the folk approach allows that folk racial terms might actually purport to refer to social kinds that exist outside of the domain of the biological sciences. Those possibilities will be explored below; all that is being advocated at the moment is that the referents of racial terms will depend in part on folk usage.

Two more points should be stated explicitly. First, the kind of conceptual analysis defended here does not deny that changes in the world or new discoveries of empirical fact—at either the microscopic or macroscopic level—might necessitate a change in how we think about the meanings of our terms. The folk approach is not inconsistent with Putnam's (1975a) intuitions that scientific discoveries and theoretical developments might reveal our ignorance and mistaken judgments about the nature of the referents of many of our terms, and that changes in empirical fact—such as lemons changing from yellow to blue—might also cause us to revise our existing definition formulations (and, given extreme enough changes, a change in meaning itself (Putnam 1975a, 148)). So all that I want to claim is that what is being revealed in such acts of revision is that we are changing our understanding of *our* terms' meanings, rather than the meanings of scientists' specialist terms. Second, non-folk concepts may be independently interesting, so we may want the conceptual resources to talk about both, such as when scientists tell us that while we ordinary folk normally think of 'liquid' as referring to the property of flowing, science instead understands 'liquid' in terms of crystalline structures that allow glass to count as a liquid. The point urged here is merely that we'd be equivocating if we switched between scientific and ordinary senses of our terms in the middle of the race debate without somehow marking this switch.[8]

This clears the way for responding to a third foreseeable objection to the folk approach, about conservatism: one might worry that if folk usage determines the meanings of racial terms, then we cannot improve (or otherwise change) racial discourse. We'd seem to be stuck with whatever folk usage says, no matter how corrupt, or racist, or confused it might be.

Of course, this would also be a problem for the history-trapped HET, but in any event I don't think it's much of a problem for the folk approach (cf. Jackson 1998a, 44–47). For a concrete illustration, consider being mixed race. For much of the nineteenth and twentieth centuries, in most parts of the U.S., being mixed race was not an option

---

8   For more discussion of how to conceive of differences between scientific and folk understanding with respect to the case of 'liquid' (couched within a broader defense of descriptivism), see Jackson (1998b, 215). As Jackson elsewhere (2001, 661) puts the present point, "we need to *start* with the folk theory because it is the folk concept that is under discussion. But this is compatible with our concluding that some other concept is the really interesting one."

with respect to blackness and whiteness. This was most famously codified in the 'one-drop' rule, which holds that if a person has even one black ancestor (or, put more problematically, one 'drop' of 'black blood'), then that person is black. Today, however, many recognize the category of mixed race, as we will see in the next chapter.

The folk approach can make sense of this development. To (over)simplify, focus on two folk theories of race: that of the U.S. in 1909, which (often) denied the possibility of being mixed race with respect to blackness and whiteness, and that of the U.S. in 2009, which (often) accepts mixed-race identity with respect to blackness and whiteness. The folk approach, according to which the relevant meanings of racial terms are constrained by folk discourse, does not entail that because 1909 folk usage denied the existence of mixed race, we are forever stuck with that usage, such that those using folk racial discourse in 2009 are somehow confused when they describe some people as 'mixed race.' This would be to overestimate the fixing power of history with respect to racial terms. Rather, the folk approach simply says that our conception of race *changed* once we realized we had made a mistake.[9] And, just like we weren't stuck with the 1909 conception of race, we might want to change the meaning of 'race' in the future. (On that front, hang tight. In Chapter 7 I argue that such changes are warranted.) So the key thing isn't to write the folk concept and conception of race in stone. Rather, it is to identify what they are, so that we know what we're eliminating or conserving, or so that we know when we're changing the subject, or so that we know when we're even staying on the same subject but attempting to make widespread changes to our folk usage.

The final objection is that it is useless to rely on the ordinary concept(ion) of race, because there is no *single* ordinary concept(ion) of race. Some people are internally confused about race, different communities appear to work with different concept(ion)s of race, and so forth. In this respect, I have simplistically proceeded here as if there is a unified ordinary concept and conception of race, and that presumption is no better than a mere simplifying device (as we will see in the next chapter). Yet it would be too quick to think that the multiplicity of folk racial conceptions or concepts, even potentially inconsistent ones,

---

9    As Putnam (1975b, 256) puts it:

> Communication presupposes that I have a stereotype of tigers which includes stripes, and that you have a stereotype of tigers which includes stripes.... But it does not presuppose that any particular stereotype be *correct*, or that the majority of our stereotypes remain correct forever. Linguistic obligatoriness is not supposed to be an index of unrevisability or even of truth; thus we can hold that 'tigers are striped' is part of the meaning of 'tiger' without being trapped in the problems of analyticity.

undermines the folk approach to racial conceptual analysis. For, first, even HET's partisans must confront this problem, as illustrated by the debate between Appiah and Taylor over which of various incompatible historical expert theories we should privilege when following HET. Second, the fact that there are different *conceptions* of race does not entail that there is multiplicity at the basic, fundamental level of the ordinary *concept* of race, where there is arguably much shared common ground.[10] Third, and most decisively, the folk approach can accommodate any remaining multiplicity on the level of concepts in several ways. To the extent that different concepts of race are tied to different communities, that "race does not travel" (Root 2000, S631–S632), we might make the concept of race irreducibly local.[11] To the degree that there is internal conceptual disharmony within a linguistic community, that community's incoherent concept of race would mean that there are no races. Or maybe the ordinary term 'race' is simply riddled with ambiguity. Obviously, much here will hang on where a linguistic community's border is drawn and what kind of linguistic dominance a particular definition needs within a community to be *the* representative definition, and while I will have a few things to say about these questions in the next chapter, sorting these things out decisively is a task that exceeds my grasp. What is clear, though, is that the folk approach is flexible enough to make sense of folk racial conceptual apparatuses. The folk approach to racial conceptual analysis does not guarantee that there will be one unified folk conception of race, or that the folk concept of race will be coherent, or that it will have a referent. It simply guarantees that the resultant racial concept(s) and conception(s) will be the ones relevant for the race debate.

## 3.4  Which Folk?

The remaining question, then, is what the folk approach actually requires us to do by way of conceptual analysis. We want to know what the contemporary folk concept and conception of race are, but this leaves open how we should go about identifying that concept and conception. On this question, we can choose between two possible methods, both of which appeal to ordinary intuitions as the main data that will inform the analysis. As noted above, the method I advocate follows the growing movement to analyze concepts by doing empirical studies. As Jackson (1998a, 36–37) puts it:

> I am sometimes asked—in a tone that suggests that the question is a major objection—why, if conceptual analysis is concerned to eluci-

10  As argued in the previous chapter, and again see Hardimon (2003).
11  For further discussion of race's apparent non-traveling nature, see also Glasgow (2007); Mallon (2004).

date what governs our classificatory practice, don't I advocate doing serious opinion polls on people's responses to various cases? My answer is that I do—when it is necessary.

The alternative, the armchair method, is the main methodological approach followed by those in the philosophy of race who do not adhere to HET.[12] According to this approach, all that conceptual analysts need to do is reflect on their own intuitions about three things: the purported intensions of our racial terms (theoretical intuitions), the groups the analysts think are properly categorized as racial groups (categorical intuitions), and their ways of racially classifying individuals (possible case intuitions).[13] The armchair method, then, is to identify one's intuitions on these three fronts and make the generalizing claim that one's own intuitions represent the views of most everyone else, or at least the views most everyone else would have if they were to engage in sustained, critical, and informed reflection on the matter.

But while the armchair method might work for some questions, it is not conclusive for analyzing racial concepts. In addition to a growing body of empirical evidence suggesting that we should always be distrustful of universalizing armchair intuitions,[14] there are two well-worn reasons to worry that the professional conceptual analysts who purport to codify folk theory do not constitute a representative sample of the population. First, insofar as one's background might influence one's intuitions about race, the demographic makeup of academics should give us pause about whether we can adequately represent the broader public's thinking about race. Second, there is the old concern that philosophers' intuitions are distorted by too much philosophizing, to the point that they do not represent what the 'average person' would say. In

12  The armchair approach is utilized either wholly or in part by Hardimon (2003), Linda Martín Alcoff (2006), J. Angelo Corlett (2003), and Lawrence Blum (2002). Some, such as Blum (who devotes an entire chapter to history), take history into account in coming up with their analyses, but their ultimate verdicts on what race is often seem to be grounded in armchair reflection alone. I too have (hastily) worked within the armchair approach in Glasgow (2003, 2006). Some of the kinds of problems for it that I will discuss are also evoked in Haslanger (2005).

13  I will continue to use the language of 'possible cases,' but of course I include here actual cases as well.

14  For evidence that intuitions about reference vary from culture to culture, see Machery, Mallon, Nichols, & Stich (2004). For similar results with respect to intuitions about epistemic concepts, see Weinberg, Nichols, & Stich (2001). For more widespread considerations that societal and cultural differences can affect our metaphysical and epistemic intuitions, as well as our cognitive processes, see the psychological review presented in Nisbett, Peng, Choi, & Norenzayan (2001). See Stich & Weinberg (2001) for greater detail on some of the problems with the armchair method. (See also Jackson (2001) for clarification that he agrees that the armchair is not decisive.)

short, data from one person, especially professional philosophers, are never as rich and reliable as data from many and diverse people. We've been correct to think that we should be analyzing concepts, but thinking that we are each adequate sources of the data to be analyzed exhibits a certain regrettable methodological solipsism. So, with the possible exception of very thin intuitions about race, I think we should leave the armchair once in a while.

In this spirit, the experimental approach joins philosophers with social scientists to explore the nature of ordinary racial discourse. We'll actually go into the field to examine how ordinary people think about race and use racial discourse, in order to generate raw data for conceptual analysis. The participants will be asked questions about racial classification and meaning, and the results will be compiled and analyzed into the folk concept and conception of race.

Thus I maintain not only that what we think about our terms' referents may be altered on the basis of empirical change or scientific discovery, but also that it's still appropriate to call conceptual analysis 'conceptual analysis' when it recruits data on discourse usage gathered in an empirical, *a posteriori* manner. Some seem to disagree, on the presupposition that conceptual analysis is essentially a priori: "philosophy should eschew the goal of providing 'conceptual analyses', and should give up the idea that its own methodology is aprioristic" (Graham and Horgan 1994, 228—Graham and Horgan thus favor what philosophers call an anti-apriori kind of 'ideology'). For my part, even when what we're doing is empirically informed, it still seems as though we're analyzing concepts. Similarly, some portray experimental philosophy's privileging of social scientific data as anathema to the use of 'intuitions' in philosophy. As I see it, it's not that we must choose between intuitions and data, but that we must choose between using some analysts' intuitions and a more 'democratic' selection of intuitions *as* the data to be used in our analyses.

Beyond this, it only remains to urge that we identify all three of our possible case intuitions, theoretical intuitions, *and* categorical intuitions. We need more than merely theoretical intuitions, because, as Stephen Stich and Jonathan Wienberg (2001) report, recent work in cognitive science shows that often our classifications of individuals are not guided by some *theory*; we are often guided by exemplars of other items in the category. Thus we must look at intuitions about possible cases as a way of identifying how we think about race, or would think about race if we were to reflect on how we classify concrete individuals.

Many advocates of the folk approach seem content, at least with respect to the conceptual domains that interest them, to make possible case intuitions the final court of appeal. Jackson (1998a), for example, privileges possible cases in determining the meanings of terms, and Machery and colleagues (2004) seem to give special priority to possible case intuitions in trying to determine how we think about reference.[15] But, it seems evident that with racial terms, as with some other kinds of terms, we try to reach reflective equilibrium between our theoretical, categorical, and possible case intuitions. For example, intuitions about possible cases affect and are taken to warrant modifications to our theories (such as when perspicuous mixed-race identities push us to eliminate the (one-drop) rule that having one black ancestor is sufficient to determine one's racial identity as black). By the same token, though, our theoretical intuitions sometimes affect our possible case intuitions ('Of course Steve Martin's character in *The Jerk* can't *really* be black; after all, at the very least if your biological parents are white, then you are white'). Finally, our categorical intuitions often affect and are affected by both possible case intuitions and theoretical intuitions ('Can Latinos/as count as a race—as distinguished from an ethnic group—if their phenotypic features are shared with members of all other races; or, does the very classification of groups like that as races mean that racial classifications involve more than phenotype alone?').

All three kinds of intuitions are thus relevant to determining the shape of our racial concepts. This may be different with other terms, such as 'knowledge.' Limiting our intuition-based data about 'knowledge' to possible case intuitions (such as intuitions about Gettier cases) might be warranted because we've got a pre-existing grip on our theoretical and categorical intuitions about knowledge. In any case, with 'race' it seems clear that we don't have a very firm grip—we make, as we will see, radically conflicting possible case, theoretical, and categorical judgments about race. In these domains, attending to the way in which race figures in our practices, institutions, and norms should be rich sources of conceptual data, as Haslanger (2005) points out.

The virtues of the experimental approach mean that we need a research program according to which we empirically identify, sort, and analyze our many intuitions about race. If we do this, we can be confident that we'll be analyzing racial discourse in a way that really captures ordinary usage. Adopting the experimental approach, then, will generate analyses that are properly applicable to the race debate's ultimate question of whether we should eliminate or conserve public racial discourse and practice.

In the next chapter, I engage this kind of approach by examining some empirical data about ordinary ways of thinking about race. Before getting to those data, however, I need to manage expectations a little by noting up front that the data we do have are frustratingly incomplete.

---

15  Though Jackson does privilege possible case intuitions (at one point he calls them the "bread and butter of conceptual analysis" (p. 56)), he also grants that in some cases "before we know what the best theory says ... we have no paradigm cases for the term" (p. 35).

We will see some psychological studies that have probed the nature of race-thinking, but as the book moves forward we will run into parts of the race debate for which the relevant empirical studies simply have not yet, to my knowledge, been completed. When we come to those points, I will have to call on *some* data, and so I will mostly fall back on the philosopher's favorite, armchair judgments about possible cases, that is, thought experiments.[16]

With respect to this fallback maneuver, the arguments put forth in this chapter mean three things. First, although armchair reflection may be the best we can do when we have no other data, it does not generate data that is robust enough to be the *final* court of appeal. Second, however, as Graham and Horgan (1994, 223) suggest, even armchair analysis generates *some* relevant data, such that "thought experiments really *are* experiments." So while the sad-sack solipsism of armchair data is wanting, it is nonetheless *one* piece of information we can use in identifying the boundaries of the concept of race. Finally, what this again means is that such data are sometimes best conceived of not as *diagnostic*, but as *predictive*. When I rendered a judgment on the various ways to think about the Twin Earth Thought experiments entertained in Chapter 2, my judgments are most conservatively construed not as decisively reliable diagnoses of how everyone else in my linguistic community would judge those cases, but as my best attempt at predicting how they would judge those cases from informed and reflective positions. And predictions, of course, can turn out to be false. In this spirit, then, while gaps in the experimental data must be plugged by armchair reflection, the plugs I propose below are tentative, and the ultimate verdict may be that they fail to keep the water out. If my intuitions turn out to be idiosyncratic, then so much the worse for the arguments that they purport to support. And in that spirit, it would be inappropriate to ask the reader to do anything other than consult her own intuitions about those cases and see if my own judgments seem strange.

Of course, we can all hope that experimental research on those as-yet unstudied possible cases will be completed some day. In the meantime, since our own judgments are the most we can go on when the data run out, we, all of us concerned with the race debate, must proceed on that basis surely, if provisionally. But before we get to any more armchair reflections, we are now well positioned to see at least *some* of what the folk actually do say. And that, in turn, will position us to finally address the question of whether 'race'—in the ordinary sense—refers to anything real, and whether racial discourse should be conserved, eliminated, or, as I will ultimately argue, reconstructed.

16  These data should not be thought to be the *only* data we might use. As Naomi Zack pointed out to me, we could also use media analysis, for example.

# 4 The Contours of Racial Discourse

## 4.1 Racial Thinking, Conceptual Analysis, and the Debate

Imagine that placed before you are drawings of two adult humans, one who by all appearances is white and one who by all appearances is black. One is a man and one is a woman (it doesn't matter which). After examining these sketches, you are asked to say what race their child would be, were they to have one.

So many commentators have issued statements about how we ordinarily think about race that it is utterly astonishing that questions like this were only first asked in controlled empirical research settings in the 1990s (Hirschfeld 1996). Studies based on these kinds of questions can provide a rich set of data about how ordinary racial discourse and thought operate, and so in this chapter I want to examine some such experimental data.[1] One claim for which I want to argue is that the data are consistent with the armchair analysis presented in Chapter 2, that race at least partly purports to be centered on visible traits. Care must be taken in making this point, though, for we will also see a substantial strain in the empirical literature showing that individual racial identities are sometimes thought to be sensitive to social pressures. Recall why this is relevant: in order to know whether race is real, we're going to have to sort out whether, and in what ways, race purports to be biological, social, or (somehow) both. Moreover, certain strains of race-thinking are more decidedly unjustifiable than others; if those unjustifiable elements are non-negotiable constituents of the concept RACE, then race's illusory status will be locked into its definition. So we need to see

---

1   The phrase 'experimental data' is not entirely appropriate when used in this way to refer to data gathered in a manner consistent with the norms and practices of the social sciences, which social scientists would no doubt be quick to point out is broader than what they normally consider experimental research. Despite this shortcoming, however, 'experimental philosophy' has become the label for philosophy that attends to data gathered in a manner consistent with the practices and norms of the social sciences.

not only whether race purports to be biological or social, but also the ways in which it is supposed to be biological or social.

Before getting to the data that can help us untangle these knots, a preliminary issue must be dispatched: why should we care how we think about race? Even *granting* the last chapter's main thesis, that if we want to know how we think about race we should consult empirical studies rather than relying solely on historical experts or armchair intuitions, why does how anyone *thinks* about race matter? What matters for the race debate, according to this objection, is finding out whether 'race' refers to anything real, and for that we need to identify the concept of race, but to do those things we don't need to spend much time looking at how we think about race. After all, we didn't say that there was no earth just because everyone thought the earth was flat, and we don't say that race is illusory just because many people used to think that the races could be hierarchically ranked in terms of native intelligence or moral status. In a word, we can be *wrong* about what race is. We can be very wrong. So maybe we should just leave thinking about race behind before departing the station.

Lurking in the critical neighborhood here is Mallon's caution (discussed in Chapter 1) that if we rely, whether explicitly or tacitly, on a controversial theory of reference, we'll end up with a more controversial theory of race than we want. This threat looms presently to the extent that if we rely on ordinary thinking about race, we might unwittingly commit ourselves to a controversial theory of reference. If, in particular, we commit ourselves to a descriptivist theory of reference, according to which the referent of 'race' is whatever satisfies (if anything satisfies) the description of race that we would ordinarily give— or, more accurately, the best description that can be teased out of data on ordinary race-thinking—we'll incur the displeasure of fans of nondescriptivist theories of reference, such as one that holds that 'race' just refers to the things we talk about when we use words like 'race,' even if it turns out that those things fail to satisfy the description we ordinarily associate with race. Consider, by way of analogy, 'atom.' Atoms used to be uniformly thought of as indivisible particles, so if we took a simple descriptivist approach to the reference of 'atom,' we might have been tempted to say that all and only indivisible particles are atoms. However, after our science made some progress, we learned that the things we were calling 'atoms' were actually divisible. In light of this inconsistency, we, or scientists anyway, faced something of a linguistic crossroads: does 'atom' refer to indivisible particles, or to those divisible things we'd been calling 'atoms'? The weight of history points us down the second road: we call those divisible things 'atoms' and acknowledge that we were wrong to think that there were no subatomic particles— that is, indivisibility is not a conceptually non-negotiable element of ATOM, despite our nearly univocal belief to the contrary.

Cases like this are sometimes taken to lend credibility to non-descriptivist theories of reference.[2] Thus there is a significant, and significantly complex, controversy here, occupation with which threatens to stall our main project of attending to race. However, recall that Mallon's caution can be heeded if the referent of the term in question is fixed independently of the correct theory of reference. (Even those who are mistaken about the correct theory of reference, whomever they may be, can know who 'Al Gore' refers to.) And non-negotiable truths—truths exposing core components of our concepts—may, in principle, be stated without recourse to a controversial theory of reference.

So the proper and relevant scope of consulting data about how we ordinarily think about race is this: data are just data. From empirical or armchair data we can draw inferences about the content of our racial concepts. These inferences are, like all inferences, fallible; our data can be suggestive without being decisive; and we can be thoroughly and seriously mistaken about the meaning of 'race,' just as we were about 'atom.' But, whether or not you're a descriptivist, you should agree that linguistic practices constrain both meaning and reference. For descriptivism, we'll look to what we say about race in order to come up with a description that can be semantically tethered to 'race.' And for non-descriptivism and its frequent companion semantic externalism, according to which the references of many names and natural kind terms are partly settled by the world rather than entirely by what we think (such as 'atom' turning out to refer to a divisible particle), the part of the world that's relevant is determined by our linguistic practices. Even according to non-descriptivist views, 'atom' refers to a certain kind of divisible particle only because we use 'atom' to talk about that kind of particle. The upshot is that these disputes in the philosophy of language don't impinge on the fundamentally intuitive point that if you want to know what a term means, or to what it refers, you need to know how we use the term. We might be mistaken in our statements that purport to give a definition or fix the referent of the term in question—a possibility that will require significant attention below—but the only evidence that we're mistaken is that those statements are, when considered in conjunction with the way the world is, inconsistent with some *other* element of our linguistic practice. The reason we were mistaken to say that 'atom' referred to indivisible particles is that we were also using 'atom' to refer to things that, as it turned out, were divisible.

Thus, if use constrains meaning and reference in this way, then when identifying the meaning or referent of 'race,' we need to identify how

2   While descriptivism sometimes takes a bad rap in cases like these (and similar cases are sometimes used to motivate an anti-descriptivist approach to ethnic terms (Nuccetelli 2001, 2004)), see, for example, Jackson (1998b) for a compelling argument that descriptivism can handle many such cases.

we use 'race' (and related terms). The previous chapter aimed to establish that we can best find out how we use racial terms by consulting experimental data. Those data will then be used to generate inferences about the content of the concept of race. As with all inferences, these are capable of generating false conclusions. But they are not wrong simply for being made. Whether or not they succeed will hang on the substance of the inferences themselves. We can be mistaken about what is non-negotiable, and while the data will unquestionably tell us about the ordinary *conception*, or folk *theory*, of race, the extent to which they tell us about the *concept* of race or the *meaning* of 'race' is a more delicate matter, since multiple conceptions of race can fall under any single concept of race. But we can get back to that later, after having had a look at some data.

## 4.2 Some Data

There are several respects in which race might ordinarily be thought about in (what we doing theory can label) biological ways. At the 'thicker' end of the spectrum, biological race-thinking might include the essences posited by what Taylor (2000, 2004) calls 'classical racialism,' that is, heritable clusters of phenotypic, intellectual, moral, cultural, and aesthetic properties or capacities. Alternatively, it might just be committed to thinner essences, including heritable and unchangeable clusters of simply phenotypic and genotypic traits. Or our visible traits might gain some purchase on biological race-thinking in non-essentialist ways (Strevens 2000). Biological race-thinking might also include thicker and thinner notions of ancestry, from the one-drop rule to a more general rule that one always has the same race as one's ancestors (with some qualification(s) to be included about how to classify people with ancestors from different races). This is as good a place to start as any.

### 4.2.1 Ancestral Race-Thinking

In an obvious sense, we normally insist that one has the same race as one's parents, but for our purposes we need to ask the slightly different question of whether it is *possible* to have a different race than one's ancestors. We also need to know if, as the one-drop rule suggests, we conceptually tether race more tightly to one set of ancestors than to another. Smedley and Smedley contend that we do: "North Americans *define* as Black anyone who has known African ancestors, a phenomenon known ... as the 'one-drop rule'.... There is no socially sanctioned in-between classification, even though the last census of 2000 permitted individuals to identify two or more racial ancestries" (2005, 20, emphasis added). Though this rule presents a very narrowly circumscribed understanding of race, many hold that the one-drop rule is, if not part of the *definition* of 'black' (or contained in the concept BLACK) at least very *common*, in the United States (for a representative sample, see Boxill 2001; Fish 2002; Gil-White 2001b; Gracia 2007b, 3; Hirschfeld 1996, 1998; Omi & Winant 1994; Sundstrom 2001; Zack 1993; 2002, 74). However, the data compel us to paint a more complicated picture.

## The One-Drop Rule

This chapter opened with a snapshot of Lawrence A. Hirschfeld's (1996) groundbreaking studies, in which participants were presented with pictures of a black person and a white person and then asked what race their offspring would be. He found that adults, at a rate significantly greater than chance, said that the child of one black and one white parent, as depicted in those pictures, would be black.[3] This might be taken to support the one-drop rule, but if we speak strictly, it seems to at most support a *sufficient*-drop rule, according to which some sufficient amount of black ancestry is enough to determine one's race as black. It does not indicate that having merely one or a few remote black ancestors is sufficient to make one black, since the study's participants were not told what proportion of the black parent's ancestors were themselves black, and the fact that the parent in the picture unambiguously 'looked black' might have suggested to participants that it was a significant proportion.

So, to take a step back, how can we directly test the prevalence of the *one*-drop rule, the rule that having one black ancestor—or, if we want to construe the rule a little more broadly, a small percentage of black ancestry—is sufficient to make one black? In a study I conducted with Julie Shulman and Enrique Covarrubias (Glasgow et al. in press), we tested the one-drop rule's acceptance by presenting participants with a version of the widely discussed case of Susie Phipps. At least as far as we are usually told, Phipps grew up thinking she was white, and she was ordinarily classified as white. As an adult, she discovered that she was actually legally classified as black, because she had a few remote black ancestors, enough so that Louisiana law classified her as black. She sued to have this classification changed, but ultimately the Louisiana and U.S. Supreme Courts denied her petition. This and similar legal cases are the evidence usually, and reasonably, deployed by those who argue that the one-drop rule is alive and well in the United States of America. And this rule is one of the more unjustifiable elements of race-thinking: it is extremely unlikely that there is any

---

3    A great deal of Hirschfeld's work concerns how children engage in racial classification. I am only concerned with his studies involving adult participants, as these are presumably more evidential of linguistically competent uses of racial discourse.

principled reason for classifying someone with only one or two remote black ancestors as black. If, then, Smedley and Smedley are correct that the one-drop rule is part of the *definition* of 'race,' race won't be real, and anti-realism will win the game before we get out of the first quarter.

But since the law might not actually reflect ordinary thinking on this matter—it is sometimes outdated, and it is always subject to distorting political pressures and individual judgment—we thought it might be useful to see what folks actually say about this kind of case. Here's how we worded it:

> Susie is a middle-aged woman. She "looks white" to the average person on the street. She was raised to believe she was white. Her co-workers and friends all think of her as white. Now, in her mid-40s, she discovers that she has a couple of black ancestors, such that her great-great-great grandparents consist of two black people and 30 white people.

We then asked participants to tell us whether Susie is white, black, mixed, or sometimes white and sometimes black (or the always useful 'None of the above'). Now if the one-drop rule is in effect in any significant way, a substantial number of respondents should have chosen 'black.' But out of 449 adults who live in the United States, only 2.2 percent chose this response. That's no typo. Far from being part of the *definition* of 'race' in the United States, these results suggest that the one-drop rule isn't even part of the ordinary *conception* of race in the United States. This inference is supported by other cases we used, as well. For instance, we also presented participants with the case of 'George,' who has *all* black ancestry but invents a machine to change his appearance so that he looks white. A much larger number, 51 percent, said that George was still black after his transformation, but this is a strikingly low number if the one-drop rule is supposed to be part of the definition of 'race.' More on George shortly. (And, credit where credit is due: many of our cases, including George but not Susie, were inspired by some thought experiments discussed by Charles Mills (1998, ch. 3).)

Before proceeding, though, we should complicate things a little. It would be too quick to infer that because participants in discursive tasks like these don't judge that, say, Susie is black, people never use the one-drop rule. As Linda Martín Alcoff (2006) goes to great lengths to show, our racial categorizations are often a function of how we visually *perceive* one another, and perceptual tasks might not track discursive tasks (Gil-White 2001a, 2001b; Glasgow et al. in press). A telling example is prominent at the time of writing, during the 2008 U.S. presidential campaign: despite the common knowledge, at least among the media, that Barack Obama's mother was someone who would be ordinarily classified as white, and despite the fact that there is no undistorted reason to say that he looks 'more' black than white, he is routinely described by members of the media as black. So, to the extent that those members of the media are operating with ancestry-sensitive criteria for assigning racial membership to individuals, they appear to be prioritizing his black ancestry over his white ancestry. Nevertheless, despite the existence of contexts in which at least a sufficient-drop rule may be operative, the results from the discursive task do tell us that people can coherently talk about race without presupposing the one-drop rule. So at this point, realism is still viable: race won't be an illusion on the grounds that the bankrupt one-drop rule is part of the ordinary U.S. concept of race, because people who don't subscribe to the one-drop rule can still have that concept.

### Ancestral Race-Thinking Beyond the One-drop Rule

A more general way of understanding race-thinking is simply that we are ordinarily thought to have the same races as our ancestors (Appiah 1996, 77; Gracia 2005; Hardimon 2003, 446; Hirschfeld 1996; Kitcher 1999; Sarich & Miele 2004). This alleged aspect of race-thinking—a version of which was labeled 'H2' in Chapter 2—is particularly significant from the realist's perspective, since, as we will see in more detail in the next chapter, some contemporary realists like to say that races are real as ancestrally related populations. And although we now have good reason to drop the one-drop rule, this doesn't mean that race isn't often thought of as, at least in part, a function of one's ancestry. Indeed, even the mere *ability* of people to predict the offspring of the people in Hirschfeld's pictures, whatever their response, may suggest that one's race is ordinarily thought to be unavoidably tied to one's parents' race.

However, not all of the available data suggest widespread endorsement of the rule that one has the same race as one's ancestors. While it was stipulated that 'George' has all-black ancestors, 41 percent of respondents said that George was *not* black after his transformation (and this excludes those who said 'None of the above' in this case). But if two-fifths of people can deny that George is black, it's hard to see how it's *conceptually* true that one must have the same race as one's ancestors (unless these matters are settled by majority, of course, a question that will be taken up later in this chapter).[4] And this kind of

---

4   Note that this may have something to do with the *kind* of change George underwent, namely one where his visible features were *themselves* changed. As Boxill (2001) notes (although we don't have experimental data to back up this armchair observation), we normally wouldn't say that someone who put on makeup to look like a member of another race really *is* by virtue of that merely cosmetic change a member of the other race. If this judgment is widespread, then this is evidence that, while your ancestry might not single-handedly determine your race as a conceptual matter, it might so long as you don't undergo a deep constitutional change. Cosmetic changes aren't enough.

result is not isolated to categorizations of people as black. Fifty-one percent of respondents denied that 'Mark'—who has all-white ancestry but is adopted as an infant by a black family and grows up self-identifying and being identified by others as black—is white. And even in the case of 'Dan,' who has wholly white ancestry and is raised white but integrates himself into a black community as an adult, 38 percent deny that he is white.

Now, at the same time, there is obviously a good deal of variation in these responses: for the 41 percent who say that George is not black, 51 percent judge that George is black. Similar complements are in place for Mark and Dan. And there is still the matter of Hirschfeld's data, where people predict that the child of a white and a black parent will be black. So as a preliminary and careful assessment, it seems we should say this: significant numbers appear to think that one must have the same race as one's ancestors, but significant numbers also appear to judge that, at least in extraordinary circumstances, it is possible to have a race that is not the same race as one's ancestors. I thus want to say that one's ancestry does not as a matter of definition determine one's race, which comports with our earlier conclusion that H2 should be jettisoned from the concept of race.

### 4.2.2  Essentialist Race-Thinking

You don't have to read race theory for very long before stumbling upon something that says that the ordinary concept of race is committed to essentialism (for a sample, see Gil-White 2001a; Hirschfeld 1996, 1998; Smedley & Smedley 2005, 19, 22; Yzerbyt, Rocher, & Schadron 1997, 41; Zack 2002, 97). Hirschfeld (1998, 338), for example, writes that "Allport (1954) describes racial thinking in mid-twentieth-century North America as essentialist and there is little reason to believe that the concept is less part of contemporary thinking in the United States." Or as he elsewhere puts it, "the impulse to essentialize is fundamental to *all* commonsense theories of race" (Hirschfeld 1996, 58, emphasis added).

Now in order to evaluate this claim, we need to know what, exactly, is meant by 'essentialism' and 'essence.' These terms can, of course, be used to mean several things, and Nick Haslam and colleagues have charged that in the psychological literature on race, 'essentialism' has been used in so many different ways that we must be careful to define it from here on out, or else we run the risk of not being able to disentangle its various elements (Haslam 1998; Haslam, Rothschild & Ernst 2000, 2002). In this spirit I will say—again, following a significant strain in psychological writings—that a representation of race is $\psi$-essentialist just to the extent that, *inter alia*, it holds or presupposes that one has various heritable, unchangeable racial features that are fixed no later than the moment one is born. (I'll use the construction 'ψ-essentialist' because while this understanding of 'essence' is common in the psychological literature, essences can also be understood in other ways, one of which will show up in the next chapter.)

This definition of 'ψ-essentialism'—simply, of course, an operationalized definition, but one that is useful given its frequency in the relevant psychological literature—is open to thinner and thicker conceptions. So classical racialism will thickly say not only that we are born with unalterable racial ψ-essences, but also that these essences are composed of or generate several kinds of traits, including visible physical characteristics, intellectual aptitude, moral aptitude or status, cultural capacity, and beauty. A thinner conception might say that our racial ψ-essences are composed only of visible traits. Let us begin by examining the extent to which we have displayed a propensity for countenancing thin racial essences.

## Thin Essences

Hirschfeld (1998, 339) inferred that because race-thinking has an ancestral component, it also has a ψ-essentialist component. In so doing, he seemingly relied on a premise that traits transmitted through ancestry are thought to be based in ψ-essences (Gelman & Wellman 1991). But this inference has been challenged: we might have traits, even traits with causal powers, that are transmitted from our ancestors but that are not based in essences (Machery & Faucher 2005b; Strevens 2000; debate may be found in Ahn et al. (2001) and Strevens (2001)). Although this is not the kind of reasoning employed in those challenges, we can imagine, for example, that the participants in Hirschfeld's study thought that while the child of an interracial couple would be black, this is only because Americans classify such children as black, and that if U.S. classifications worked differently (say, determined such a child to be mixed race or white), the child would have a different race. If this is the case, patterns of racial classification that prioritize ancestry do not necessarily presuppose that our race is a ψ-essence that we simply inherit from our parents; they could also allow non-essentialist social practices of classification.

So where else might we find proof that ordinary racial thinking is ψ-essentialist? In a survey presented to undergraduates, Haslam and colleagues (2000, 2002) disambiguated features associated with essentialism into multiple components: discreteness, uniformity, informativeness, naturalness, immutability, stability, inherence, necessity, and (in Haslam et al. (2000) only) exclusivity. They then asked the participants to rate several categories, including racial categories such as 'black people' and 'white people,' as well as 'Asians' and 'Hispanics,' which they classified as ethnic groups but which others classify as at least partially racialized groups (Alcoff 2006, ch. 10; Blum 2002, 152–154; Haney López 1995, 2005), for each of these components. After examining responses to all of the categories (not just race and ethnicity), it was found that there are actually two dimensions to thinking often described by academics as 'essentialist.' The first is a *natural kind* dimension, which combines naturalness with necessary traits, immutability, discreteness, and stability. The second is an *entitativity* dimension (that is, a dimension such that members of the kind are treated as coherent and unified entities, but not necessarily natural ones), which combines informativeness, uniformity, inherence, and exclusivity. Although the elements *within* each of these two dimensions of essentialist thinking cleave together, as dimensions they come apart, and, interestingly, the racial and ethnic groups Haslam and colleagues inquired about were rated highly on the natural kind dimension, but not on the entitativity dimension.[5]

These responses should not be discounted. If people think that race is natural, immutable, stable, and discrete, and that it can be defined in terms of necessary traits, then perhaps there is an essentialist element to the ordinary concept of race. However, not all data confirm this hypothesis. For example, the claim that one's race is, by definition, unambiguously natural, stable, and immutable is challenged by the fact that many assert, with apparent competence, that George can change his race.[6] If one can at least *conceivably* change one's race, then it is not *conceptually* true that one's race is a fixed ψ-essence installed at birth.

*Thick Essences*

Doubt has so far been cast upon the uniformity with which ordinary race-thinking is committed to thin racial essences, and if we don't normally represent race as involving thin essences, we won't represent it as involving thicker essences either (since thick essences entail thin essences). This prediction finds confirmation in the empirical literature. By showing that race isn't understood in an entitative way—that race is not predominantly thought to feature inherence, informativeness, uniformity, or exclusivity—the data from Haslam and colleagues suggest

---

5   The instrument used in their "Essentialist Beliefs Scale" was not worded to ask directly whether a participant thought a given category was, say, natural or discrete. Rather, they worded items more descriptively. For example, the item for naturalness was worded, "Some categories are more natural than others, whereas others are more artificial"; and the item for necessity stated, in part, "Some categories have necessary features or characteristics; without these characteristics someone cannot be a category member" (Haslam et al. 2000, 117–118).

6   Again, see Glasgow, Shulman, & Covarrubias (in press) for further details and relevant cases.

that even if we are tempted to describe ordinary race-thinking as essentialist, we should do so in a circumscribed manner, where a significant entitative component is not included as a matter of definition. Moreover, Condit and colleagues (2004, 260) found that while people often link race to our genes, they link personality and behavior to non-genetically determined choice. This is not to say that people don't harbor racist beliefs, or don't make stereotypes about other races. (On the contrary, the same research showed that participants were "quite willing to rank races hierarchically, stating that some races exhibit particular undesired characteristics as a group" (Condit et al. 2004, 264).) It's just to say that when they did view races as having negative characteristics, they didn't attribute it to genetics or other biological features beyond individual choice. Again, then, thick essences seem not to be part of the *concept* of race, even if some believe that they exist.

### 4.2.3 Phenotypic and Social Race-Thinking

What else might show that our race-thinking is biological? The final possibility I want to consider is that race is thought to be a matter of physical appearance, and perhaps a matter of the genes that underlie our visible traits.[7] When asked whether a person is a member of her race *because* of (any combination of) visible features, social ties, and/or personality traits, the most frequent choice—though by no means the only one, at a rate of approximately 50 percent—is to select visible traits alone as determinative (Shulman & Glasgow in press). Focus group research provided by Condit and collaborators (2004) has also shown that race is commonly understood as a function of one's physical appearance and that appearance is commonly understood to result from genetics. And while focus group data reported by Dubriwny et al. (2004) reveal that geography is perceived as an important source of human variation, those same data show that physical characteristics seem to be core parts of the definition of race for several of their participants. Indeed, this is thought by the authors to be one of the main points of distinction between the ordinary and scientific understandings of race, and some participants were explicit that race is not determined by geography, a finding that nicely comports with the analysis, given in Chapter 2, that excludes H3 (geographic origins) from, and includes H1* (visible traits) in, the ordinary concept of race. And, again, the research conducted by Haslam and colleagues (2000, 2002) showed participants who rated black people and white people highly on

---

7   One other kind of evidence I don't consider here is that race-thinking appears to mirror other kinds of thinking about biological categories with respect to inferential patterns (see Machery & Faucher n-d).

a 'natural kind' dimension of essentialist thinking, according to which these categories are thought to be discrete, natural, immutable, histori-cally stable, and to have necessary features. If these are thought to be elements of specifically biological, rather than more broadly natural, kinds, this research too supports the thesis that race is ordinarily con-ceived of as biological.[8]

Nevertheless, important strains of ordinary thought also take race to be partly a matter of social practices, even practices that can in principle reverse the relevance of phenotype to the determination of an indi-vidual's race. The same research from Condit et al. (2004) showed that while participants understand individual race to be largely a matter of physical appearance, this is defeasible—as one participant put it, in cap-turing the phenomenon of racial 'passing,' "[s]ome people you can't tell by color" (256; cf. Dubriwny et al. 2004, 189). Similarly, when Dubri-wny and colleagues (2004, 187) asked their focus groups, "What do you think is generally meant when people use the term 'race'?" and fol-lowed this with probes about whether race is defined in terms of culture, geography, heredity or genetics, color, and religion, they found that race is conceived of in a "multifactorial" way, that is, such that race is "defined" to include cultural elements—including a history of discrimination—in addition to genetic and phenotypic elements.[9]

Here it is also worth recalling cases like that of 'George.' When participants held that George was still black after using his appearance-changing machine, this suggests that a change in one's visible appear-ance (in fact, a change in appearance *and* social relations) is not considered to be enough to change one's race. This is, again, evidence that race is ordinarily thought of in biological terms, and other cases (such as the case of Dan) confirm this suggestion. However, the other responses to the case of George, along with responses to other cases, suggest that ordinary race-thinking is more complex than this. When participants were told that 'Anatole' had undergone no physical

8    Actually, four of the five items—immutability, discreteness, stability, and containing necessary features—could also be true of social categories. However, while it has been suggested that the fifth, naturalness, might be read in a manner consistent with social influences, naturalness in their study was contrasted with artificiality (see the wording in note 5 above), which is presumably a hallmark of social kinds.

9    It is a live question whether different answers to these types of questions are more fre-quently given by people who self-identify with different races. Condit et al. (2004) and Dubriwny et al. (2004) found that self-identified African Americans were more likely to emphasize the importance of culture (including practices of discrimination) as a determinant of race. In Shulman & Glasgow (in press) we found no pattern like this. In Glasgow et al. (in press), self-identified white participants were more likely than self-identified non-whites to reject the one-drop rule, to reject the criterion that ancestry solely determines one's race, and to accept that one's race is at least partly socially determined.

changes but integrated himself as a member of the white community, only 2 percent said that Anatole was white before this shift, but 23 percent said that he was white after, suggesting that for these participants social relations and self-identification—non-biological factors—can fully determine one's race. So biology doesn't seem to be the *only* element in the *concept* of race, at least when that is understood as a kind of property born by individuals rather than as a group (a distinction that will be significant below).

## 4.3 The Ordinary Concept(s) and Conception(s) of Race

Perhaps the only obvious conclusion to be made from inspecting these data is that ordinary race-thinking is a mess. (That, plus the conclusion that more research needs to be done.[10]) We can say *some* things, of course. For instance, we now have strong evidence that the one-drop rule is *not* part of the concept of race. But it is no less true in experimental philosophy than in armchair philosophy that it is easier to use thought experiments to rule propositions *out* of a concept than to rule them in, and the big problem we seem to face is in fixing the positive content of the concept RACE. Many people seem to think that race is tied to ancestry, but then there is a sizeable chunk that seems to think that one's race does not necessarily have to be the same as the race of one's ancestors. Many seem to think that phenotype is crucial, but many also think that phenotype isn't necessarily indicative of one's race. Given the evidence we have seen, there is little reason any more to think that thick racial essences have widespread currency, and although the thinner idea that race is unchangeable seems to have some purchase on folk intuitions, it does not hold decisive numbers in its grip. Many, in fact, seem to think that one's race can be determined by social relations, although many disagree with that claim as well. Thus there are really two

---

10 One sometimes hears the objection that asking people what they think about race overexposes the data to social desirability effects; that is, roughly, that participants will say what they think they should say rather than what they really think. There are three points that soften the impact of this objection, however. First, even if existing data do not reveal ordinary race-thinking in a perfectly transparent way, they are the best (the only!) empirical data we have. Second, there are established ways of reducing desirability effects, such as by asking the participants not what they think about race but what they think people normally think about race, or by collecting responses in ways that maximize anonymity, such as internet surveys. Many of the studies discussed above take advantage of these methods. Finally, the studies do show a wide array of responses, which suggests that at least many people were not afraid of giving undesirable answers to various questions. For instance, some studies also measured racist attitudes (to see in part whether or not different conceptions of race were more likely than others to be accompanied by racist attitudes), and many participants did not shy away from giving answers that are classified as racist.

problems here: race, particularly the race of an individual (as opposed to racial groups, a concept about which we have much less experimental data), seems to be determined by a collection of radically different, sometimes inconsistent criteria; and there is widespread disagreement as to what the determinative criteria are. These two problems leave us with one question: Once all the data are in, what should we say that the concept of race consists in? When faced with such a robust diversity of race-thinking, if we want to shoot for a complete analysis, that is, an analysis that specifies every component of the concept of race, four choices present themselves. A fifth option will be to settle for an incomplete analysis. To begin with one of the former options, though, let's consider giving up.

### 4.3.1 Incoherence

Perhaps, given the diversity of race-thinking, 'race' is defined in such a way that it includes contradictory propositions: that one always has the same race as one's ancestors, but also that one's racial identity need not always be anchored to one's ancestry; that it is set by a $\psi$-essence, but that it is changeable; that it is always a matter of one's biology, but also that it can be determined by one's social relations; and so on. Ian Haney López's (1995, 193) suggestion that races both exist and are "contradictory" notwithstanding, there is nothing, not even race, of which it can be true both *that p* and *that ~p*. (Unless there is something to be said for dialetheism, the view that contradictions can be true, but let's keep things simple and assume standard logic.) So if we take all or most of the elements of race-thinking that gain a sufficiently large plurality of adherents and conjoin them as the contents of the concept of race, race will not be real because RACE will be incoherent.[11]

I have to admit that I'm a bit partial to this way of diagnosing the conceptual terrain. Of course, I've already let slip that I'm an anti-realist, so it's no big loss to my view if it turns out that race is not real because RACE is incoherent, and with that as the dialectical background, the incoherence diagnosis is tempting in light of the seemingly irreconcilable of ways of thinking about race.[12] In fact, given that our understanding of race has been shaped by morally disastrous practices, such as slavery, conquest, genocide, domination, and exploitation, which

---

11  One currently fashionable way of specifying the content of a concept is just to list all the platitudes associated with it. The diversity of race-thinking examined above suggests that either there are no platitudes about race or that there will be contradictory platitudes.

12  Some anti-realists, such as J. Angelo Corlett (2007, 226), succumb to this kind of temptation.

were not exactly marked by coherence and justification, it really would not come as a shocking surprise if RACE turned out to be incoherent.

That being said, if there is another way of analyzing RACE, we shouldn't be *too* quick to embrace the diagnosis of incoherence. From the dialectical position I occupy, that of defending anti-realism, it would be better to make realism as strong as possible than to unnecessarily stack the conceptual deck against it. And in general it seems desirable, other things being equal, to 'save the phenomena' and to preserve our discourse: if there is a way of running things so that race turns out to be real, that would be in some conservative respects better than if it turned out not to be real. Given these desiderata, let us turn to whether realism can be given at least an initial boost by coming up with some other diagnosis besides incoherence.

### 4.3.2 Tyranny of the Majority

One option is to go with majority rules: whenever inconsistent answers are given to a question about race, the answer that wins the most endorsements is the one that has a legitimate claim to being part of the content of RACE. Or perhaps this standard is too strict. Consider again the case of George, where 51 percent said that after using his appearance-changing machine, George was still black. If we go with a simple majoritarian approach, then that means the other 49 percent are contradicting themselves.

This is a very strong claim. It is not just that the 49 percent are *mistaken* in thinking that George is not black. It is that when they assent to the proposition *that George is not black*, they are assenting to a contradiction. Conceptually it would be no different than assenting to the proposition *that I am a married bachelor*. (It might be a more understandable mistake, but it would be 'equally' inconsistent.) This seems like a dubitable assessment, committed as it is to the claim that the 49 percent minority simply don't know how to properly use words like 'black.'

This problem might be alleviated if we moved to a 'super-majority' kind of approach, where a proposition can have a legitimate claim on being part of the concept only if it has a sufficiently large number of assenters. Presumably it must also gain the right *kind* of assent—by people who are relevantly informed, for instance. If people largely agreed that atoms were indivisible, but were uninformed of the science showing that atoms are, in fact, divisible, we wouldn't take their agreement-in-ignorance as decisive in setting the content of the concept ATOM. But one of the claims of Chapter 3 was that 'race,' as concerns the race debate, is a folk term, rather than a term of art like 'atom,' and one of our guiding principles is that the average adult is linguistically competent, which supposes that they have much of the relevant information. This is not, again, to deny that we can make mistakes (that thesis will be considered below under 'Revisionism and Externalism'). But it is to say that folk linguistic practices are given a place of privilege in setting the content of the concept of race. This means that people have, by and large, at least *some* relevant information, not about the scientific details about race, but about how concepts like BLACK or WHITE can be deployed. (Recall that even if the scientific details end up upending some proposition that we believe about race, this is only because those details are pertinent to some *other* aspect of our linguistic practices.)

Now surely some version of the super-majority approach will be compelling, even trivial perhaps. If 99 percent of people non-negotiably insist *that p*, and 1 percent deny this, there will be good reason to suspect (defeasibly, as always) that those in the minority are confused about something. But few of the data examined above are subject to such extreme super-majorities. Recall that 23 percent said that after integration into the white community, Anatole was white. Now these participants might be wrong. But it is still counterintuitive to say that they are *conceptually* confused, that they *contradict* themselves when they endorse the proposition, *that Anatole is now white*. (Given that only 2 percent said Anatole was white prior to his transformation, we can infer that approximately 93 percent of that 23 percent held that Anatole was not white before the transformation; were they deploying 'white' incorrectly then, too?) A super-majority approach, if it settles for anything less than trivial super-majorities as determinants of conceptual truths, is still counterintuitively committed to saying that these people are incompetent with respect to using the word 'white.'

In insisting that some proposition is non-negotiably embedded in a concept, we set up a linguistic wall. We say that those on the other side of the wall are either contradicting themselves or using their own language. They are talking past us, who are having a conversation over here on *this* side of the wall. The majoritarian approach requires us to say that those in the minority, those who think that Anatole is white, either don't understand the meaning of 'white' (even though they deployed 'white' correctly when they said that Anatole was not white before his integration), or mean something by it that is different from what the rest of us mean by it. In this way, we face the same choice we faced in Chapter 2. We can say either that the majority and the minority are *disagreeing* about race, or that they are simply talking past one another. Conceptual majoritarianism steers us down the latter road, but in many cases that seems like a dead end. *Of course* people can sensibly disagree about race in these ways: they have different conceptions, and this means that the concept of race must be thin enough to accommodate the diverse panoply of racial thought. Once we seek to accommodate that plurality, once we adopt nothing stronger than a trivial super-majoritarian approach, we can only say that the concept of race includes *very* thin elements, thin enough to be common to *all* of these conceptions.

### 4.3.3 Ambiguity, Partial Reference, and Clusters

For the same reasons, we won't want to go with the conclusion that most of the participants in the various studies noted above are deploying distinctive concepts of race, where some possess a biological concept, $RACE_B$, and others possess a social concept, $RACE_S$; where some utilize an essentialist concept $RACE_E$, and others don't; where some deploy an ancestral race concept $RACE_A$, but others don't. If this were true, then none of the respondents would be disagreeing with each other about what race consists in, and what race George or Anatole is. Instead, they would simply be talking past each other, confusingly using the same word-forms to express different propositions. It is not too much of a stretch to say that this sometimes happens, but it seems unlikely that we are all missing each other's point with the frequency found in the studies reviewed above. Saying that we have multiple concepts—that words like 'race' are ambiguous—in all of these ways would be tantamount to saying that we are simply babbling past one another when we talk about race, rather than having a linguistically sensible conversation. That seems implausible. What is more plausible is that we use the same concepts but disagree about the nature of race.

Now a variant on this position would be to say that 'race' is a term of *partial reference*, like the philosophically favored example of 'jade,' which refers partly to jadeite and partly to nephrite (each of which bears similar superficial properties that can fool the naked eye into thinking they are identical—hence the term coming to refer to two different kinds of thing). They are two different kinds of mineral, and so "there is really no such thing as jade, only jadeite and nephrite" (Griffiths 2004, 902). So maybe 'race' is used in some contexts to refer to a social kind of thing and in other contexts to a biological kind of thing. It's not that different *people* talk past one another when they use race in these varied ways; instead, it's that *all* (or a sufficient plurality of) competent language users use 'race' as a term of partial reference, to refer to different things in different kinds of cases. In fact, cluster concepts are plausibly the limit case of partial reference terms, and it has been suggested that RACE is a cluster concept (Mosley 1997; Outlaw 1996a, 1996b). If RACE is a cluster concept, then no one property is necessary for a person to be, say, Asian, and several properties might be individually sufficient to be Asian. To return to our cases, then, perhaps one can be Asian if one has a certain kind of ancestry, but also if one has the right kind of appearance-changing machine, and so on.

Despite their relative unpopularity, cluster analyses do have the virtue that they can accommodate those concepts whose instantiations seem to have no single unifying trait, and that might seem to do the trick of accommodating the diversity of racial thinking that has proven to be a thorn in our analytic side. However, things aren't that easy, for the problem embedded in the diversity of racial thinking is not so much the various ways of using racial terms as it is the widespread *disagreement* and *inconsistency* contained in our racial discourse. The classic case of a cluster concept, Wittgenstein's example of GAME, is compelling because we can agree that so many different games—hopscotch, rugby, Texas Hold 'Em, solitaire—are in fact games, even though they seem to have nothing else in common other than being games. But our problem with analyzing race-thinking isn't that irreducibly different kinds of people seem to be Asian or black or Latino/a or white. It is that being Asian or black or Latino/a or white is, according to ordinary ways of thinking, a matter of contradictory criteria *even in the same cases*: ancestry, but not ancestry; phenotype, but not phenotype; inherited essence, but not inherited essence. This is why incoherence looms as a real threat. Saying that RACE is a cluster concept won't defend it against that threat. Thus one problem with this move is that, in a departure from our usage of 'jade,' different people use 'race' differently in the *same* cases.

A second problem is that it dooms realism from the start. Because it picks out two different mineral kinds, 'jade' does not mark out a real mineral category (though jadeite and nephrite are, individually, minerally real). It marks out a category we have contrived, imposed on the world, defined by a boundary that we have gerrymandered for our classificatory convenience. The same thing will be true of race, if 'race' is just a category we have contrived to apply to two different—social and biological—kinds of things. This, like the incoherence option, may very well be true, but it dooms racial realism from the start, and I'd like to give realism some more air before sealing its fate.

### 4.3.4 Revisionism and Externalism

A more viable strategy is to say that we sensibly disagree about race, and that while few of us are *conceptually* confused and contradicting ourselves, many of us can be wrong. Perhaps it will turn out that, as a matter of fact, one's race is never determined by social relations, for example. A *revisionist* view holds that while we might say *that p* is true of race, we can be mistaken, and it might turn out *that ~p* is true of race. It might even turn out that we are mistaken about some seemingly non-negotiable truths about race; recall that putting significant semantic authority in folk's hands does not mean that folk are infallible, any more than putting it in a scientist's hands means that the scientist is infallible. And revisionism is, among other things, a way to make the concept of race coherent: while people ordinarily think *that p* is true, in other contexts (say, where they are more informed about the way the world is) they would not think this, so we can say that *that ~p* is something to which they would assent when in a properly reflective and informed position. Once we build the goal of consistency into the relevant contexts, it is tempting to say that ordinary people would assent to a revised set of claims about race that would allow for RACE to be a coherent concept.

Revisionism is in principle compatible with a variety of semantic theories, but it comports nicely with externalism, which, recall, holds that the meanings of terms are not always entirely fixed by what we think about the objects of those terms; sometimes it may be determined by factors external to the mind, such as the history of the term's use, or the nature of the things we talk about when we utter those terms, or the sociolinguistic context in which we utter them (see, e.g., Appiah 2007). Now semantic externalism is hardly an uncontroversial theory, but it is at least plausibly animated by cases such as 'water,' where 'water' might mean $H_2O$ even for those who don't know that it refers to $H_2O$, even when the entire linguistic community doesn't associate $H_2O$ with water (Putnam 1975b).

An anti-realist might try to argue against semantic externalism on principle, but to do so would be to throw to the wind Mallon's caution against assuming controversial semantic principles. A safer bet would be to see what kinds of things might be said if one were tempted to be an externalist or a revisionist and to evaluate each proposal on its own merits. What this tells us, though, is that revisionism will be motivated only if there is some *reason* to offer a revision to what people ordinarily say about race. It cannot merely be that we want the concept of race to be coherent; we must have reason to say that it is coherent in a certain *direction*, perhaps so that it turns out to be a social kind of thing, or a biological kind of thing that is not contingent on social relations, or perhaps so that one has to have the same race as one's ancestors, despite what people often say about George. Our immediate difficulty, one that will be resolved later on, is that at the moment we don't know what reason we might have to revise our claims about race in any one direction. To know this, we have to know what plausible realist proposals have to say about the way the world is and how it lines up with our racial discourse. Perhaps, after considering those realist proposals, we will decide that race can be understood in a uniformly social or uniformly biological way, despite the fact that both options garner some dissent. So if there is a way to revise our currently inconsistent set of claims about race and still be talking about *race* and comport with the facts of the world, this will be compelling reason to revise our understanding of race. So this option will have to wait. It won't be until after we consider plausible realist proposals that we will have all the reasons for revision before us. Revisionism is put on hold until Chapter 6.

### 4.3.5 An Incomplete Analysis

I think the best we can do at this point is to settle for an *incomplete* analysis of RACE, one that makes a few specific claims about the concept of race and even fewer positive claims about its content. We can say that race-thinking seems to involve both biological *and* social elements, something I will henceforth refer to as the apparent *biosocial complexity* of racial discourse. We can say that phenotype is in some sense central to race, without going so far as to say that one's race will always be dictated by the way one looks. We can say that one's race at times might turn out to be a function of one's place in a matrix of social relationships. We just know at this point that race-thinking involves both social and biological elements, that visible traits and social relations sometimes seem relevant to determining a person's race.[13] Perhaps after we get our realist proposals on the table, in the next two chapters, we will have reason (in Chapter 6) to adopt a revisionary analysis that will allow us to come up with a more decisive specification of the concept of race and possibly eliminate some of the complexities. And perhaps we will, as research progresses, obtain more decisive data about the contours of ordinary race-thinking. But we are not at either of these points yet, so complexity is the best we can do, at least for the moment.[14]

We can close, then, with a reexamination of Chapter 2's thin analysis of the concept of race, understood as a kind of group. According to this thin analysis, which was motivated by considering some Twin Earth thought experiments, races are (H1*) groups of human beings distinguished from other human beings by visible physical features of the relevant kind that the group has to some significantly disproportionate extent. This appears to be consistent with the data given here. Because it focuses on races as groups, H1* allows that some individuals might

13   Further evidence for the biosocial complexity of race is that once we look past the 'black–white binary,' we find that rac*ism* operates not only on our physical traits but also on non-physical traits, such as culture or whether a race is perceived as 'native' to a country, as argued by Alcoff (2006, ch. 11). For further discussion, see, for instance, Sundstrom (in press, ch. 3).

14   Ron Sundstrom suggested to me that at this point we might pragmatically revert to using historical expert writings to settle the disagreement between the folk and to simplify the complexity of their answers. However, I would, first, reiterate that we cannot even recognize which historical experts are using the relevant concepts of race until we have some sort of grip on our concept of race (that is, I would rehash the arguments of the previous chapter), and, second, note that historical expert usage appears to be biosocially complex as well, so that won't solve our current problem even if it were otherwise a sound approach.

not have the physical features that are disproportionally typical of the group. The criteria for belonging to a race might, recall, come apart from what makes a group a racial group, so even if H1* is correct, that leaves room for variability and social relations in the assignment of individuals to racial groups. Thus we can keep the thin analysis while taking seriously the other complex ways in which we ordinarily think about individual racial identity. More than that, the two seem to dovetail to some degree, since the experimental data clearly reveal that phenotype is central even to thought about individual race, possibly more central than any other element.

The move from thinking about individual racial properties back to thinking about the nature of racial groups is crucial in part because our next questions are whether we have reason to say that race is real, and whether in so saying we have to revise some of the things people say about race, and whether in so revising we end up with something that is still recognizable as *race*. From this point forward, then, we move from focusing on methodological and conceptual issues to focusing on the Ontological Question: Is race real? In asking this question, I will be oriented towards asking whether *races* or *racial groups* are real. Here I follow the principle that "[r]ace-thinking is about kinds, called races, and only derivatively about individuals, who thereby have racial identities" (Taylor 2004, 17; cf. Zack 1993, 70). That is, nobody has a race if there are no racial groups. So, while our understanding of individual race should inform our understanding of racial groups, if it turns out that there aren't any racial groups, it will follow that race is an illusion. I will begin, in the next chapter, with an examination of whether we should say that race is biologically real. (A hint as to my answer: No.) Chapter 6 will explore whether race might be socially real and, upon suggesting that it is not socially real and therefore not real in any sense, it will pay off this chapter's sizeable promissory note, that of giving realist revisionism more substantial consideration. At that point the case for anti-realism will be closed. But this will only open up a new problem. Anti-realism seems to motivate the elimination of racial discourse, but there are also, as we will see, some strong reasons to be wary of such a proposal.

# 5  Breaking Nature's Bones

A relief map of North America will show the Rocky Mountains, the Great Plains, the Sonoran Desert, and the Canadian Arctic Archipelago, but no political entities, no Mexico, no United States, no Canada, and no Sonora or California or Yukon Territory. (For those you will need a political map.) In this way, maps represent the world in a manner that helpfully captures the difference between geological entities and political entities. Even when we isolate an island, or a collection of islands, that perfectly aligns with a political state, such as New Zealand, the islands and the state are two different things. In short, political entities are not items in nature's suitcase. We can point to a line in the ground and say, 'This is where Mexico begins and the United States ends,' but such lines are written upon nature by us. The claim of this chapter is that the concept of race is similar to political concepts to the extent that it is written onto the world by us (cf. Kitcher 2007). If this is correct, then perhaps, on the one hand, race is real in some other, non-biological way. Maybe it is a real social construction in the way that political entities, like California, are real social constructions. Or perhaps, on the other hand, it just isn't real. These two options will be considered later. For now, our task is to see whether race is biologically real.

## 5.1 How Race Might be Biologically Real

### 5.1.1 Kinds of Kinds, Real Reality

Determining whether race is a biological kind of thing requires taking a moment to sort out what it is for something to constitute a real biological kind. Sometimes this is put in terms of a contrast between natural kinds and social kinds. In one sense this is a perfectly reasonable contrast: there are kinds of things that are in nature itself, and then there are kinds of things that we create through social interaction alone. However, here I will adopt a plausible and historically influential alternative understanding of natural kinds, recently characterized by Edouard Machery (2005, 446) in the following helpful way:

[T]he notion of natural kind singles out those classes about which nonaccidental, scientifically relevant inductive generalizations can be formulated. With this notion, one draws a distinction between two kinds of classes: those about which inductive generalizations can be formulated, e.g., atoms, and those about which no or few generalizations can be formulated, e.g., things that weigh more than 124 kg. Thus, the members of a natural kind are supposed to share nonaccidentally a large number of ... scientifically important properties (or relations) beside the properties (or relations) that are used to identify them.

The guiding motivation behind this (Millian) understanding of natural kinds is that any kind of thing that does *not* enable inductive generalizations will be mostly useless in the activities of science. But notice that, so understood, not all natural kinds are kinds studied by the natural sciences; social kinds can also be natural kinds in this sense. We can make many inductive generalizations about universities or nation-states by virtue of the properties that the members of each (non-accidentally) share, even though universities and nation-states are not studied by natural scientists. Additionally, while many natural kinds (such as gold) might have non-relational essences, sets of intrinsic properties that are necessary and jointly sufficient for the bearer of those properties to be a member of the kind in question (atomic number 79), some natural kinds do not. Other mechanisms, such as the relation of common descent, can also explain why members of a kind tend to share so many properties about which we can generate inferences (Machery 2005, 448).

On this understanding, then, natural kinds should be contrasted not with social kinds, but with *superficial* or *gerrymandered* kinds. Gerrymandered kinds will be kinds, such as *things that weigh more than 124 kg*, whose boundaries we directly impose on the world. They are the products of classifications we make, as opposed to kinds that are demarcated by the world itself. Now this doesn't mean that things that weigh more than 124 kg are not in the world itself. Instead, it means that the *kind* composed of those things is a mere classificatory convenience, and the telltale sign is that its members don't have much in common other than the features we use to identify them as members of their category. Thus consider an example from one prominent advocate of this understanding of natural kinds, Ian Hacking (2005) (following Mill): since horses have many properties in common other than the properties that are used to identify them as horses, and white things do not, *horse* is a natural kind, while *white thing* is not.

So understood, races are almost surely not natural kinds by virtue of any biological facts: there is little reason to think that there are any races, properly so-called, whose members share many biological properties beyond those used to racially classify them. It might thus be objected that by adopting the understanding of 'natural kind' that I have adopted, I have rigged the dialectic so that biological racial realism comes out false. That is, it might be objected that even if putatively biological races are not natural kinds in our operative sense, they are still real biological kinds simply by virtue of there being a *few* biological traits shared by members of each race, such as skin color, perhaps, or a certain small section of our genetic code, or a certain slice of our ancestral relations. Indeed, if current taxonomy strives not to explain or predict much other than "the history of human populations, their patterns of migration, and their degrees of reproductive isolation" (Andreasen 2004, 435), any attempt to demand that biological categories do more than this—that is, to demand that members of a race have *any* distinctive, shared, and non-relational traits in order for the race to count as biologically real—will attract some serious suspicion (Dupré 1981; Kitcher 2007; Mosley 1997). As an alternative to appealing to shared intrinsic properties, or even just similarity *tout court*, these days many demarcate biological categories in terms of their *histories*, so that we are members of, say, a species because we are members of the right kind of reproductively isolated population (Sterelny and Griffiths 1999, section 9.2). Thus an ancestor and a descendant in a species (or other taxon) might have completely different properties other than that of being part of the same lineage, which is to say that, at least in principle, they might not be genetically or phenotypically similar in any respect.[1]

So as a point of dialectical charity, until the end of this chapter, where I will return to the Millian approach to see whether race might be a natural kind by virtue of its position in a nexus of generalizations germane to disease and medicine, I am going to give up talk of natural kinds and adopt the relatively weak constraint that a kind will count as a biological kind only if it has *some* biologically principled basis. The next question—What counts as having a biologically principled basis?—itself surely groans under the weight of controversy, of which I also want to steer mostly clear. Will I merely negatively say, with even some realists (e.g., Arthur 2007, 60), that a kind is not biologically principled if it is biologically arbitrary, which is to say that the biological facts do not give us sufficient reason to mark off that kind. For example, because all the biological facts that we might learn about goldfish, dogs, and parrots will not be sufficient to tell us that they are particularly

---

1   However, many think that in order to be marked out as a distinct species, the species must by and large bear *some* distinctive intrinsic properties, even if some individuals within the species do not share some of those properties and even if those properties can evolve. Among others, a couple of very helpful overviews of the history of, and current problems facing, biological classification, in a way that brings into stark relief the respects in which conventional kind-talk does not comport well with biological and taxonomic practice, are (Ereshefsky 2001, chs 2–3; Sober 1993, ch. 6).

prone to human domestication, the category *household pets* is not a kind germane to the biological (Griffiths 2004, 905).[2]

In maintaining that a kind is not biologically real if the border drawn around it is biologically arbitrary, I am also presupposing a certain notion of 'real,' and in my conflict-avoidance mood I don't want to stage any battles over this presupposition. So although I will continue to use 'real' in this way, if you prefer to understand 'real' in such a way that even kinds whose borders are not fixed by facts within a domain (e.g., the domain of biology) can be real kinds of that domain, hopefully we can all at least agree that the arbitrariness criterion used here is spot-on that there is no *biology-driven basis* for such classifications (cf. Brock & Mares 2007, section 3.2).

Now some hold that multiple biological classifications are equally legitimate. John Dupré's (1981, 1999) 'promiscuous realism' accepts that we have various (although not unlimited) legitimate classificatory principles, and therefore various classificatory systems, none of which is privileged by the world.[3] Similarly, Philip Kitcher's (2007) classificatory pragmatism holds that the concepts we bring to bear in dividing up the world, and therefore the taxonomies that result from such endeavors, are not dictated by the world itself, and are legitimate only insofar as they serve purposes whose benefits, on balance, outweigh their costs. While I have some sympathy for these kinds of views, I am not going to argue that, as a general matter, we cannot find any privileged borders in the biological world. It would be a gross understatement to say that the questions to which promiscuous realism and classificatory pragmatism speak are complex and contentious, and if my arguments are on track, entering that hornet's nest is unnecessary for the task at hand. Nevertheless, in their spirit, I will make the more narrowly circumscribed case that specifically *racial* borders are products of our conventions rather than elements in the architecture of the biological world. That, as I see things, means that race is not biologically real.[4]

2   Contrast this principle with one from Barbujani (2005)—with whom my view otherwise shares a considerable amount—which says that an arbitrary classificatory system is not *useful*. My claim here is that arbitrary lines of demarcation might often be quite useful in allowing us to understand, investigate, and simply get along with some domain of the world—perhaps so useful that we should continue to use them in some contexts—but they do not reflect any division *in* that domain.

3   Dupré, however, does not want to say that biological categories, like species, are on that ground not real; hence the 'realism' in 'promiscuous realism.'

4   At one point Risch and colleagues (2002, 4) hold that "it is difficult to conceive of a definition of 'biological' that does not lead to racial differentiation, except perhaps one as extreme as speciation." They don't tell us what would be less extreme, but note that criteria for classificatory legitimacy less "extreme" than speciation are highly controversial among those who try to figure out what counts as a legitimate, real, biological category. Often the line is drawn at speciation precisely because it seems less arbitrary.

### 5.1.2 Three Ways of Being a Realist about Biological Race

While philosophers are fond of saying that scientists increasingly doubt that race is biologically real, biological realism has been gaining ground in recent years. In fact, it has been several decades since it's been this good to be a biological realist. Recall that there appear to be three ways in which they try to make their case.

According to the *superficial theory*, race is something that can be more or less straightforwardly read off of the way we look. We have obvious, visible, phenotypic traits. Some of those traits, such as one's sexual organs, indicate one's sex. Other traits, such as skin color, indicate one's race. Moreover, it is arguable that there are just a few races, although here the theoretical waters get a little murky. For proponents of the superficial theory (sometimes called a 'typological' view of race), we can quibble about those details later. Race is, in any case, obvious.

One reason to think that races are biological kinds is that those obvious, superficial, phenotypic traits are themselves biological. But another is that they are tied to genetic markers that we can use to sort people into ancestral groups. This link suggests two further tacks for biological racial realism. Rather than appeal to visible traits at all, races might be biological by virtue of their genetic markers. So on this view, when we racially classify people on the basis of their visible traits, we are tapping into what is most appropriately unpacked as a genetic truth: we form different races insofar as each race has a distinctive set of genetic traits. Call this view *genetic racial realism*.

Now a related, sometimes conflated, theory holds that races might simply be ancestrally linked groupings whose members may or may not share certain distinguishing phenotypic or genetic traits (more on this below). According to this view, *populationism*, races are breeding populations; that is, populations or clusters of populations of people who reproduce at a significantly higher rate with other members of the population than with those external to the population, a behavioral pattern of reproductive isolation that usually over long periods of time ensures some non-insignificant degree of genetic distance between the isolated population and external populations.

Thus in the one view, race is something that can be read directly off of our visible physical traits; according to the second theory, race is a matter of our genetic endowments; and in the last view, races are a function of breeding relations. If any of these is vindicated, biological racial realism gains the upper hand in the race debate. And it is not hard to see why any of these theories might be compelling, for they are naturally connected. At this point, it is presumably more or less conventional wisdom within many societies that our genetic endowments are in substantial part inherited from our ancestors and that our visible traits are in large part the expression of our genetic endowments. So if race is thought to connect to visible traits, it should also be thought to connect to genes and therefore ancestry, and therefore to the breeding populations from which we are spawned. And something in the neighborhood of this line of thought is not altogether uncommon, as we saw in the previous chapter.

While importantly different from one another, these realist theories share some virtues. None commits itself to the kind of doomed science race studies used to bandy about, such as that involving different kinds of 'racial blood.' Moreover, none commits itself to there being some sort of deep essence to race. These accounts, at least in broad outline, refrain from positing that our physical traits or ancestry cleave to traits other than the physical or the ancestral. In particular, none of the realist views under consideration now necessarily posits any correlation between the physical or the ancestral, on the one hand, and the moral, intellectual, cultural, or aesthetic, on the other. These days it hardly (though occasionally) needs mentioning that, even if race turns out to be biologically real, biological race does not determine moral status or aptitude, intellect, or beauty. Racist views have been so common in the history of scientific thought that contemporary biological realism should be acknowledged for its independence from such doctrines.

Given these virtues, then, we should distinguish between two more basic ways of understanding race biologically, and collect the three new-wave realist theories on the more plausible side of the divide. On the less plausible side is classical racialism, the view that races carry a *robust* set of distinctive traits. It is fair to say that many have been at pains to show specifically that race *in the classical racialist sense* is not real. This is an important task, and one that has been ably completed by others. It is also as close to a settled debate as we see in academia: there are no races in the classical racialist sense. However, we have seen that the concept of race is thin enough to allow that there might be races even if there are no robust racial essences. So although most serious people who make their living working on race already agree that classical racialism is false, several people still present serious arguments that race in some thinner sense is biologically legitimate. It is on these more viable contemporary accounts that we should now be focusing our attention: Why should we say that race is not biologically real even in one of these thinner ways?

## 5.2 The Ways We Look

### 5.2.1 The Superficial Theory

Anti-realism will be a non-starter if race's biological reality is as obvious as the superficial theory says it is. Armand Marie Leroi (2005) articulated fairly well some hard-to-dispute claims (also see Sarich and Miele 2004, 207–208):

- People have different visible traits, including skin color, facial features, and hair types.
- These different traits are often clustered, so that, say, different skin colors tend to co-vary with different facial features.
- The different clusters can be correlated with different ancestral origins, so that we can just look at many people and justifiably say, 'It's highly probable that many of your ancestors came from Europe, or Africa, or Asia, or Australia, or the Americas.'

Of course, most anti-realists are reasonable people. We acknowledge that people look different from one another and have ancestors who came from different places. So if we can endorse those truisms but still deny the biological reality of race, something else must be the issue of contention. Put one hackneyed way that we have inherited from Plato, the question at hand is whether a system that subdivides us into races based on our visible traits "carves nature at its joints," or whether it instead breaks nature's bones by imposing a gerrymandered classification scheme upon humanity, just as our political boundaries impose a contrived scheme upon the *terra firma*.

### 5.2.2 *The Arbitrariness Objection*

Perhaps the most compelling argument—one that is at least as old as Blumenbach and as popular as any—against the superficial theory begins with the premise that the difference between alleged races is one of gradation, and so there are no biological lines between them. If we look at skin color, for instance, it is not as if everyone has one of five different skin colors. Rather, people occupy very many different locations on a spectrum of shades, from very light to very dark. Similar points are true of our facial features and hair types. Once we recognize this fact, which I will call the *fact of continuity*, it is hard to deny that any system of racial classification based on visible traits must be imposed upon nature by us. We can designate points on the melanometer as the locations of our borders, but those designations are not determined by our biology, and if that is true, then racial categories are, just going off of visible traits, arbitrary. Thus it seems that the superficial theory posits things that don't exist, namely sets of visible traits that are differentiated in biologically non-arbitrary ways. So the fact of continuity generates the *Arbitrariness Objection* to the superficial theory.

Racial realists, and those interested in biological categories more generally, sometimes maintain that the presence of a vague boundary between two categories does not mean that the difference between those categories is illusory (Andreasen 1998, 204; Sober 1993, 147–148). The line between being bald and being hairy is vague, but, they say, we shouldn't conclude from just that point that nobody is really bald or hairy. I think we shouldn't be too quick to uncritically accept this controversial kind of claim, but I don't want that to slow us down, for the point is commonsensical enough to at least be granted to the realist for the sake of argument: even when the boundaries are vague, that doesn't by itself mean that there is no difference outside of those boundaries.

So we shouldn't conflate the Arbitrariness Objection with the objection—the Vagueness Objection—that is the foil for this kind of realist response. The Vagueness Objection seizes upon the fact of continuity and argues that when the boundary between different points on a continuum is arbitrarily drawn, the difference between them is not real. The Arbitrariness Objection is more modest. It, unlike the Vagueness Objection, allows that we really have, say, different skin colors. What it denies is a more specific claim of the superficial theory, namely that we fall into non-arbitrarily demarcated groupings based on visible traits like skin color, and it denies this because our differences on these fronts are nearly perfectly continuous. Thus, just as the Vagueness Objection is arguably too quick to reason that, because the change is gradual, there must be no difference between the different parts on the continuum, the superficial theory moves too hastily from the point that there are real differences between individuals on the continuum to the conclusion that those different points can be bundled according to biologically non-arbitrary boundaries. So the central and distinctive claim of the Arbitrariness Objection, even when we focus on just one visible feature such as skin color, is that because there is no biological reason to draw the boundaries between racial groups that we draw, racial groupings based on distinctive visible traits are biologically arbitrary as *groups* (Zack 2002, 43).[5]

---

5   Zack seems to grant to the biological realist that if the commonsense divisions of a continuously varying trait like skin color were *orderly*, they would capture biological divisions. (She then supplies the further argument that the commonsense division of races is not orderly, since, for example, not every black person has darker skin than every white person.) I think Zack concedes too much here; I think that because an orderly but perfectly continuously varying trait has no biological lines of demarcation (something with which Zack agrees), it is an "insurmountable problem" for the superficial theory (something with which Zack disagrees).

   Many maintain that for a racial division to be biologically legitimate, it must be based on more or less *perfectly* discretely separated categories (cf. Barbujani et al. 1997, 4518; Blackburn 2000, 8; Keita & Kittles 1997, 537). This discreteness criterion might be imported as a rule embedded in the concept of race. It is telling, on this score, that research has shown that people often conceive of races as stable and discrete (Condit et al. 2004, 257). However, this research does not tell us whether the discreteness of race is only part of the ordinary conception, rather than the concept, of race. In any case, the dialectical power of the fact of continuity, as I see it, lies in the fact that continuity entails arbitrariness. So could proponents of the superficial theory abandon the claim that races are discrete groups whose lines of demarcation are written into the biology, as, for example, Sarich and Miele (2004, 209) attempt to do? (It should be noted, though, that Sarich and Miele here present the reader with

Keeping our eye squarely on the Arbitrariness Objection, the problem generated by the fact of continuity is only compounded when we add in more than one visible trait, such as hair texture or facial structure. These additions are crucial for the superficial theory, since groups defined by only one visible trait, such as skin color, do not map very well onto our racial classification systems (Blackburn 2000, 10). However, multiplying phenotypic racial traits has the result, not only that considered in isolation they too gradually shift on a continuum, but even more problematically that, as has also been long pointed out, they correlate with one another in no particular order, throwing the alleged features for biological racial reality into an unorganized mess, one that highlights that we *choose* to organize racial categories around various similarities. In short, there is little if any concordance between skin color and other traits, a phenomenon that we can refer to as the *fact of discordance* (e.g., Blackburn 2000, 12–13; Brown & Armelagos 2001; Cooper et al. 2003; Diamond 1994; Fish 2002; Graves 2001, ix; Keita & Kittles 1997, 537; Shreeve 1994; Taylor 2004, 50–51; Zack 2002, 56). Once again, the discordance problem makes it hard to deny that the clusters of phenotypic features we select as the basis for our racial categories are set off from one another in a gerrymandered fashion, rather than a fashion decided by biology itself.[6]

---

apparently contradictory propositions. While they emphasize that categories don't have to be discrete (see also p. 211), elsewhere (pp. 25, 163) they accept that the ordinary concept of race—which they are expressly trying to vindicate—is such that racial categories are by definition discrete.) The (further) problem is that Sarich and Miele provide no biologically motivated criterion for where to draw the line between gradually shifting visible traits. Without such a criterion, they might have a response to the Vagueness Objection, but not to the Arbitrariness Objection's claim that while racial divisions are responsive to biological traits, those traits are demarcated in biologically unprincipled ways. Now at one point Sarich and Miele write that "questions of 'How many races are there?' and 'How should we classify them'" are not only not productive but also "wrong" and less than "valid" (Sarich & Miele 2004, 209–211). Their first reason for thinking this appears to be that the answer to those questions will depend on our criterion of sorting accuracy. In response it should be noted that, first, that is part of the anti-realist's point—the criterion for sorting accuracy is not given by any biological facts—and, second, we also need to know *where* (not just *how often*) we should draw the lines of demarcation, and the answer isn't given by the biological facts themselves. Their second reason is that they take the truly productive questions to be "how races came to be and the extent to which racial variation has significant consequences with respect to function in the modern world." Well, sure, those are interesting questions, but the supposition, *that race is real*, is a separate proposition, the truth of which Sarich and Miele are also supposed to be proving.

6   The very plausible explanation for the fact of discordance is that different traits are subject to different evolutionary pressures, and so are not selected for at the same rate and in the same direction (Brace 2003, 61). See Brown & Armelagos (2001) for a helpful review of this topic. In addition, some racial markers, such as skin color, seem to have developed through independent processes of selection in different populations, and thus different populations can find themselves bearing *convergent* traits,

One feature of racial classification shines a particularly bright light on the superficial theory's fault-line: different cultures sort the races differently, and no one criterion for sorting seems more biologically principled than the others. The old guard U.S. racial classification system used the one-drop rule, and this is biologically arbitrary, as advocates for mixed-race identity among others have long insisted: biologically speaking, those of mixed black and white ancestry could just as sensibly, arguably more sensibly in many cases, be classified as mixed race or white, and are classified as such in other societies (Blackburn 2000, 6; Zack 1993). And it is not just mixed racial ancestry that illustrates the arbitrariness of local racial classification schemas; different communities can differ widely on this front (Fish 2002). Indeed, it is readily apparent why the racial lines of demarcation that we draw onto our visible traits are set differently in different societies: they often arose under the influence of various social and political pressures that were not dictated by the biology alone. For example, the one-drop rule effectively increased the number of African-descended slaves and crudely attempted to rationalize a corrupt notion of 'white purity,' while a higher quotient of American Indian ancestry (at least a quarter) has been required for one to be officially recognized by the U.S. as an American Indian, effectively *reducing* the number of indigenous Americans (Sundstrom 2001, 287–288, n. 5).

Now it is worth stressing that, even if *we* choose where to divide humanity along lines that are not carved into the biology of the world, that doesn't mean that traits like skin color are any less biological. Those are things *in the world*. They are not inventions, like basketball or journalism or airplanes, and they are not things we have merely imagined, like the powers of witchcraft. So anti-realism should not be interpreted as claiming that purportedly racial traits have no biological basis. Rather, anti-realism claims that even though these are biological features, races—*racial groups*—are not biologically real. Recall again this chapter's favored analogy: even though political borders are

---

such as the similar darkish skin color found in some Sub-Saharan Africans and aboriginal Australians (Bamshad et al. 2003, 587; Bamshad & Olson 2003; Bamshad et al. 2004, 601; Tishkoff & Kidd 2004, S21). In what is supposed to be a realist response to Diamond's discussion of the discordance problem, Sarich and Miele object that

> the discordance issue [Diamond] raises applies within groups as well as between them. He is dismissive of the reality of the Fulani-Xhosa black African racial unity because there are characters discordant with it. Well then, one asks in response, what about the Fulani unit itself? After all, exactly the same argument could be made to cast the reality of the category 'Fulani' into doubt.

(2004, 165–166)

To which the unambiguous reply should be, *Precisely.*

superimposed on natural things—we can point to a piece of dirt and say, 'There's the line between the U.S. and Canada'—those political borders are not part of the natural world. Similarly, while racial borders are superimposed upon our bodies, those borders, and by extension the classes of things marked off by those borders, are not part of the biological world. Certainly, at least, that seems true when the boundaries of those groups are fixed according to our visible traits.[7]

## 5.3  Genetic Racial Realism

Genetic racial realism takes a different approach and holds that race is biologically real by virtue of its correlation with our genetic material. Here's how Sarich and Miele (2004, 23) put it: "If 'race' were a mere social construction based upon a few highly visible features, it would have no statistical correlation with the DNA markers that indicate genetic relatedness," which it does. I want to dispense with this view quickly, as its fortunes seem tied to our next view, populationism.

If, on the one hand, our genetic material is racially relevant because it tracks our visible features, then the facts of continuity and discordance will likely be true of it, too. This kind of point will be important below: racial categories use visible traits, and visible traits can be correlated with genetic material, but this does not guarantee that when we take those traits (and therefore the DNA markers with which they correlate) and assimilate them into categories, we are not creating the categories. We could similarly divide humanity into people 6.4 feet and above, 5.7 to 6.3 feet tall, 4 to 5.6 feet tall, and so on, and in so doing divide ourselves according to traits which are to some degree biologically heritable. Such categories do wrap themselves around real biological facts, just as the category *things that weigh more than 124 kg* applies to physical facts, but for all that we are imposing them on the world, gerrymandering it for our purposes.[8]

---

7   What about trying to identify a paradigmatic member or set of members as typical of each race and then saying that any member of the same race is simply a deviation from type? Hull (1998, 358) asks, with regard to the case of the species *Homo sapiens*, for whom Carolus Linneaus was honored as paradigm: "In what sense is a relatively short, blue-eyed, blonde, male Swede in any sense a typical human being?" The same, no doubt, could be asked of any alleged racial paradigm. As Hull also observes, "Too often, it seems, the deviants outnumber the normal cases."

8   It has been suggested to me that discrete breaks on the genetic level might correlate with clinal differentiation on the visible continuum, as the correlation between the two levels is only *statistical*. Of course, it would be an extraordinary coincidence if the genetic level gave us clear breaks where we happen to partition our species racially on the visible level, a coincidence that should exceed credulity given that different communities select different points of partition. In any case, in §5.4.4 we will see reason to doubt the existence of biologically principled discrete breaks at the genetic level.

If, on the other hand, the significance of "genetic relatedness" lies in the evidence it provides for the proposal that different races are ancestrally demarcated breeding populations (as other comments from Sarich and Miele suggest), then it appears to be at its strongest as a proxy view for populationism, which is the subject of the following section. So I want to subsume our consideration of genetic realism under our consideration of populationism. Indeed, the evidence that we can be partitioned into groups based on our genetic traits—the evidence that there is genetic clustering—is also the most compelling evidence that we fall into breeding populations. And, to the extent that the evidence is the same, it is hard to see how appealing to genetic similarity is going to do much more work than can already be done by appealing to lines of ancestry.

Before moving on, however, a brief word is in order regarding one last argument from Sarich and Miele (2004, 31–32, 50): different cultures have sometimes independently arrived at roughly similar racial classifications, and the tendency to organize humans racially might even be hardwired into our cognitive system, as evidenced by childhood development of racial thinking. Much has been said about the alleged evolutionary basis of racial thinking, but for our orthogonal purposes the short answer is this. Anti-realists can grant that we are hardwired to think in racial terms. (That, in fact, would nicely explain why we have so consistently bought into the illusion!) Thinking that race is real doesn't mean that race is real. No matter how awesome the fact that we all came up with the same ideas, it does not entail that these ideas reflect an independent biological reality. Even when everyone believed that the world was flat, and even if we were predisposed to believe this due to our evolutionarily determined ocular capacities, the world was not actually flat. So just like the Flat Earth Society, Sarich and Miele had better come up with an independent, extra-cognitive argument for the biological reality of race. The most likely source of such an argument is populationism.

## 5.4 Populationism, the Mismatch Objection, and Beyond

### 5.4.1 Populationism and the Race Debate

While it has been in the ether for several decades, lately different versions of the view that races are breeding populations or clusters of breeding populations have been getting sustained defenses by philosophers (Andreasen 1998, 2000, 2004, 2005, 2007; Arthur 2007, ch. 2; Kitcher 1999), natural and social scientists (Burchard et al. 2003; Mayr 2002; Risch et al. 2002; Sarich & Miele 2004), and even some popular writers, such as one of the *New York Times*' science journalists (Wade 2006, ch. 9). While populationists disagree among themselves on some crucial details, the basic picture calls on populations whose members reproduce at significantly higher rates with each other than with those outside the group.[9] As a result of their relative reproductive isolation, each breeding population should eventually bear distinctive genetic and ultimately phenotypic traits. And science, only recently being able to use as evidence genetic markers that number in the thousands (Shriver et al. 2004), seems to have made good on this theory's promise: Sub-Saharan Africans, Europeans, East Asians, Pacific Islanders, and Native Americans appear to be continentally based, ancestrally defined populations with unique genetic clusters. That is, with enough genetic information, and depending on the study in question, science is capable of genetically sorting individuals into some combination of East Asian, Sub-Saharan African, European/West Asian, Native American, and New Guinean/ Melanesian ancestral groupings with an astonishing degree of accuracy, with less success rates for populations that have seen more admixture, such as samples from southern India (Bamshad et al. 2003; Rosenberg et al. 2002). And here's the punch-line. Since many taxonomists now believe that the best way to understand species is as ancestrally defined populations distinguished in terms of the reproductive isolation they experience (rather than any visible similarities distinctive to their members), then if you believe species are real, you should also believe that races—who experience fewer, but not insignificant, rates of reproductive isolation—are also real.

Again, different versions of populationism require different facts of breeding populations—that they are (or are not) evolutionarily significant, that they must contain (or do not necessarily contain) distinctive genetic or phenetic structures, that they would have to (or not have to) remain reproductively isolated even when given ample opportunity to interbreed, and so on—and the relevant differences will emerge shortly.[10] For now I only want to note that, in broad strokes, there is

---

9   For simplicity, I will henceforth talk of breeding populations and omit talk of clusters of breeding populations.

10   The fact that two populations happen not to have interbred is not evidence that they *would* not interbreed, which is arguably the key biological criterion here (Kitcher 1999). But since some populationists only require that there should not have been interbreeding, I will assume this weaker criterion. Furthermore, while Risch and colleagues (2002, 3) think that race has "potential meaning" because "it defines an endogamous group," that is, it picks out a group that is geographically and reproductively isolated, many—including some populationists—in fact deny this and maintain that "nothing like reproductive isolation exists for subspecific groupings" (Hull 1998, 363). So some of the controversy over populationism seems to trade on how much reproductive isolation is required for groups to count as legitimate biological units: for some, human populations have swapped enough genetic material that they are not isolated to a sufficient degree to count as separate breeding populations (cf. Keita & Kittles 1997, 536; Pigliucci & Kaplan 2003, 1164; Romualdi et al. 2002; Sarich & Miele 2004, 131); for Andreasen (1998, 214), the slow evaporation of reproductive

much to be said in favor of this view, not least that it has the support of some impressive recent data. (For further review, see Race, Ethnicity, and Genetics Working Group 2005.) So the stage seems to be set for a realist advance: if the data show that there are biologically real breeding populations, and if these populations are races in the relevant sense, then we might have good reason to say that race is biologically real.[11]

As is no doubt clear by now, 'in the relevant sense' is going to do a lot of work here. One thing that is sometimes said is that even if race in the ordinary sense is not real, the reality of human breeding populations means that 'race' in some biologists' sense is real. Andreasen (2005) has called attention to this maneuver by suggesting that the scientific and the lay concepts of race might be *autonomous* (if in some way related historically, prior to their divergence), or as we might instead put it, independent from one another (cf. Arthur 2007, 82–84; Brown 2004; Pigliucci & Kaplan 2003). In this case there must be literally two different concepts of race, in the way that the term 'bank' can mean either a landmass alongside a river or a financial institution. It is worth re-emphasizing, then, that the concern of the race debate—the concern of *this* book, anyway—is whether race, as defined within the constraints of ordinary use, is real. If scientists use 'race' in a way that deviates from the way it is used by the folk, such that, say, a group of people who reproduce exclusively with those in the right cocktail party circuit or profession count as a race on the scientific but not folk definitions, then 'race' can be defined in (at least) two ways: a scientific way, and a way constrained by folk usage. Now as a separate matter, we have seen that folk might defer to scientists in ways that give scientists some of the authority to identify the reference of even folk racial terms, and new discoveries of biological facts might alter how we characterize the definition of the folk term 'race,' but whether or not either of these possibilities materializes, our focus is only on folk racial concepts. If 'race' (like 'force field') can be a term of art with a meaning that deviates from

---

isolation means that race is "disappearing"; and for Kitcher (1999, 94, cf. 95, 115, n. 9), racial classifications are not biologically warranted if the mixed-race population fails to remain "relatively small." (As discussed above, Kitcher (2007, 301) has more recently suggested, in a pragmatist vein that dovetails with some arguments I will put forth below, that in part because there are many ways of carving ourselves, none of which are uniquely privileged by the biological world itself, our taxonomies are imposed upon the world by us.) Clearly what counts as sufficient reproductive isolation is not an easy issue, and just as clearly, populationists could help their cause if they sorted out this issue in a non-controversial way. I'll also proceed as if there is some good answer to this question.

11  Even paradigmatic anti-realists such as Appiah sometimes admit that at least on some theories of reference, 'race' seems to refer to populations (Appiah 1991, 7; 1996, 72–73). But in that case he thinks it better to talk in terms of populations, rather than race (Appiah 1991, 12, n. 9).

its folk meaning, then that deviating meaning—even if it consists of a *closely related* concept—is for others to discuss. Our topic is whether folk racial discourse should ultimately be conserved, eliminated, or reconstructed, and so we want to know whether *it* is vindicated by the biological facts.[12]

### 5.4.2 The Mismatch Objection

With attention focused squarely on the ordinary concept of race, a number of us have pressed various versions of what Mallon has called the "Mismatch" Objection to populationism. The basic idea is that the breeding populations identified by science and the (intensional) meaning of the term 'breeding population' match neither the groups picked out by ordinary racial discourse nor the ordinary (intensional) meaning of the term 'race.' Consequently, breeding populations might be real, but they are not races in the relevant sense.[13]

The first point of mismatch can be approached by noting that within each breeding population there are huge gradations in skin color (Wade 2006, 184). More generally, populationists like Nicholas Wade are quite upfront that "the genetic definition of race … has nothing directly to do with any physical attribute" (Wade 2006, 188; cf. 193–194). Since genetic attributes are surely physical attributes, presumably this is a mis-statement; what Wade must mean is that his account of race does not directly correlate with physical features that are *visible to the naked eye*—what I have been simply calling 'visible traits.' However, as we have seen, skin color, among other visible traits, appears to be a core component of ordinary racial concepts. Thus there appears to be a mismatch: racial groups are conceptually organized in part by skin color, while human breeding populations are not.

So the first step in launching the mismatch argument is to insist that Neil Risch and colleagues (2002, 4) are incorrect when they state that "[r]acial categorizations have never been based on skin pigment, but on

---

12   It is worth observing here that some scientists seem to think race is not real in part because they use 'race' in the way that the rest of us use it.

13   Though few put the argument quite this way, and though different people emphasize different details of the mismatch and take it in different directions, variations on the mismatch theme may be found in Appiah (1996, 71–74); Blum (2002, 143–144); Condit (2005); Feldman et al. (2003); Glasgow (2003); Hirschfeld (1996, 4); Jorde & Wooding (2004); Keita et al. (2004); Keita & Kittles (1997, 538); Montagu (1964b, 7); Witherspoon et al. (2007); Zack (2002, esp. chs 2, 4, and 5). To be sure, even some of those whose data to an extent ratify human breeding populations or who think there is *some* viable non-folk concept of race agree that there is a substantial mismatch between the facts of biological populations and ordinary racial discourse (e.g., Bamshad & Olson 2003; Bamshad et al. 2004, 601; cf. Pigliucci & Kaplan 2003, 1166).

indigenous continent of origin." To this extent the experimental and armchair data are in, and they indicate that visible features such as skin color have proven more crucial to racial categorizations than other factors, including continental origins. This partly explains why, in their research with focus groups, Condit and colleagues (2003, 2004) found that lay understandings of race do not map onto credible continental clusters. (Note that to identify such a mismatch is not to say that geographic origin is wholly irrelevant to the lay understanding of race (Condit et al. 2004, 258).)

This divergence, indeed, gets us to other points of mismatch. Consider a compelling way of putting one such point from David Hull (1998, 364–365):

> Several groups of people who are considered Caucasoids by anthropologists would rouse all the anxiety and hostility in ordinary white racists that blacks do. Their skin is black. They look black. But technically, they are Caucasoids. But such observations are not likely to persuade the members of the admissions committee of an all-white country club.

More generally, racial terms are applied to individuals in a way that does not map onto how science applies breeding population terms to individuals.

In addition, the very populations that are identified as genetic clusters don't always map onto commonsense racial categories.[14] On that score, Risch and colleagues themselves observe that people generally self-identified in the 2000 census as members of only one race when the genetic picture is actually one of widespread admixture, and they note that "the U.S. census would also not merge Chinese with New Guineans," as their data on continental clusters require (Risch et al. 2002, 5–6). For a further example, consider that the data suggest that Hispanics are not a race, and are instead the result of an admixture of scientifically validated breeding populations (Risch et al. 2002, 3, 5–6; Wade 2006, 185; cf. Bamshad et al. 2004, 607).[15] But in the United States, some 42

---

14  For a model of how we can deviate in phenotype from our genetic populations, which can explain how we pick out both individuals and groups in ways that do not match their genetic clusters, see Witherspoon et al. (2007, 358).

15  Tang and colleagues (2005) found genetic clustering for Hispanics, but their sample was limited to Mexican Americans from one location in Texas. It remains to be shown that the entire population of Hispanics form a distinctive genetic cluster. I should add that while many researchers who work on these questions (e.g., Condit et al. 2003; Wade 2006, 185) seem to classify Hispanics or Latinos as a linguistic group, members of this group use multiple languages, and non-members speak those languages, so the grounds for classifying it as a linguistic group are shaky at best (see, e.g., Gracia 2000, 9–10; 2005, 15; Nuccetelli 2007, 143).

percent of Hispanics on the 2000 census said they were of a race other than the ones listed, which later research showed was mainly the case because they considered *Hispanic* to be their race (a categorization disallowed by the census) (Navarro 2003; cf. Condit et al. 2003). Later research also showed that if asked the open-ended question of what you take your race to be, a true majority of Latinos will racially identify as Latino (Haney López 2005, 46). Given the widespread phenomenon of claiming a racially distinctive Latino identity, Haney López suggests dividing up the conceptual terrain so that there are black Hispanics, white Hispanics, Asian Hispanics, American Indian Hispanics, and ... here's the point ... *Latino* Hispanics. Now if it would be conceptually non-negotiable for a significant chunk of our linguistic community to give up their own racial identity of being Latino, populationism will almost certainly fail, so long as it cannot find a coherent biological basis for saying that Latinos constitute a race.[16]

To be sure, the categorical mismatch doesn't end there. The data also combine, for example, Europeans, Middle Easterners, and Asians west and south of the Himalayas into one race (e.g., Risch et al. 2002; Rosenberg et al. 2002)—which at least on the surface seems to run against some mainstream ordinary American classifications, including those that do not classify South Asians as white (Blum 2002, 151; Fish 2002, 124) and that have increasingly 'racialized' Arabic peoples as non-white (Alcoff 2006, 258; Taylor 2004, 147). Examples like these—and there are still others, such as that there is actually *more* genetic diversity within Africans than between Africans and Europeans and Asians (Yu et al. 2002), which entails that if we want to use genetic diversity to say that Africans are racially different from Europeans or Asians, whether we use that diversity to indicate genetically defined groupings or as evidence for distinct lineages, we would also have to say that Africans do not themselves constitute a race—render populationism highly susceptible to the mismatch argument. So despite *some* points of correspondence and despite some assertions to the contrary (e.g., Mountain & Risch 2004, S52; Risch et al. 2002, 3; Sarich & Miele 2004, 25; Tang et al. 2005, 268, 273; Wade 2006, 184), scientifi-

---

16   You don't have to look very far to find instances of the racialization of Latinos, and it is not just a matter of self-identification. To again turn to the U.S. presidential elections, the media and pollsters regularly represent (people whom they usually call) Hispanics as a racial voting bloc whose voting preferences are to be distinguished from those of racial groups like blacks and whites. As my appeals to these kinds of cases indicates, while some, such as Hardimon (2003, 450), believe that the concept of race is not in itself tied to any particular set of racial categories, I think this will actually be a more context-sensitive matter of how negotiable the various categorizations are to the relevant set of language users.

cally identified breeding populations seem not to correspond very well with ordinary racial categories.[17]

Not unrelatedly, some studies have shown that you will get different populations depending on the genotypes you select, and while this might give populationists hope for a match, it seems to show that there is no principled way of carving humanity into different large-ish populations. For example, Romualdi and collaborators (2002) found that one set of data generated evidence of a Eurasian group and two roughly global other groups, while another lumped together Africa and Oceania. Thus, with each study differing in priorities, genetic material, and—even when the *same* data set is examined across studies—simply unique assumptions, different studies sometimes fail to match not only common sense, but also each other (Barbujani 2005; Barbujani & Belle 2006; Lao et al. 2006). Guido Barbujani and Elise Belle (2006) take this inconsistent clustering to be evidence of what I call the fact of continuity. The scent of arbitrariness is in the air.

### 5.4.3 The Elusive Match

But even if science has so far given us only mismatching populations, it is worth asking whether populationism might find a more *theoretical* device to secure the right kind of match. To see how such a proposal might work, consider two kinds of populationism. What I will call *constrained* populationism holds that for populations to count as races, the members of those populations must by and large share various visible traits of the relevant kind. This version of populationism is accepted by some (e.g., Kitcher 1999), but many populationists, including Andreasen, Wade, and Mountain and Risch (2004), do not commit to this constraint. They insist that for a breeding population to be biologically real, its members need not share any visible (or genetic) traits at all; they must simply conform to certain specified breeding patterns. Thus, *unconstrained* populationism maintains that races can be populations without having *any* roughly distinctive visible or genetic traits.[18]

---

17  Some versions of populationism seem to suffer from the mismatch problem particularly badly. For example, Sarich and Miele (2004, 172) judge that the Dogon, Teita, and Bushmen (their terms) are distinctive races, as are people from Athens and Copenhagen (p. 210), but most of these groups don't seem to qualify as races as ordinarily conceived (presumably at least in part because these groups do not have readily identifiable distinctive visible traits). Of course, Sarich and Miele are entitled to use the word "race" however they want. But their central and explicit aim is to vindicate the *ordinary* concept of race, and so they cannot soundly replace ordinary race-talk with some other kind of talk.

18  Unconstrained populationism, insofar as it does not appeal to genetic clustering, is going to have a hard time coming up with any decisive evidence that there are races (evidence we need if we are to conclude that race not merely *could* be real, but *is* real). Of course, there are other kinds of evidence, such as the linguistic or archeological

Now there is reason to adopt unconstrained populationism: it appears that the only way to have a biologically privileged and noise-free classification system is to *simply* limit it to mapping branches of descent and exclude all reference to similarities of intrinsic properties. But while its freedom from the problems plaguing the superficial theory is unconstrained populationism's key to enhanced plausibility, the cost of that freedom is that it now seems to wander too far from the ordinary concept of race to be relevant. That is, it is what generates the Mismatch Objection.

Beyond what we have already seen, clearly non-racial populations that are reproductively isolated would seemingly have to count as 'races' on unconstrained accounts (Appiah 1996, 73; Blum 2002, 144; Kitcher 1999, 103–104). That is, economic classes, peasants, the Amish, or Ivy Leaguers who work with and socialize (and therefore reproduce) at a distinctively high rate with fellow Ivy Leaguers would have to count as races, a posit that violates the conceptual constraint that races must have phenotypic profiles of the relevant kinds.

Perhaps a thought experiment from Chapter 2 best makes the point: if the global water supply was infused with an agent that instantaneously changed all of us to look roughly like the Dalai Lama, it seems intuitive to say that there is no longer any racial difference between us. (As one focus group participant memorably judged the idea that visible appearance is eliminable from the concept of race, "...someone probably wasn't being 100 percent honest if they said color wasn't one of the first one or two things that popped into their head [when asked about race]" (Dubriwny et al. 2004, 189).) But unconstrained populationism implies otherwise. It says, counterintuitively, that even though we would look the same, our ancestors' breeding patterns mean that we would comprise different races.[19] On this count, let me borrow one other case from Dupré (1981, 88):

---

records, but the most compelling evidence, if it is ever to be found at all, is likely to be found buried in the genetic record. Given this common evidence, while their commitments are always distinctive, arguments that appeal to genetic evidence on behalf of populationism sometimes come hand in hand with arguments on behalf of genetic racial realism.

19  Putnam (1975a, 1975b) famously maintained that if there were a mutation and tigers lost their stripes, we would still say they were tigers. Putnam's intuition concerns a scenario in which, first, tigers are the only species that undergo a change, and, second, they still bear visible marks that distinguish them from other species. A species-level scenario comparable to the race-level scenario we are considering would, instead, be one in which *all* species (or perhaps only all mammalian species) underwent a change so that they all looked more or less the same—say, so that all mammals looked and behaved like humans. Is a tiger that is altered to look and behave exactly like Bill Clinton still a tiger? I'm inclined to say 'no,' to say that the 'tiger' has at that point become a human being. And Putnam seems to agree, at least at times (1962, 660). In any case the view I advocate here converges with Putnam's view that while the world

If, say, a chicken began to lay perfectly ordinary walnuts which were planted and grew into walnut trees, I would not wish to refer to this result as the production of a grove of chickens. If accepted, this intuition shows that the right ancestry is not a sufficient condition for taxon membership.

Dupré uses this thought experiment in the service of a much broader agenda than we have here, but the point holds equally well in the narrower case of race: if all the members of R₁ exclusively produced an entire generation that for some reason looked exactly like members of *another* race, R₂, we wouldn't be inclined to say that the new generation and its descendants were R₁s. We would say that we had seen R₁s produce a generation of R₂s. If anything can be learned from such examples, it is not only that ancestry is not sufficient for the generation of a race, but also that morphology apparently matters a great deal.[20]

If these intuitions are on target, then populationism can comport with the ordinary concept of race only by accepting as a pre-existing theoretical commitment the constraint that breeding populations must preserve the relevant visible characteristics to count as races.[21] That is, the only form of populationism viable for the race debate is constrained populationism. So, is there any theoretical, non-*ad-hoc* reason to expect that our breeding patterns might yield visibly distinctive breeding populations so as to converge with our folk racial categories?

can determine (and convey via science) the referents of our terms, it does so only within the constraints of our referential intentions. Once the world strays too far from our intentions regarding some term—such as with a Clintonian 'tiger'—the world no longer supplies a referent to the term. Regarding a closer case from Putnam (1975a), of lemons changing from yellow to blue, we should say the same thing: if *all* lemons looked and behaved exactly like a blue lemon, distinguishing between blue lemons and non-blue lemons would no longer make much sense, and in Putnam's privileged sense of meaning, focused on stereotypes, the meaning of 'lemon' would change insofar as its stereotype would change.

20  It is sometimes held that ancestry is sufficient, since, for example, people who do not have the morphology typical of their race can 'pass' as members of another race; seemingly, the only reason we nonetheless classify them as members of their race is their ancestry. This is, recall, a point at which the difference between an individual's race and a racial group becomes important. It seems that for some individuals, ancestry is sufficient to give them their racial identities; it is consistent with this, however, that distinctive ancestry alone is not sufficient to make an otherwise indistinguishable group a distinct race.

21  Note that these intuitions expose points about morphology being central to the *concept* of race, in which case it is insufficient for populationists to insist that morphology isn't irrelevant to the science of race because scientists can use morphology to *indicate* reproductive isolation (Andreasen 2004, 436–437; 2005, 99). Populationists need to further *require* that specifically racial breeding populations have distinctive morphologies, but the very point and purpose of unconstrained populationism, its very liberation from similarity-based forms of classification, means that it cannot (and aims not to) show that.

Here Kitcher (1999, 106) makes an intriguing proposal: since our breeding patterns are structured by social norms, including some societies' rules against interracial intimacy, our belief in, and attitudes about, racial categories might influence reproductive behaviors so that we would end up falling into breeding populations that do match ordinary racial categories. In this case, "while the concept of human races may have biological significance … the explanation of the mating preferences [that generate races] may have no biological significance" (Kitcher 1999, 107).[22]

In order to believe this proposal, we need solid evidence of low inter-population reproductive rates. Kitcher (1999, 98–100) presents some evidence that there is low interracial marriage in the United States, particularly between blacks and whites. (One assumes that a low rate of inter-population marriage means low inter-population reproduction, although social taboos, family pressures, racism, and violence have clearly pushed many interracial reproductive events out of the institution of marriage, so that evidence of interracial reproduction is very likely conservative.) However, there is much less inter-population reproduction elsewhere: within the United States, Asians and Latino/as appear to be mating with blacks and whites at much greater rates—one estimate has Hispanics in the U.S. marrying non-Hispanics at a rate of 70 percent (Cantave & Harrison 2001; Kitcher 1999, 116, n. 18; Will 2003). More generally, Joshua R. Goldstein (1999, 399) estimates, for example, that by 1990 (almost two decades ago now!), the American family was such that

> [o]ne in seven whites, one in three blacks, four in five Asians, and more than 19 in 20 American Indians are closely related to someone of a different racial group. Despite an intermarriage rate of about 1%, about 20% of Americans count someone from a different racial group among their kin.

Furthermore, current data suggest that African Americans have on average around 80 percent African ancestry, in a range that spans from 20 to 100 percent, while approximately 30 percent of European Americans have less than 90 percent European ancestry (Shriver et al. 2003).

To look not just at static time-slices but also at longer term trends, the black-white intermarriage rate shot upward to some 700 percent between 1960 and 2000, from 51,000 to 363,000. More generally, the number of interracial marriages appears to have grown from 150,000 in

---

22  While in this earlier piece Kitcher articulated a way in which constrained population-ism might be run, recall that he has recently expressed some skepticism about racial realism, including skepticism towards the idea that breeding patterns will trend towards isolation (Kitcher 2007).

1960 to 1.46 million in 2000 (Cantave & Harrison 2001). To be sure, this rate of growth over four decades is hardly a revolution in itself,[23] but the skyrocketing absolute number of the increase is evidential and no doubt at least partly enabled by social changes that have taken place in that time and that show little sign of abating. Finally, and perhaps most tellingly, interracial children's "rate of growth since the early 1970s is 260 percent compared to 15 percent for monoracial persons" (Blum 2002, 174).

So if we are admixed to such a significant degree and trending towards increasing admixture, it is unclear that many among us fall into real breeding populations that match our racial classifications. And, it is worth adding, in many areas outside of the U.S., such as Brazil, physical appearance has been shown to be a decidedly *poor* indicator of ancestry (Parra et al. 2003). Some populationists, such as Andreasen, think that races are real in principle but disappearing—or already gone—precisely because of these trends. The fact that levels of reproductive isolation differ at different locations led Kitcher (1999, 100) to entertain the possibility that there might be races in some locations but not in others, but by now you will have anticipated that I think that this too seems to pick out a notion of 'race' that is just not the notion of race we ordinarily work with. Assuming the right reproduction frequencies, it would mean that you could have a race if you're in Mississippi, but not if you're in Rio or Oakland. Since you might fall within one isolated group in one place and another in another place, it also means that local breeding patterns might change your race as you take a trip from the one location to the other.[24]

So given the facts as we currently know them, populationism seems to have little chance of surviving the Mismatch Objection. However, given the rapid advances of science, we should acknowledge that it is at least *possible* for the Mismatch Objection to someday succumb to future research in population genetics showing that our concept of race *perfectly* picks out scientifically identified breeding populations. (Science is progressing so rapidly in this area that I fear that by the time these

---

23  In the United States over the same period, the population alone increased by about 1 percent each year, with increased levels during the trailing years of the baby boom. See http://www.census.gov/popest/archives/1990s/popclockest.txt.

24  There is some limited evidence (Dubriwny et al. 2004; Glasgow et al. in press) of folk usage accepting what race theorists are fond of noting, namely that your race can apparently change depending on the location you're in—that your 'race does not travel' (a controversial phenomenon discussed at length in Glasgow 2007; Mallon 2004; Root 2000). However, to the extent that it is true, this evidence and theory seems mostly confined to the point that different locations use different systems of racial classification, and *this* is why your race might change; it does not say that your race might change as a direct result of who has been reproducing with whom in various locations.

words reach the bookshelves, even this sentence will be out of date.) So while I remain enthusiastic about the force of the Mismatch Objection, it also would not hurt to imagine what we would want to say if there was such a perfect match.[25] For this, we will have to head into new territory.

### 5.4.4 Beyond the Mismatch Argument

Unarguably outdated scientific theories of race, such as classical racialism, failed to comport with the facts as ascertained by the most advanced science. If the Mismatch Objection is correct, populationism fails to show that its populations comport with the commonsense concept of race. The current question is whether, even if there were a *perfect* match between ordinary race-talk and the biological facts about breeding populations, such populations would actually constitute real biological kinds, or alternatively would still be gerrymandered, with borders superimposed on nature by us. The answer, I think, is that they are gerrymandered.

It is a safe assumption, and was granted above, that some aspect of our heritable genetic material underlies the visible traits we commonly use to classify the races. So, for all the whiz-bang science behind populationism, and for all the serious effort it has taken to get its sophisticated and impressive results, it should not have come as a massive surprise that if we can utilize visible traits to make rough-and-ready folk racial classifications, we should be able to find some genetic markers that correlate with our folk racial classifications. And, under the entirely uncontroversial premise that we inherit much of our genetic material, it should not come as a surprise that those genetic traits can provide evidence that we have fallen into various breeding patterns. I will call this proposition—that members of ordinarily identified racial groups to some degree share certain genetic markers that may in turn be tied to various ancestral populations—the *Unsurprising Result*. Fans of the Mismatch Objection maintain, of course, that those ties are too slippery to sustain the ordinary concept of race, but again let us put aside this worry and imagine that the Unsurprising Result instead generated a *perfect* match between scientifically identified human populations and races, as defined by ordinary use.

---

25  This possibility is also worth considering in light of the fact that the Mismatch Objection has its detractors. For a criticism of details in my own earlier presentation of the mismatch argument (Glasgow 2003), see Andreasen (2005). Chapter 3 above effectively constitutes part of a response to Andreasen, but for the rest of the response see my contribution to Allan Hazlett, ed., *New Waves in Metaphysics* (Palgrave-Macmillan, forthcoming).

Despite its intuitive force and the way it is called into service by the recent wave of biological realism, the Unsurprising Result seemingly has one unfriendly implication for populationism: if folk racial groups are demarcated by visible traits in biologically arbitrary ways, the Unsurprising Result should mean that the breeding populations that putatively correlate with the visible traits to which our folk classifications are sensitive are also demarcated in biologically arbitrary ways. If the contagion of arbitrariness infects biological racial realism at the visible level, it should also spread to its genetic bases and to the patterns of breeding that give rise to those bases. Hence the unfriendly implication: if populationism is going to maintain that there *is* a match between its populations and race, then it is seemingly committed to selecting biologically arbitrary groups as races.[26]

Briefly put, populationism faces a dilemma. Breeding populations either sufficiently match ordinary racial classifications or they do not. If they do not, then populationism falls to the Mismatch Objection. If they do, then populationism falls to the Arbitrariness Objection. On this second horn of the dilemma, the short story is that moving to the genetic or ancestral as opposed to the visible level does not by itself guarantee that the resultant division of humanity is a division that marks legitimate biological kinds, any more than a division of humans by general height categories tracks principled biological categories. So even if we imagine that we could coherently divide humanity according to not just one visible feature but a complex set of them, and even if the division we ended up with matched ancestral groupings that bore a corresponding set of genetic markers, that wouldn't mean that those divisions are biologically principled kinds. For that, we need to know that these populations are set off from one another via some biologically principled criterion.

Like many short stories, this is too quick. Several studies have been able to identify at least some continental populations and use a person's genetic profile to very reliably sort her into those populations without knowing her self-reported racial identity (for some recent examples, see Lao et al. 2006; Witherspoon et al. 2007). This leaves us with a puzzle. On the one hand, if our folk racial classification schema is biologically arbitrary, and if our folk division is, in principle and to some significant

---

26  Despite our dialectical presumption in this section, note that none of this presupposes that there will be no variation between breeding patterns, genetic profiles, and clusters of visible traits. Of course, the claim here is not that the arbitrariness will be exactly the *same* at the genetic and visible levels: genes don't have shades in the way that skin colors have shades. Instead, the idea is that as we go from individual to individual and population to population across roughly geographical lines, we will mostly see slight, non-discrete changes in genetic makeup, such that those that are very far apart will be very different, but neighbors will be not so different. The genetic analysis will show largely, if not entirely, *clinal* differentiation (Livingstone 1964).

extent, reducible to ancestral populations with distinctive genetic traits, then a genetically identified population classification system that *does* match the folk system of racial classification should be biologically arbitrary too. And yet, on the other hand, it seems that scientists can use various genetic markers to infer biologically demarcated human populations.

It is tempting to resolve this puzzle by noting that little is known about the genes that control physical appearance, and that the genetic markers used to identify breeding populations have not been shown to be the direct causes of physical appearance (Mountain & Risch 2004, S51; Wade 2006, 188; Zack 2002, 41), in which case the arbitrary lines of demarcation drawn within the continua of visible traits might not be the genetic lines that are observed in the identification of breeding populations. However, we are supposing for the moment that even if those lines are not identical, there is at least a correspondence between folk classifications and populationist classifications, and it would be an utterly astonishing coincidence if our arbitrary visibly based folk classifications happened to correspond perfectly with an entirely non-arbitrary classification system whose structure is hidden in our genes. Utterly astonishing coincidences are not satisfying solutions to puzzles.

A more plausible solution appears to lie in the details of how the science has been done. The arbitrariness of our phenotype-based racial classification schemes is evidenced in large part by the fact that when we line up all of humanity, we find a continuum of skin colors, hair textures, and so on. So to see if this fact of continuity is also true of genetically identified population classification schemes, we need to get a whole swath of genetic samples from continuous and global locations and then see whether the cut-off lines between purportedly racial continental populations are biologically grounded or whether the genetic variation is continuous. The suspicion that we will find continuity should be piqued by the observation, acknowledged even by died-in-the-wool populationists like Risch and Wade, that there are, at least, "intermediate groups" found at the geographic and genetic boundary between two races, such as Ethiopians and Somalis between those to their north and south or South Asians between East Asians and Europeans, where the lines between the populations are blurred.[27] Suspicion is also warranted by the fact that as geographically intermediate regions are added to the data, the genetic markers used to identify continental clusters become less powerful, in which case "the inclusion of such samples demonstrates geographic continuity in the distribution of genetic variation and thus undermines traditional concepts of race"

---

27  It is unclear, of course, what biological justification there is for calling them "intermediate," but that is what they are often called.

(Bamshad et al. 2003, 587).[28] So what do high degrees of inter-population admixture mean for the population clusters that, we are assuming for the sake of argument (and contrary to fact), match our folk racial categories?

A recent paper from David Serre and Svante Pääbo (2004) undertook to examine this very question (cf. Jorde & Wooding 2004; Lewontin 1972). In response to research purporting to show that humanity clusters neatly into continental clades, Serre and Pääbo investigated how the samples for this research were isolated, in part for the very reason that this kind of research sometimes intentionally excludes admixed people or assumes that no individual sampled by the study comes from multiple lines of ancestry (e.g., Bastos-Rodrigues et al. 2006), and that, when people of mixed ancestry are included, science, understandably, has much less success in accurately assigning them to a single genetic cluster (Bamshad et al. 2003, 2004). They found that when the research sample is composed of people from "the extremes of continental land masses," you will see a little admixture but a lot of clustering that suggests large, continentally based, relatively discrete units. However, when the sample is composed of geographically diverse people, what results is a picture of genetic differentiation that exhibits little continental discontinuity, that displays gradual change along roughly geographical lines, and that includes a substantial amount of mixed ancestry for just about every individual, where the "admixture … changes continuously with geographical distance without any major discontinuities" (Serre & Pääbo 2004, 1683). This suggests that a more complete picture—one that relies on representative continuous as opposed to unrepresentative discontinuous sampling—at most allows one to say that "individuals can be assigned to *culturally predefined* populations on the basis of their genotypes" (Serre & Pääbo 2004, 1683, emphasis added; cf. Ramachandran et al. 2005). And this plausibly resolves the puzzle: the fact of continuity seems alive and well even at the levels of ancestry and genes, as would seem to be the natural consequence of the Unsurprising Result.[29]

---

28  (Cf. Bamshad et al. 2004, 601; Barbujani 2005; Barbujani & Belle 2006; Barbujani et al. 1997, 4518; Blackburn 2000, 14–15, 17; Bowcock et al. 1994, 456–457; Gannett 2004, 341–342; King & Motulsky 2002, 2343; Tishkoff & Kidd 2004, S25). For discussion of the blurriness of boundaries when intermediate groups are considered, see Burchard et al. (2003); Risch et al. (2002, 3–4); Rosenberg et al. (2002, 2382); Wade 2006, 184–185). Also relevant here is evidence of genes that have been swapped across entire continents for some time (Barbujani 2005; Romualdi et al. 2002).

29  Here I have focused on the fact of continuity and put the fact of discordance to one side. At this point, though, it may not be surprising to note that when Barbujani and Belle (2006) looked at the same data set as the one used by Rosenberg and colleagues (2002) (whose original study has been used as so much ammunition by populationists), they found that discordance exists on the genetic level, much as it does on the visible level.

The debate doesn't end there, however. Noah Rosenberg and colleagues (2005) followed up on the research from Serre and Pääbo,
finding it based on an insufficient amount of data. Considering consid-
erably more data, Rosenberg and colleagues not only did not find that
a less geographically random sample resulted in more genetic clustering, but in fact found that such a sample resulted in *less* clustering.
This result is noteworthy, but care is in order here. First, this study
tested the fact of continuity by seeing if there were more discontinuities
among non-random samples than among random samples, but the
samples themselves were not consistently taken from globally continuous regions. Thus their admittedly probative evidence doesn't tell us
how many dis/continuities we would find if we examined a continuous
swath of samples from around the globe. At present, we apparently
don't have a truly representative, continuous set of samples, and until
we do, populationism cannot be vindicated (Handley et al. 2007). The
importance of this point is testified to by the fact that Rosenberg and
colleagues confirmed yet again that 'intermediate' populations for
which there *were* samples—such as in Pakistan and western China—
did not reveal discontinuities between the populations they ostensibly
separate (Eurasians and East Asians), a result that likely holds globally
(Witherspoon et al. 2007). Second, what Rosenberg and colleagues
measured was distance between populations, rather than individuals.
As we will see shortly, this is significant, for what we in the race debate
need to know is whether there is continuity from individual to individual, not just from population to population, in order to know
whether the fact of continuity means that our racial groupings of individuals are arbitrary. Third, for the Arbitrariness Objection to call the
fact of continuity into service, it does not require that there be *no* discontinuities, such as at some geographic barriers like the Sahara and
the Himalayas (Handley et al. 2007), but only that there be continuous
links from population to population, and again, from individual to
individual.

Furthermore, Rosenberg and colleagues confirmed what nearly all
studies in the current generation of research have found, namely that
although different levels of classification are not equally statistically
robust, the populations identified in any give study depend on how
many genetic clusters the researchers tell their computer programs to
find. This suggests that while we maybe *can*—again (counterfactually)
assuming a perfect match—find genetic clusters that correspond to
racial groups, *we* have to decide how many clusters we are going to
look for, and thus getting a racial rather than non-racial set of clusters
is underdetermined by the biological facts; to get the data to give us
particularly *racial* populations, *we* must impose certain constraints on
the biological world, gerrymandering it for our purposes (Kitcher 2007,
304–305). As L.L. Cavalli-Sforza and colleagues (1994, 19) noted prior

to the recent populationist surge, so long as it is up to us whether to be "lumpers," who see fewer, larger populations on the biological scene, or "splitters," who see many, smaller ones, the taxonomy of race is biologically underdetermined.

Lastly, perfect assignment of individuals to populations is not tantamount to a demonstration that we do not as a whole make up a continuous population. Indeed, while Witherspoon and colleagues have shown that if many thousands of loci are used to assign an individual to a population, no individual will be genetically more similar to those outside of her population than those within her population, measures of similarity used to identify populations and individual proximity to them are based on similarities found within the population as a whole, not within each individual (Witherspoon et al. 2007, 357). Demonstrating that the last person in population α has more of population α's genetic markers than those of any other population does not demonstrate that that person is closer to the first person in population α than the first person in population β, in which case the last person in α and the first in β might very well share more lines of ancestry or genetic material with each other than each shares with several others in 'their own' population. I may have more of my population's genetic markers than the markers of any other population, when that commonality is understood as a relation between my genetic profile and some sort of (say) average or aggregative genetic profile for each candidate population, but that doesn't mean that I have more in common genetically, or ancestrally, with each *member* of my population than with anyone outside of my population.

Given these points, it remains likely, if not decided, that if we line up humanity, we can group ourselves in various ways without being required to say that those groupings reflect genetically or ancestrally discontinuous distinctions. Now it is sometimes said that even if there is a continuum of traits or of reproductive patterns across the globe, or even just across one continent, this does not mean that the populations at the extremities of the continuum are not distinct races (Andreasen 2004, 440 n. 7; Kitcher 1999, 98). Scientists sometimes offer demurring criteria, such as the criterion that populations fail to constitute subspecies (and therefore races) either when they geographically and reproductively overlap (Mayr & Ashlock 1991, 44) or when they gradually meld into one another (Mayr & Ashlock 1991, 98–100). But beyond the appeal to scientific practice, it seems to me that there are two problems with hitching the populationist wagon to the claim that populations at the extremes constitute real races, both of which stem from the fact that this tells us nothing about the people between the extremes.

One problem is that if, as an attempt to deal with the arbitrariness in our lines of demarcation, we say that each extreme is bounded by a really wide and fuzzy border, then the races will have indeterminate membership. And if the races have indeterminate membership, then many people—all of those within the fuzzy border zone—will have an indeterminate race. Note that this is not to say that they are *mixed* race; it is to say that their race is *indeterminate*—there is no fact of the matter as to what race they are. The other is that all the people between the two boundaries, that is, those who are neither surefire members of the extreme races nor located within the indeterminate border zones, would have *no race at all*. These implications violate what appear to be platitudes, that everyone has some race or some combination of races, and no one has an indeterminate race or no race at all. In short, we might be able to clearly identify each end of the line, but any way of sorting the points in between is not dictated by the line itself.

## 5.5 Race, Medicine, and Explanatory Vindication

A final question will be whether, *even if* we could come up with a biologically principled way of dividing humanity into breeding populations that matched races as defined by ordinary usage (as it seems we cannot), we would be able to infer much from these results. Recall that in order to do much science, scientists will need to make inductive generalizations about these populations. So, even putting aside the problems that have so far installed considerable dents in populationism's armor, are many scientific generalizations forthcoming about the populations studied? I have been arguing that races are not *biological* kinds, but a plethora of scientific generalizations that ineliminably feature race might vindicate races as natural kinds.

Now race does appear to figure in some inductive generalizations related to disease susceptibility and medical treatment, such that different races might be more or less susceptible to various genetically based diseases or more or less responsive to certain treatments, such as drug regimens (Bamshad & Olson 2003; Risch et al. 2002, 4; Wade 2006, 182–183, 194–195), and from this some conclude that race is biologically real (e.g., Arthur 2007, 78).[30] Realists sometimes also question how, if there are no races, forensic scientists can identify a corpse's 'race' from just a bag of decomposed bone fragments or identify a suspect from a sliver of DNA (Sarich & Miele 2004, 23). Up until this point we have seen that race seems not to be biological, so it should turn out to be somewhat confusing if there is a biological link between biological race and disease and medical treatment. Can the anti-realist say anything to avert this confusion?

---

30  In his more moderate position, Hacking (2005, esp. 108–109) maintains that the connections between race and, say, the leukemia antigen mean that race is a statistically significant, meaningful, and useful category.

The first thing to say is that anti-realism is at least *consistent* with any finding that connects 'races' with forensic and medical facts.[31] Scientists can reconstruct real biological properties of the individual corpse or suspect, and, knowing that such properties tell us where that individual falls in our socially constructed set of racial categories, scientists can tell us that this corpse or suspect has the thus-and-so properties that place it in a gerrymandered category we call 'white' (or whatever) (Barbujani 2005; Shreeve 1994). In a like manner, an archaeologist could tell from key *physical* properties that a decomposed human-made structure is the remnant of a stadium (or temple or house or whatever). The properties are physical, but the stadium they compose is not itself a category for the geological sciences. It is, quite literally, a human construction. In the same way, the anti-realist can say that when any given genetically based disease is said to be common in a race, this is just a paraphrased way of saying that it is common among people whom *we have categorized* as a race, rather than one that is demarcated in nature.

What is more, at least many of the links between race and disease that have been uncovered actually link disease and race-*related* but *non*-racial environmental factors, such as political pressures, cultural practices, environmental toxins, access to health care, education, economic resources, and diet (Condit 2005; Graves 2001, ch. 11; Keita et al. 2004; Kitcher 2007, 315; Race, Ethnicity, and Genetics Working Group 2005, 524–525; Root 2000, 2001; Schwartz 2001; Serre & Pääbo 2004, 1683–1684). For example, while Leroi points out that in America black men have higher rates of hypertension, there is good reason to think that higher rates of hypertension among African Americans are not due to anything specifically biological about race: people of African descent living elsewhere do *not* have higher rates of hypertension, and people of non-African descent living elsewhere, such as Russians, *do* have higher rates of hypertension, all of which suggests that African Americans' higher rates of hypertension are caused by something unique about America (such as, perhaps, the stress its persistent racism can cause) (Cooper et al. 2003; Shreeve 1994).

Of course, the failure of this one example does not entail that there might not be some other correlation between race and biologically interesting factors. But that puts the burden on realists, and it is a burden that is almost impossible to shoulder as a way of demonstrating that race is a scientific category. The kind of shelter in which you live can affect the likelihood that you will experience respiratory illness, and the kind of work you do can affect whether you will get a repetitive stress injury, but *well-ventilated house-dwellers* and *ten-key*

---

31 The second thing to say is that many purported racial differences in drug therapy have been debunked (Cooper et al. 2003).

*data-enterers* are not scientifically real kinds. To establish that race is relevantly different than being a data-enterer we would have to see that race is biologically real and that its correlations with disease and drug functionality are not mediated through something non-scientific. That is, it would have to be shown not only, first, that there are populations that are demarcated by biologically non-arbitrary criteria and that more or less match our racial categories (contrary to the arguments above), but also, second, that some diseases are significantly linked to some of these populations, third, that these diseases significantly link *only* to one of the populations (otherwise, the disease-susceptible population would be orthogonal to the racial population), and fourth, that this link is based in the *biological* profile of the race in question, which is an extremely hard thing to demonstrate given that it means ruling out every other potential influence on disease, many of which are hidden from the eyes of science and will remain hidden for the foreseeable future (Burchard et al. 2003; Risch et al. 2002, 11; Root 2001, 27–29). Presumably the height of the hurdle set by these four criteria explains why we haven't seen decisive evidence of causal links between biological race and disease.[32]

Finally, consider the sobering numbers about how likely it is that we might identify links between specifically racial populations and disease.

32  Many of the studies purporting to link races to various medical conditions identify the subject's racial population by non-genetic 'proxy' methods: they ask the subject to self-report her race or ancestry, or the researchers themselves make the racial or ancestral identification without obtaining genetic information (Cooper et al. 2003; Foster & Sharp 2002). But to establish a conclusive link between breeding populations and any given medical condition, we need *direct* (as opposed to proxy) evidence that the subject with the medical condition in question comes from a population that is supposed to be uniquely disposed to it and that is a race. And it is no coincidence that the mismatch problem looms large here. Consider, for example, that, in illustrating the medical import of race, Wade writes "The Pima Indians are particularly susceptible to diabetes" (Wade 2006, 182). Even without questioning the medical facts in this assessment, we should ask for the grounds on which the Pima Indians are classified as a race. Wade presents no data that suggest this is an ordinary racial category, and it seems to me that it is not. Perhaps *Indians*, or *Native or Indigenous Americans*, is a commonsense racial category, but *Pima Indians* does not appear to be. (Of course, this is, in the experimentally enthusiastic spirit of this book, a prediction more than anything, a prediction that when we look at ordinary classificatory practices *Pima Indian* will not turn out to be classified as a self-standing racial category. I hope that the reader puts credence in this prediction, but also that someone tests it.) This mismatch echoes what Wilson and colleagues (2001) found, namely that there are possible drug response differences between different populations, but also that the responsive populations did not match folk racial categories (e.g., Ethiopians largely fell in the same population as Norwegians). Generally speaking, medical conditions and genes, such as the hemoglobin S allele that provides resistance to malaria, higher risk of Tay-Sachs disease, and cystic fibrosis, are not tied to *racial* groups, contrary to what is sometimes advertised (Barbujani 2005; Brace 2003; Condit 2005; Cooper et al. 2003; Serre & Pääbo 2004, 1683–1684).

We have known, since Richard Lewontin's seminal article, "The apportionment of human diversity" (1972), that the genetic difference between alleged continental clusters is very small. This has been confirmed repeatedly over the years, such that only a small percentage (approximately 3 to 15 percent on most studies) of humanity's unique genetic diversity exists between races and/or populations (depending in part on what criterion the study uses to define races and/or populations) (see, e.g., Barbujani et al. 1997; Hoffman 1994; Shriver et al. 2004, 283–284; see also Brown & Armelagos (2001) for a review; and Long & Kittles (2003) for a critique of the statistical methods found in many such studies). This is a percentage, again, of our *unique* genetic diversity, which is only about 0.2 percent of our overall genetic material, which means that the likelihood of people from two different 'races' differing at any given gene is probably somewhere between 3 to 15 percent of 0.2 percent. That isn't much.

Some point out that this small proportion of our genetic makeup might be responsible for our racial differences, and so its paltriness doesn't show that race is not real. But that doesn't speak to the current issue. The current issue is simply that once we subtract from this already small percentage the 'junk' DNA that has no function whatsoever (generally thought to make up the lion's share—north of 90 percent—of our genetic material), plus the genetic material that is used to identify the different populations, presumably very little of this already tiny slice of our genetic material will be left over to render individuals within any alleged racial population *uniquely* susceptible to some kind of disease. This is particularly compelling given that "[a]ccumulated small differences in common alleles will yield differences in population risk only if a disease is caused primarily by interactions among multiple loci, and this is both mathematically and biologically implausible" (Cooper et al. 2003; cf. King & Motulsky 2002, 2343; Race, Ethnicity, and Genetics Working Group 2005, 525). So, just going off the numbers alone, it seems highly unlikely that, even if humanity could be non-arbitrarily carved into biological racial populations (which it cannot), these populations would uniquely feature in more than a very small number of inductive generalizations about genetic predispositions to disease.[33]

---

33  It is worth adding that since there is so much inter-population admixture, for any given individual, just knowing a population from which she comes can often be inadequate to assess risk of disease. The susceptibility to disease is assigned to the population as a whole, within which a very wide range of ancestry and thus genetic disease susceptibility is found (Bamshad et al. 2004, 606). What is medically useful is less knowing a patient's population than knowing the *proportions* of her various ancestries. It is also worth adding that right now there are very few confirmed associations of specific alleles with specific diseases (Bamshad et al. 2004, 606; Foster & Sharp 2002). Surely we will need more, and better grounded, causal associations before they could even begin to play an effective role in forming generalizations involving race.

Instead, it is likely that racially relevant genetic material is just what we should suspect it to be, namely either non-functional or relevant only to the superficial traits we associate with race, such as hair texture or skin color (cf. Pääbo 2001; Schwartz 2001). Indeed, given that our superficial traits are discordant, we have even less reason to expect that genetic traits that match our visible racial traits will be concordant with medically relevant genetic traits (Root 2001, 23). This, I should stress, is not to say that we shouldn't conduct research that seeks to link groups ordinarily classified as races and disease, for such links are often based in social causes, such as, again, access to health care or proximity to toxins, and it is indisputable that such environmental factors are linked to ordinarily identified races. I also would not say that there are no populations with genetic predispositions to certain diseases, but I do doubt that much, if any, genetic susceptibility will be tagged to racial populations.

## 5.6 Conclusion

To return to the question of whether races are biologically real, I take all *prima facie* plausible forms of biological racial realism to face fatal trouble with either the Arbitrariness Objection or the Mismatch Objection. If this is right—if, in the end, race is not biologically real—we have two options. We can say, on the one hand, that race is real as some non-biological kind of thing, in the way that some might say that political states are real. Or, on the other hand, it remains open to us to say that race simply is not real. The next chapter continues the case for anti-realism.

# 6 Constructivism, Revisionism, and Anti-Realism

Plenty of folks from a wide array of disciplinary perspectives embrace the proposition that race is constructed and real at the same time, and we will see that this view, constructivism, is appealing in various ways, particularly given that race fails to be a biological kind. I will now argue, however, that constructivism is flawed, that race is importantly different from apparently real social constructions like California. The broader upshot is that, since race is not socially real, and since as argued in the previous chapter race is not biologically real, race just isn't real. Of course, if I am going to maintain a steadfast anti-realism and insist simultaneously that we shouldn't eliminate race-thinking outright, I've got my work cut out. The project of showing how these two positions may be reconciled is tackled in the following chapter. Here I first lay out the constructivist options, and explain why, in the end, they aren't decisive. Since we will then have our two main forms of realism on the table, we will also be in a position to make good on the promissory note issued in Chapter 4 and consider revisionist versions of each. If, as I will argue, revisionism cannot rehabilitate realism, the final piece of the anti-realist puzzle will be in place. In order to motivate things properly, I begin with the debate between eliminativism and constructivism.

## 6.1 The Constructivist Response to Eliminativism

While there are several variations on the eliminativist position, perhaps the most common route to eliminativism is as follows:

(E1)  If race is an illusion, then racial terms should be eliminated from public discourse.

(E2)  Race is an illusion.

Thus,

(E3)  Racial terms should be eliminated from public discourse.

Now E1 should cause an eyebrow or two to arch. At most, the illusory status of race will generate *one* reason to eliminate racial discourse, and we should allow that there might be other, contravening reasons to keep it around. In light of this possibility, I will ultimately target E1 in order to create space for reconstructionism. However, constructivists train their criticisms on E2. I am just the latest in a string of anti-realists who endorse something like the following argument on E2's behalf:

(A1)   Race is an illusion if there is no adequate biological basis for our racial categories.

(A2)   There is no adequate biological basis for our racial categories.

Thus,

(E2)   Race is an illusion.[1]

The constructivist response to this kind of argument is to reject A1 and maintain that race is socially real even if it is a biological fiction. Put succinctly, the idea is that the true nature of race lies not in biology, but in the sociohistorical relations that have been produced by widespread, significant, and long-standing race-based practices. Now right off the bat, proponents of this view face at least two theoretical hurdles. First, they must offer a defensible general ontological framework according to which things that are not proper objects of study by the natural sciences (i.e., things that fall under irreducibly social categories), can be considered real. Why should we say that *anything* that is socially constructed is nonetheless real? I here want to grant this first, more general claim that socially constructed kinds and entities can be real, for not only is it intuitive that journalists and California are real, but also there is little disagreement about this within the race debate. That is not to say that there is no disagreement; hyper-materialists will deny adamantly that social kinds are real. Rather, it is just to say that in our dialectical context, non-constructivists can (and sometimes do) grant to constructivists that, in general, there are socially constructed kinds of things in the world. As Taylor (2000, 122) points out, even Appiah allows the general reality of social kinds when he argues that while races are not real, racial identities—which are themselves social kinds—

---

1   This simplifies Appiah's (1992; 1996, 71–74) extended arguments, but it represents his point of divergence from constructivism. See also Graves 2001, esp. 195, and Zack 2002, 3.

are real.[2] Given this background, I am going to assume that social kinds can be real.

Within the race debate, then, the contentious issue concerns a second, more specific question of whether *race* is one of these social kinds. Many point to the roles that race plays in our lives—in marital status, housing, education, employment, criminal arrest and conviction rates, wealth, access to health care, exposure to environmental toxins, and so on—as evidence that race is as socially real as any other social category, such as *wife* or *student* or *journalist*. Obviously, there are various ways one might go about spelling out the details, but whatever social facts are recruited into this picture, the basic idea to constructivism is that race is a social construction in the way that monetary value is entirely social but apparently real. And generally the constructivist's developmental story is that races came to be, and continue to be, social kinds because we acted as if race was real, and since the racially oriented norms and beliefs by which we divide and sort our race-conscious selves affect the lives of anyone who is 'raced,' which is to say pretty much all of us in the United States, our race-based practices have corralled us into social races (e.g., Alcoff 2006, ch. 7; Gooding-Williams 1998; Gracia 2005; Haslanger 2005, 2006; Mills 1998; Outlaw 1996a, 1996b; Root 2000, 2001; Stubblefield 2005; Sundstrom 2001, 2002a, 2002b; Taylor 2004).[3]

Given the various ways in which racial concepts are tied to visible traits, it is important that constructivists generally accept that our racial discourse is to some extent tethered to biology. It is a testament to his intellectual legacy that on this question many constructivists see themselves as continuing a tradition pioneered by Du Bois, taking as their starting point, for example, not only the frequently cited constructivist passage that "[t]he black man is the person who must ride Jim Crow in Georgia," but also the claim that "the physical bond is least and the badge of color relatively unimportant save as a badge; the real essence of this kinship is its social heritage of slavery; the discrimination and insult" (Du Bois 1984 [1940], 153, 117).

Within the constructivist family, there are two ways of taking up Du Bois' claim that race involves *both* a visible 'badge' and a set of socio-historical relations. On Boxill's (2001, 31) and Sundstrom's (2002a,

---

2   The general thesis that non-physical kinds are real is often motivated by considerations independent of race, such as taking the social and biological sciences seriously in a world where social and biological facts might not be reducible to physical facts. For the situation of racial constructivism within this more general theoretical orientation, see Root (2000); Sundstrom (2001, 2002a, 2002b); Taylor (2000; and 2004, esp. 90–92, 110–112).

3   Some of those mentioned here might balk at being called either a realist or a constructivist, but they fall into those camps as I am using the labels.

105) version of this view, physical features such as skin color are merely (fallible) racial *identifiers*, while what *makes* one a member of one's race just are the social practices to which one is subject and in which one participates.[4] Reshuffling some of these details but falling into the same Duboisian tradition, others elevate visible features to the level of racial membership criteria. Jorge J.E. Gracia understands races as 'families' such that every member of a racial group shares a common line of descent and "has one or more physical features that are (i) genetically transmittable, (ii) generally associated with the group, and (iii) perspicuous" (Gracia 2005, 85), where these physical features are "selected from a socially constructed list" (Gracia 2005, 98; cf. 148).[5] Similarly, Outlaw's (1996a, 1996b) "socio-natural kinds" approach holds that each race is marked by some *roughly* distinctive biological features and is also socially constructed, in two ways: first, each race is also marked by various non-biological, cultural features, and second, the biological features associated with each race have that association only insofar as our beliefs, norms, and practices "conscript" those biological properties into racial service (Outlaw 1996a, 21). To be a member of any given race, then, you will need to have a sufficient number of a socially determined cluster of biological and cultural properties, none of which is individually necessary for being a member of the race. While coming from a different theoretical orientation, Alcoff's (1997, 69; cf. 2006, esp. ch. 4) analysis of race as "a particular, historically and culturally located form of human categorization involving visual determinants marked on the body through the interplay of perceptual practices and bodily appearance" also privileges our visible traits as what gives us our (socially constructed) races. Finally, Taylor's view (explicitly allied with Outlaw's in broad strokes if not details) is that races are populations constituted by social forces that give meaning

4   Boxill doesn't go quite so far as to say that these socially constructed races are real (in Boxill 2001), but recall that in Boxill (2004, 209, n. 2) he writes, "[t]he existence of race as a social construct is not controversial."

5   Gracia regularly maintains that there are no properties or features shared by all members of each race, and that instead what joins them are relations. I am using 'properties' (and 'features') in the wider sense that includes the possibility of *relational* properties (e.g., the property *being a daughter*). (Despite the strong emphasis he places on the difference between a shared-property view of race and a relational view of race, in at least one place Gracia (2007a, 97) takes relations to be a subspecies of properties, and he is willing at times to talk about racial features (e.g., Gracia 2005, xxiv).) A contentious element of Gracia's view that one must have at least one of the visible features that are distinctive of one's race is that it leads him to deny the phenomenon of passing, such that if one can 'pass' as a member of some race, then one doesn't really pass at all—one *is* a member of that race (Gracia 2005, 91). See Glasgow (2007), Gooding-Williams (1998), and Mallon (2004) for discussion of the claim (made by Michaels (1994)) that constructivist accounts that fail to account for passing are inadequate.

to visible traits and ancestries in a way that links those populations to distinctive probabilities for various "life chances" (such as the chance to live in a healthy environment or receive a first-rate education) (Taylor 2004, esp. 85–87, 107–112).

Thus, on the one hand, Boxill's and Sundstrom's kind of constructivism has it that our biological features are at most racial indicators, while what *makes* a (say) black person black—our *race-makers*, if you will—are a network of social practices and policies, such as the Jim Crow-era policy that such a person must be seated in the segregated train car; and, because perception of our visible biological features affects how we are treated, those biological features co-vary, but only co-vary, with the social facts that make us members of various races. On the other hand, for folks like Alcoff, Gracia, Outlaw, and Taylor, our race-makers include either socially recruited visible features and lines of ancestry or those socially recruited biological facts plus some other social facts about us.[6] Either way, by preserving the notion that race is in some sense tied to the physical, these constructivist conceptions of race seem to be consistent with the idea that races are (H1*) groups that are distinguished from other human beings by visible physical features of the relevant kind that the group has to some significantly disproportionate extent. Constructivism thus appears to be powerful enough to both make sense of the fact that our racial categorizations are driven by social practices and preserve the relevance of the visible differences that we take to racially divide us.[7]

## 6.2 The Centrality of the Biological

The nearly univocal anti-realist judgment is that whatever might exist as a reality that has been constructed by our race-based practices isn't race, because race is conceptually required to be biological. In the

---

6    For the intra-constructivist argument that the Outlaw-style idea of a socio-biological kind is incoherent, since biological and social kinds have distinctive features due to their being objects of distinctive sciences, see Sundstrom (2002a, 105–106). In this way, the sociobiological kind account might have to posit that 'race' is, like 'jade,' a partial reference term.

7    Various important details are needed to make these accounts fly. For instance, in order to deal with the fallibility of visible traits as racial indicators, Boxill (2001, 33) writes that we should amend Du Bois' account to say, not that a person is black if he has to ride Jim Crow in Georgia, but that "a person is black if he would have to ride Jim Crow in Georgia *were his ancestry known to the conductors*" (emphasis added). This counterfactual formulation allows the constructivist to say, not only that those who lived under *de jure* segregation in the U.S. were black if they would have had to ride Jim Crow, but also that those who do *not* live under such segregation are black so long as they would have had to ride Jim Crow *had* they found themselves in legally segregated Georgia.

extreme version, Lawrence Blum (2002, chs 5, 7–8) holds that race is not only supposed to be biological (specifically, somatic and ancestral), but also something that carries connotations of unequal value and capacity and of inherent behavioral and temperamental differences, connotations that, though weakened over time, frustratingly persist. Certainly, if that is what 'race' is supposed to refer to, then race is an illusion, not a social kind. In a similar but decidedly less extreme fashion, the reason I want to deny that race is a social kind is that 'race' (and cognate and related terms) purports to refer to something biological, something which, it turns out, does not exist. This semantic position, that race purports to refer to something at least partly biological, rather than a global hostility to social kinds, is here the motivation for A1.[8]

Again, constructivism deserves its due for acknowledging the depth to which biology permeates racial thinking. Boxill (2001, 31–32), for just one example, notes that not every socially constructed group counts as a race. To constitute a race, Boxill writes, biology must factor in somewhere:

> the belief that people are members of a biological race ... is essential to the social construction of the races. Without such a belief, cultural, ethnic, or class prejudice may result in the social construction of certain classes of individuals, but these classes will not be races.

In this kind of way, again, constructivism seems capable of finessing the fact that our race-talk often centers on biology: as long as it is not conceptually non-negotiable that races are biological, constructivism can accommodate any other belief that links race to biology.

By this point it will come as little surprise that I think that the beliefs seen by Boxill as so central to race-thinking are so central that they are actually conceptually non-negotiable. Constructivists are surely right that our race-based practices (including not least our race-talk) have

---

8    For other accounts that racial terms have inextricably biological meanings, again see also not only Appiah (1996, Part 1; Zack 1993, 1995, 1997, 2002, 2007), but also Corlett (2003); Michaels (1994). The subtleties of Blum's view require careful interpretation. On the one hand, his explicit and repeated conclusion, based on his analysis that race is ordinarily understood and/or practiced as something inherent and value-laden, is that race is not real. At one point he says that the very *concept* of race is tied to racism (2002, 206 n. 21). On the other hand, at other times he allows that the inherentist, value-laden understanding of race is not the *only* possible or even operative view of race (e.g., 2002, 205 n. 16). This latter claim would suggest that race, on some non-inherentist and value-neutral conception, might still be real, but this is a possibility he does not evaluate.

influenced us and sorted us into social groups. But why should we say that those groups are *races*? Appiah got us to think about this question in terms of witchcraft: in using the language of 'witch,' we didn't sort ourselves into witches and non-witches, because our witch-talk was predicated on a conceptually non-negotiable but factually false belief, namely that there were people who cavorted with the devil. Similarly, our race-talk is predicated on a conceptually non-negotiable but factually false belief, namely that we fall into biological races. This contrasts with decisively social kinds, like professional kinds. When we talk about being a journalist or a teacher, there is no false belief (negotiable or not) that the biological world contains these kinds. So, on this anti-constructivist position, our racial identifications might produce sociohistorical facts and even social collectivities of some sort, but, as a conceptual matter, those social collectivities do not constitute races.

I do not mean to deny that constructivism rightly taps into a core part of racial discourse. Above we saw that this discourse is biosocially complex, such that the ways in which individuals are racially categorized is sometimes sensitive to various social practices and relations (though even with respect to ascription of individual racial identity our visible traits seem to play a central role). Nevertheless, I believe that the experimental evidence presented in Chapter 4 and the armchair evidence presented in Chapter 2—though not, strictly speaking, inconsistent with constructivism—strongly suggest that talk of *races* is an attempt to talk about biologically based groupings: the concept of race requires not merely that races be tethered to various visible traits by virtue of one or another of our social conventions, as constructivism's interpretation of H1* has it, but that those traits purportedly sustain race independently of our practices.

We can put this another way. The experimental evidence we do have suggests that people see visible traits like skin color as conceptually central to race, and Chapter 2's armchair excursion suggested that visible traits are *all* there is to determine a race. Thus constructivism seems to heavily revise our understanding of 'race,' and consequently we need to ask whether that revision is so heavy that it no longer represents 'race' in the ordinary sense. I want to approach this question of revision indirectly, via a few more thought experiments that directly target the sorts of constructivism being considered here.

Begin with the kind of theory that makes your race a function of the probabilities that you will die at a certain age, or face incarceration, or live far from environmental hazards, and so on. This kind of constructivism—probabilistic constructivism—requires that each race have its own statistical profile, detailing the distinctive rates with which various socially malleable facts, such as those listed above, are true of its members. Now imagine

120 Constructivism, Revisionism, Anti-Realism

> *Utopia.* Our society (or even the whole world), with all its racist baggage, finally comes around. It is no longer true that being white is a point of access for getting better car loans, that being Latino means having a much greater than normal chance of dying in a workplace accident, or that being an indigenous American means being more likely than most other Americans to live one's entire life in extreme poverty. In short, there is no longer any difference between various races with respect to any of the social statistics probabilistic constructivists might use to individuate the races. Society is perfectly racially egalitarian.

Probabilistic constructivism implies, counterintuitively, that Utopia contains no races, that, in fact, racial equality is impossible. Of course, it might turn out, as a matter of contingent fact, that such a utopia is psychologically impossible—we might be cognitively cursed to treat people of different races in different ways, thus generating different statistical profiles for each race. But even in that case (even if constructivism required us to be pessimistic in this way!), I want to say that we can at least *conceive* of a world where there is no social statistical difference between the races. Probabilistic constructivism, by contrast, distinguishes races by various social statistics, so it has to say that the moment we arrive at an apparently racially egalitarian state of affairs, races become non-existent, and individuals go from being raced to non-raced. This seems to depart from the commonsense concept of race. Maybe race was illusory all along, but the disappearance of racial inequality doesn't entail the disappearance of race. Equivalently, if all the world's anti-racists got fed up and banded together to colonize some distant, uninhabited planet with an egalitarian society, they don't lose their races the moment their ship is launched. In short, to the extent that we believe that 'racial equality' is not an oxymoron, that it is at least a conceptual possibility, we are conceptually committed to the proposition that races are not constituted by their distinctive social statistical profiles.

Our next version of constructivism holds that the relevant social facts lie not in disparities in housing, education, health care, and so on, but simply in the fact of racial categorization itself. So if the mere fact that we racially categorize ourselves and each other is crucial to this kind of constructivism—categorical constructivism—then we need to see if there are any cases where we keep our races despite the fact that we don't engage in the activity of racial categorization, as in

*Disaster*. Everyone above the age of ten months is being killed by a virus that itself will expire as soon as it kills the last person who is more than ten months old. In a furious effort as they await their doom, the remaining scientists devote themselves to finding a device that can keep the infants alive until they are old enough to survive on their own.

Categorical constructivism suggests that as soon as the last non-infant dies—as soon as the practice of racial classification stops—all the infants in Disaster stop having races. There will be, at that point, no races on Earth. Now, as an anti-realist, I am comfortable with the idea that there are no races. But I find it counterintuitive that whether or not there are races depends on whether the last non-infant has died. I also find it counterintuitive that if, years later, these children, now teenagers, learn of their parents' racial classification system and subsequently adopt it for themselves, they will become raced again! Perhaps this is my own shortcoming, but I am not sure how to get my head around the idea that an otherwise non-changing population could go from having races, to not having races, to having races again, just depending on whether some people around them think they have races. Thus a different case that has the same effect would be

*Temporary Amnesia*. We are all simultaneously struck by an agent that causes us to forget our systems of racial classification. Any time we start to racially classify ourselves, our cognitive apparatuses short-circuit. One hour later, cognition reverts to its pre-amnesiac state, and racial classification resumes.

In this kind of case, even though we have no practices of racial classification, it seems counterintuitive to say that we lose our races for the 60 minutes in question. If this is so, then categorical constructivism seems not to tap into the core nature of race.

Furthermore, consider Alcoff's (2006) fascinating brand of constructivism, according to which sensory information, and in particular the visual, is central to race. As I understand it, the basic idea is that one of the unique things about racial identities is the way in which they are constructed around our visible features, so that our race-based practices and cognitions would be nonsensical if divorced entirely from what we see; nevertheless, how these visual appearances are represented in any given society—what they signify, their *meaning* in some sense—is to some extent constructed and is not picking up on any biological fact. (Consider, for instance, that many in the United States tend to *see* people with mixed black-white ancestry as black, when in other places many such people would be seen as white or as bearing some third kind of racial identity (Alcoff 2006, ch. 12).)

My reason for hesitating about this kind of constructivism—perceptual constructivism—is probably apparent by now: we can imagine a world just like ours, except that on New Year's Eve everyone is simultaneously blinded and struck with a strange kind of racial amnesia. Do these people go from having races to being non-raced? If they regain their eyesight and memory a day later, do they go back to being raced? Perceptual constructivism's implications that they do lose their races with their eyesight, and regain it with the return of their eyesight, is far enough from my understanding of race that I don't think we're talking about race any more, at least not race in the folk sense.

Alcoff also emphasizes the extent to which others' interpretations of our visible markers, interpretations which are guided at least in part by socially constructed beliefs and values, impacts our "lived experience or subjectivity" (Alcoff 2006, 92, ch. 7). So it has been suggested, not only by Alcoff (2006, 43, 278) but also, for example, by Charles Mills (1998, ch. 3), that race might be understood in terms of unique, socially mediated subjective profiles, sets of experiences that while diverse are also to some extent similar within, and distinctive to, each race. However, we have seen that in cases like Disaster, Temporary Amnesia, and Utopia, although individuals' subjective experiences are not racially distinctive, those individuals do not, on the ordinary concept of race, convert from being raced to being non-raced (and back again!). Tommy Lott (1999, 64–66) appears to tolerate a similar kind of case, where all and only people we call 'white' manifest the "sociohistorical consciousness" that is presently manifest in all and only people we call 'black.' Although he recognizes that it is "odd," Lott thinks that the idea of "white African Americans" is no stranger than the idea of "black Anglo-Saxons." But this is where Lott's (purposeful) collapse of ethnic and racial groups appears to become untenable. It is not that there cannot be, in some sense, white ethnic African Americans or black ethnic Anglo-Saxons. It is that there cannot be white black people and black white people (which is not, of course, to say that there cannot be people who are of mixed black-white ancestry). The reason that this is so is that the swapping of two racial groups' "consciousnesses" or experiential profiles is not enough to make those groups swap races, any more than shedding their uniquely racial experiential profiles is enough to make them lose their races altogether. Group amnesia does not eliminate a race any more than individual amnesia means that the individual loses her race. I should underscore that to say this is not to endorse race's extra-experiential dimension; it is just to say that experiential constructivism fails to comport with some key thought experiments about how race operates.[9]

If my judgments about these cases are on target (and more on that shortly), then we don't want to say that whether you have a race depends on whether we can see your race, whether we happen to racially categorize you, whether you have actually had experiences based on your racial categorization, or whether there are inequalities between the races. As far as that goes, these judgments only entail that *those* non-biological facts are not our race-makers; they do not show that there is *no* social race-maker. However, when we consider that there is a gap between all of these socially constructed elements and the way race operates, and when we recall that race would seemingly vanish if our bodies all changed to look more or less the same, a generalizable pattern starts to appear: in each of the various cases meant to expose the shortcomings in constructivism, the reason that our races don't change when the relevant social facts change is that our *visible traits* don't change. This corroborates the suggestion that while an *individual's* particular race might depend on social factors, each racial *group* is, as a conceptual matter, defined *only* in terms of its purportedly distinctive visible, biological profile. And, again, since these groups' putative distinctiveness is not, in point of fact, legitimated by the biology, there are no races. Now add the plausible principle, from a constructivist, that I borrowed in Chapter 4: "[r]ace-thinking is about kinds, called races, and only derivatively about individuals, who thereby have racial identities" (Taylor 2004, 17). It follows that if there are no races, then no one is a member of any race, in which case we don't, for the purposes of determining whether race is real, need to go any further and sort out the myriad membership criteria by which individuals are assigned to different races (a task that, frankly, seems nearly impossible if the goal is to render those criteria consistent so that race can be real). All we need to know is that racial groups purport incorrectly to be biological.[10]

When we step back and look at the evolution of the race debate, a certain trend emerges. The constructivist literature which responded to

9 Mills (1998, 56–59), whose experiential constructivism hinges on our practices of "intersubjective classification," is willing to allow that if your experiences are those of an $R_1$, you might really become an $R_1$. Although I am not sure that this verdict is true (see Glasgow 2007), it is in any case compatible with the claims I am making. What is crucial for me is that if *all* $R_2$s all of a sudden have the experiences of $R_1$s, this does not make them $R_1$s, and that, for all infants who fail to have racially distinctive experiences, lacking this experience does not make them raceless.

10 One possible recourse for realists at this point is to deny that there need to be races for individuals to (derivatively) have a race. It would be interesting to see how such a proposal might be spelled out.

the first wave of anti-realism has gone to great lengths to show that race could be real as a social kind, because social kinds are real. It also demonstrated the myriad ways in which our race-conscious practices, linguistic and otherwise, have generated a social world that we ignore at our peril. Fair enough; these are important lessons learned. Nevertheless, the theses that social kinds are real, and that our race-conscious practices have created social realities, are, I submit, not a decisive response to A1 (though perhaps they constitute a response to hyper-materialists). Anti-realists can grant that social kinds are real, and they can (and should) recognize the social phenomena that our race-related practices generate and sustain, and that our racial vocabulary can be infused with meanings that go beyond the conceptual constraints on which I have focused here. That being said, what will be decisive in determining whether race is socially real is whether the folk concept RACE is constrained in such a way that it must be biologically real to be real. And, I have hoped to argue here, it is.[11]

The old point is apt here: even though social forces in colonial Salem worked to structure lives—and deaths—around belief in witches and around practices that responded to those beliefs, that wasn't enough to make witches real. The explanation for this, of course, is that 'witch' (in the colonial sense operative here) purports to refer to something that is not reducible to a sociohistorical object. If the people identified as witches did not conference with the devil, they simply were not witches, no matter what the sociohistorical facts were. And just as the ability to dance with the devil is conceptually non-negotiable when we're talking about witches (in the colonial sense), and just as having a horse-like shape and a single horn is conceptually non-negotiable when we're talking about unicorns, the claim here is that being biological is conceptually non-negotiable when we're talking about races (in the ordinary sense). Any constructivist response must show that 'race' is conceptually flexible enough to abandon all pretension of referring to biological kinds, and the cumulative conclusion to be drawn from Chapters 2 and 4 and the thought experiments considered in the present chapter is, in effect, that this cannot be shown, or, at least, that the burden is back on constructivists to put forth their own, countervailing evidence that race, in the ordinary sense, can have a referent divorced from biology.

This returns us to the dialectical landscape painted at the outset. Once biological realism is sidelined, the ontological debate largely comes down to whether racial discourse is such that 'race' can refer to a social kind or instead must refer to a biological kind. Thus, whether or

---

11  Given this dialectic it is worth observing, I think, that at least in their work which started appearing in the mid-1990s, Appiah's and Zack's racial anti-realism is similarly predicated on what they take *race* to be, not what they take *reality* to be.

not race is real is subject to a constraint that has been core to this book from the start. Call it the 'Onto-semantic Constraint,' or OSC for short:

> **OSC:** Ontological theories of race must be consistent with the best semantics of race.

Up until this point I've used a smattering of experimental and armchair evidence to argue that race operates on a complex of biological and social elements but cannot be wholly divorced from the pretension to biological reality. But what if this approach is wrong? What if, for instance, we should adopt the historical-expert approach to identifying the meanings of racial terms? As we saw in Chapter 3, because Appiah's analysis of the historical experts (largely Arnold and Jefferson, but also Shakespeare, Herder, and Darwin) reveals that they took race to be biological, he concludes that 'race' must be a putative biological concept; but as we also saw, Taylor's constructivist response to this interpretation of the intellectual history of race is to recruit such sources as Du Bois and Locke as evidence that several experts took race to be a social, rather than biological, kind. So this methodology might provide constructivism with a boost by enabling it to do an end-run around my armchair and experimental folk data.

There is much to admire in both Appiah's and Taylor's interpretations of the intellectual history of racial discourse, but, as I argued in Chapter 3, historical expert thinking about race is largely irrelevant to the race debate. What will instead constrain the meanings of racial terms is contemporary ordinary usage of them. Moreover, I think both interpretations suffer from an overly monistic approach to the meaning of 'race': each treats racial terms as if they could only purport to refer to either biological or social kinds, yet—following their *own* historical/expert methodology—their combined analyses suggest that the best account of historical expert discourse on race is that, as a group, the historical experts have purported to talk about race in a complex of *both* social and biological ways. Thus, on their own methodological principle, neither Appiah nor Taylor provides an analysis that satisfies OSC, for while each accepts that racial terms' meanings can be determined by historical expert usage, historical expert usage has actually been biosocially complex. Now since I don't believe that the meanings of racial terms are best determined by historical expert usage, I of course cannot help myself to a conjunction of Appiah's and Taylor's analyses. But notice, in what is perhaps ultimately not that great a surprise, that historical expert usage in this respect dovetails with ordinary usage, as unpacked in Chapter 4, in being biosocially complex. And so, whether you disagree with my folk-based approach in favor of the historical-expert approach or you (rightly) favor the folk approach, the fact remains that racial discourse operates on a complex of social and biological elements.

One reaction to the complexity of racial discourse is that when we face, in Taylor's (2004, 108) phrase, "competing world descriptions," we should choose the description that is more useful. Thus, since the social semantics of race are more useful than the biological semantics of race (because of the problems with finding an acceptable biological account of race), we arguably should say that 'race' refers to something social. But the pressing worry about selecting social meanings of 'racial' terms on purely pragmatic grounds, the worry that I have tried to defend in this section, is that we will no longer be talking about race in the relevant sense. That is, if folk racial discourse still carries a significant amount of conceptually non-negotiable biological baggage, then theories of race must either acknowledge that baggage or risk talking about something else besides race in the folk sense.

## 6.3  The Revisionist Rejoinder

In advancing the cause of anti-realism, I have postponed discussion of what is perhaps realism's most promising move, which can, in different ways and with different details, be useful to friends of either constructivism or biological realism. Above I called this rejoinder *revisionism.* In order to be clear about what I mean by 'revisionism,' I want to begin by contrasting it with substitutionism, which I will defend one version of in Chapter 7. Consider an exchange: Andrew defines birds as feathered animals that fly, to which Jacob responds that penguins are flightless birds; upon realizing this truth, Andrew backtracks, allows that birds can be flightless, and goes on to some other definition, such as *feathered and beaked animals.* In this exchange, does Andrew *change* what he means by 'bird,' or did the point about penguins instead expose to him that he had made a mistake in *expressing* what he had meant by 'bird' all along? It is plausible to think that he was always working with the not necessarily flighted concept, and he just didn't realize it when first trying to state a definition of what a bird is. To look at matters this way is to say that our concepts are (at least sometimes) *opaque.* It is highly unlikely that all our concepts are *transparent,* that is, that we are always aware of what we mean by any given term. Often it takes a bit of work for us to learn what our terms mean.

But then notice what did *not* happen here. Andrew didn't just change the meaning of 'bird' as he uses it. Rather, he possessed the right definition all along but wasn't able to formulate it adequately at the first try. Thus, he didn't give up his concept of what a bird was and *replace* it with something else. That would have been to *substitute* his idea of birds with some idea of birds\*. Rather, Andrew backtracked and revised his *express formulation* of his already existing, if poorly perceived, definition of 'bird.' This difference, between substitution and revision, opens the door for a powerful dialectical move from both kinds of realism.

Here again Putnam's (1975b) example is useful: just as 'water' referred to $H_2O$ even when users of the term 'water' were unaware of this, so 'race' might refer to a different biological kind than the one we think it refers to, or it might refer to a social kind even if ordinary language users don't believe this (Haslanger 2003, 2005, 2006). Once ordinary users fix the paradigm cases of a term, it is often up to the 'experts' to determine the best account of what the term refers to. Thus, the first crucial move here is to appeal to the idea that we can err in our expressions of our terms' definitions and then repair those expressions (as Andrew does with 'bird'), a move that I am calling 'revisionism.' The second is that it might be features of the world that tell us our expressions are mistaken, such as when the fact that atoms are divisible causes us to revise our express definition of 'atom' or when the fact that water turns out to be $H_2O$ causes us to revise our express definition of 'water.' Note that, as Haslanger points out, it is consistent with this second move, the move to semantic externalism—the view that our terms' referents and their common nature are to some extent 'out there,' rather than entirely 'in our heads'—to hold that the experts who have the authority to determine the way in which the world (sometimes surprisingly) provides a referent for our terms can be not only scientists but also social theorists (cf. Taylor 2004, 88–89).

Externalism is, in principle, a not only plausible but downright powerful resource for realists, and I do not wish to argue against the general externalist insights that have been gained in the philosophy of language since the 1970s. But note some limits on how externalism can be successfully used in the race debate. Recall, first, that 'race' and, say, 'water' appear to be disanalogous in important and relevant ways. If we are going to rely on the experts, we need to know who the experts are, even if it's an idealized set of experts, and what they say, or would say, about the terms in question. With 'water,' it's fairly clear that the experts are chemists and that they uniformly say that water is $H_2O$. But who are the experts with 'race'? While I am unsure how we might answer such a question and unconfident that ordinary users of racial discourse intend to defer to extra-scientific, social experts, let us assume we could come up with an appropriately constructivist-friendly set of criteria for expert selection, which would include social theorists. But it would then include not only constructivists but also anti-realists and populationists. So if we want to defer to expert knowledge of the world, should we say, with the constructivists, that 'race' refers to a social kind, or, with the anti-realists, that 'race' has been structured by social forces to purport to refer to something that turns out not to exist, or, with the populationists, that it refers to some kind of breeding population? Without expert consensus, deferring to race theorists threatens to stick us with a sort of analytic paralysis (Glasgow 2003). At the least we would need some expert tie-breaker, but it is unclear what tie-breaker would be acceptable.

Moreover, recall that we should, for the race debate, leave a considerable amount of semantic authority in the hands of ordinary users of racial discourse. As Putnam (1975b, 228) points out, while certain terms like 'gold' or 'water' arguably exhibit a division of linguistic labor, that is, their referents can best be determined by experts, other terms, such as 'chair,' do not. Lay usage fixes the entire meaning of 'chair.' It is unclear what principle we should use to determine whether 'race' is more like 'chair' or 'water' in this respect, but I submit that since we aim to determine what to do with ordinary racial discourse, we should focus on the meanings of our ordinary terms. Strictly speaking, eliminativists claim not merely that we should abandon certain words; after all, they're willing to speak of a foot 'race,' and they would not be satisfied if we replaced our word 'race' in this context with, say, 'shmace,' to cover the exact same ideas. Instead, they seek a broader rejection of a network of folk ideas, conceptions, and meanings, including intensions, associated with race. Since it is this commonsense intensional and conceptual network that is at issue, the relevant semantics for our purposes is folk semantics.[12]

I cannot emphasize enough that this does not mean that semantic externalism and the division of linguistic labor have no role to play; if folk usage intends to talk about biological kinds, then biologists will tell us what, if anything, underlies the putative kinds in folk usage, and if folk usage intends to talk about social kinds, then social theorists will have the relevant expertise. But it does mean that folk referential intentions set the limits of our investigation, since it is that discourse that we'll end up eliminating, conserving, or reconstructing. Fans of semantic externalism shouldn't find this too strange a view, for they generally hold that our referential intentions—as exposed in the elements of the relevant domain of discourse that are privileged by externalists (often paradigm cases)—constrain meaning, even when that meaning is partly determined by the world outside of the head. In order to secure relevancy to the race debate, the kind of usage on which we focus is ordinary usage.

So, with these limits in place, return to how realists might plausibly fold externalism into their theoretical structure. The constructivist could insist that while surveys might indicate that we think that racial terms refer to some partly biological reality, this is a superficial set of data that fails to deeply penetrate our opaque racial concepts and

---

12  Thanks to Jan Dowell for discussion here.

comprehensively track patterns of language use (e.g., Haslanger 2006; Taylor 2004, 87–88). Once the subjects of those surveys are informed that there is no such biological reality, they could still insist that they know the difference between, say, an Asian and a Caucasian, and upon learning that this difference could alternatively be construed as a social difference, they might say, 'Well, I guess that's what I meant all along.' Haslanger has called this kind of move a "debunking" project, an attempt "to show that a category or classification scheme that appears to track a group of individuals defined by a set of physical or metaphysical conditions is better understood as capturing a group that occupies a certain ... social position" (Haslanger 2003, 318). With regard to race, the debunking project is not a substitutionist recommendation of the sort that will be examined in the next chapter, but instead is an attempt to show that in our ordinary racial discourse we are *already* committed to a social semantics that we might not be aware we are committed to, in which case we should revise, not the definitions of our racial terms, but our faulty attempts to express those definitions in biological terms.

A new-wave biological racial realist, importantly, might tell a parallel story. She could insist that the survey answers are superficial, eliciting only what appear to be transparent conceptual data. And when informed that no biological groupings map onto the transparently identified understanding of race, but also that there are, nevertheless, other ways of grouping humans into breeding populations, the survey respondents could insist, 'That's what I meant by "race" all along.' If the revised statement of the meaning of 'race' maps onto scientifically verified breeding populations, the apparent mismatch between ordinary racial concepts and scientifically identified breeding populations will be dissolved.

So again, while the details are substantially different, both kinds of revisionism say that, sometimes at least, when we revise our stated analyses of what something is, we are not changing *meaning*. Instead, we are doing something else, clarifying, tweaking, or equilibrating the *way we are expressing* our existing meanings. With the old, faulty formulation of our analysis, we made a mistake; now we want to clarify it. We did not *really* mean to point to that one—Andrew didn't really, on further reflection, mean to suggest that all birds can fly. Rather, now that we see our mistake, we realize that we should have stated the newer, less faulty analysis.

In short, there are three things we can do when we have a faulty formulation of what an *X* is. First, the eliminativist route allows us to purge *X* from our ontology. This seems to have been what happened with WITCH, PHLOGISTON, and ZEUS. In the next chapter I will argue that the eliminativist prescription with respect to race has serious costs. Second, we can acknowledge that our concept of *X* is so faulty that it fails to refer to anything and then, as a separate matter, resolve to replace it with some proximate concept. In the next chapter I will also advocate for a version of this substitutionism. Third, as in the bird dialogue, we can offer a backtracking revision of our attempt at a definition of 'X': we can replace the malformulated definition with what Tyler Burge (1993) calls the "metaphysically correct definition," which might be hidden from us while under the spell of the malformulated definition (what Burge calls the "epistemically primary definition"). This, we are told, has been the case with terms like 'atom' and 'acid': in addition to our malformulated definition, we have some other "epistemic hooks" (Burge again) into the metaphysically correct definition, such as paradigm examples whose empirical nature tells us, only after we have erroneously bought into the malformulated definition, that our expressed definitional statements are really malformulated and should be revised to reflect the nature of whatever it is that we are hooking into.[13]

So what might be said on behalf of revisionism about race? As a first pass, note that if you think that terms are hyper-flexible and that reality always wholly dictates our semantics, then you will certainly want to be a revisionist. If what we *apparently* identify as races aren't in the world, then maybe you will want to say that the world dictates that by 'race' we instead mean something else, like 'breeding population' or 'social statistically defined population'—it's what we meant all along, we just didn't know it. However, I believe that it is more plausible to think that some of our terms can purport to refer to things that don't exist. 'Witch,' again, is a good example: we shouldn't say that what we really meant all along by 'witch' was not, as you might think, a person (who never existed) with the supernatural ability to cavort with the devil and cast spells, but, instead, a person (who did exist) *who was thought* to

---

13  In addition to Burge (1993), for discussion of 'acid' and 'animal spirit' in a context relevant to the race debate, see Appiah (1991). Burge's distinction between metaphysically correct and epistemically primary definitions might seem to map, at least in a rough-and-ready way, onto Haslanger's (1995, 2005, 2006) distinction between "manifest" and "operative" concepts. As Haslanger defines those terms, however, merely being manifest or operative does not determine that one of the two is actually correct or privileged—they are both concepts that supply the term with a meaning—and the real question for her is whether it would be to our benefit to keep the different concepts around. So, to be clear, there is a difference between, on the one hand, a term meaning two different things—one concept that is intuitive to ordinary users right off the bat (the manifest concept) and one that is hidden in their practices (the operative concept)—and, on the other hand, a term seeming at first glance to mean one thing when it really means another. It is this latter distinction on which I am focused here. As I am using the terms, then, 'revisionism' labels a kind of account that purports to give the meanings or referents of our ordinary terms, while 'substitutionism' is the label for accounts that want to replace our terms' concepts with others. ('Revisionist' is sometimes used in the way that I am using 'substitutionist' (e.g., Haslanger 2005, 23; Saul 2006).)

have the supernatural ability to cavort with the devil and cast spells (Appiah 2007, 36–37). In this way, if you agree that the world some-times fails to provide a referent for our terms, the meanings of which are partially fixed by our linguistic practices, then indiscriminate exter-nalism seems like a dead-end. When seeking to find the best fit between our discourse and the world, sometimes we need to polish our under-standing of our discourse and sometimes we need to polish our under-standing of the world, but occasionally our discourse outstrips the world, and the two shall never meet.

But this in itself doesn't undermine revisionism, for revisionism is, more basically, the view that we can make errors in stating definitions because our concepts are opaque to us, and this allows that our con-cepts will, occasionally, simply fail to pick out anything in the world. It is unclear that there is any principled difference between the times we revise our understanding of our terms to match the facts (such as with 'acid') and the times we don't (such as with 'phlogiston') (Appiah 1991, 1996, 39), but I think that the empirical results discussed in Chapter 4, the thin analysis proposed in Chapter 2, and the thought experiments utilized in this chapter heavily weight the case against revisionism. More empirical study would be useful, but until someone takes up the slack on that front, the most we can do is to appeal to the evidence we do have and to our intuitions. So ask yourself: Does it make sense to you that despite what you may have thought, when you've been talking about race you've been talking about groups whose racial difference might disappear for ten seconds even though during that time they undergo no physical change, or, alternatively, about breeding popula-tions that could actually look exactly similar to one another? When pondering that question, I think that these are interesting ways of carving up humanity into different groups, but also that those groups don't sound like races in the ordinary sense. Or better yet, predict how people would respond when presented with the cases we have been mulling over. It is less of a loss to the conceptual scheme with which I find myself, and which I believe I share with the bulk of my linguistic community, to trade away the proposition that race is real than to trade away the proposition that races are what they purportedly are simply by virtue of having the relevant kinds of visible traits. If we trade away the latter, at that point 'race' has been revised so much that it's hard to recognize as race anymore.

Now I don't mean for that to sound quick. Haslanger (2006, 93) astutely observes that:

> if the adequacy of a philosophical analysis is a matter of the degree to which it captures and organizes our intuitions, and if [revisionist constructivist] analyses are always counterintuitive, then it would seem that philosophers would never have reason to consider

> [revisionist constructivist] projects acceptable. However, this seems
> too fast. Surely philosophers cannot simply rule out [revisionist
> constructivist] analyses from the start.

I hope to have paid this concern due consideration. I want to construe 'our' broadly enough to include everyone in the linguistic community, and I want to consider our intuitions about as many categorizations, theories, and cases, real or imagined, as we possibly can, so that we might have discovered that race is not defined in biological terms even though it appears to be. That said, the constructivist must also leave an equal amount of room for anti-realists to argue that, after all of that evidence is in, revisionist constructivism still does not succeed. The points made in this chapter, along with the considerations marshaled in Chapters 2 and 4, have been aimed at making just that kind of case.

Of course, it bears repeating that my anti-realism is grounded on evidence that could ultimately prove lame. Such is the nature of making inferences based on controvertible evidence, and all our resources— theoretical reflection, thought experiments, experimental research—generate controvertible evidence. My own intuitions about the possible cases discussed above might be idiosyncratic, and, of course, we might get more, and more decisive, experimental data that contravene those I have considered. If, however, my intuitions are not wildly idiosyncratic, and if the incoming stream of experimental data continues to show a significant strain of (misconceived) biological race-thinking, then anti-realism would seem to be vindicated, leaving us with an array of difficult choices. We can erroneously stick with our faulty racial discourse. We can out-and-out eliminate our racial discourse. Or we can replace our racial discourse with some nearby discourse that better matches the facts. I will argue next for this third approach: we should reconstruct our discourse to talk about races* as social kinds.

# 7 Reconstructionism

## 7.1 The Normative Question

If race is an illusion, then racial eliminativism might seem to be our last best chance at a sensible policy. But it's not so straightforward getting an *ought* from an *is*, especially when other normative options are available. In particular, we might think that, even if there are no races, the costs of eliminating racial discourse are nevertheless outweighed by the benefits of retaining it.[1] The body of existing literature on this normative question is to my mind conclusive that we have good reason to try to preserve something like racial discourse, and so while I have little to add to that already extensive discussion, I will begin by briefly surveying some of the considerations which support that conclusion.

The imperatives that require something like racial discourse can be sorted, roughly, into political, prudential, and moral imperatives. One such political imperative is equal opportunity. Often, of course, it is a contentious matter whether equal opportunity requires certain race-conscious policies, such as affirmative action for college admissions. Many equal opportunity policies requiring racial discourse, however, are less divisive. For instance, given that the so-called "Black Okies" of California's San Joaquin Valley have been systematically denied a proportional share of public resources dedicated to poverty relief (Arax 2002), it is plausible that we should earmark some resources for that population, such as a Head Start program for equal education. And, since the disparity here appears to be a disparity between races, it appears that we cannot fulfill such an obligation without using something like

---

1  In other theoretical domains (e.g., the moral and the modal), theories that tell us to (continue to) act as if some *F* is real even though in our most honest, critically reflective moments we know that *F* is illusory—that is, that our *F*-talk and *F*-practices conspire to create a 'useful fiction'—are often labeled 'fictionalist,' though in race theory, some name this kind of view "quasi-racialism" (e.g., Taylor 2004). Just to keep things straight, note that I will be using the term 'quasi-racial discourse' as a name for discourse that mimics racial discourse fairly well, but that fails to be racial discourse.

racial terms: it's hard to say that a Head Start program should be instituted in this black community without talking about black communities.

Now consider some prudential reasons to sustain something in the neighborhood of racial discourse. Here, *racial identities*, rather than *race*, become particularly salient. As others have pointed out, a person's self-understanding can often be constructed around and crucially informed by her racial identity. Furthermore, the fact of racial oppression means that we live in a world where solidarity based in part on shared experience of racial oppression can be critically important: it can usefully provide role modeling and be a source of self-esteem, it can generate a feeling of connectedness, and at the very least it can supply the basis for important political alliances aimed at overcoming racism (Corlett 2003; Moody-Adams 1999, 420–421; Shelby 2002, 2005; Stubblefield 1995). So if something like racial identities are a psychologically and materially healthy response to living in a racist society, then it is prudentially valuable to maintain something like racial discourse, and prudentially harmful to eliminate it.[2] Beyond that instrumental value, many value their racial identities in themselves (Taylor 2004, 113), and racial identities may even operate as a source of meaning in life and of perspectives from which we come to know the world and ourselves (Alcoff 2006, chs 2, 4, 7). So for some, such as Outlaw (1996a, 34), race would be valuable even if racism were no more. As long as people perceive these values, the outright elimination of racial identities would at the very least constitute a perceived harm.

---

2   However, see Tommie Shelby's (2002, 2005) work for a compelling critique of the thought that the basis for anti-racist political solidarity needs to be a strict racial identity. The point being made here is simply that *something* like racial discourse is required to achieve the benefits of *something* like racial solidarity; put otherwise, the worry is that if we simply got rid of racial discourse and replaced it with no alternative that can do its work relatively well, some important benefits would be lost. (Shortly I will consider the extent to which anti-realists can find this way of securing prudential goods agreeable; hence the talk of *something like* racial discourse rather than racial discourse, *simpliciter*.) As a separate matter, note that if the value of racial identities lied *only* in the role they play in resisting the negative psychological impact of being racially oppressed, then presumably there would be no justification for white identity in societies that privilege whiteness. Perhaps this is a good thing: perhaps if there is no white identity, there can be no white supremacism. Marilyn Frye (2001) suggests something close to this when she holds that we ought to eliminate "whitely" ways of being, but not non-whitely ways of being. But Frye does not offer a reason to think that white supremacist ideology would not simply be supplanted by some sort of non-raced supremacism. Additionally, there seem to be some affirmative reasons to make room for white identity: white folks—at least, those who enjoy white privilege or benefit from a legacy of white privilege—have a special responsibility in eradicating racism. Indeed, some articulate white identity in terms of both recognition of, and awareness of white resistance to, white privilege (Alcoff 2006, ch. 9; Taylor 2004, 115).

Finally, knowledge of one's own racial identity can provide important resources for accurately predicting what one will experience (Taylor 2004, 113–115, 142), such as one's ability to successfully hail a taxi cab, to take the stock, and well-founded, example (Dao 2003). Now if the above arguments for racial anti-realism are sound, racial identities will be based on certain false beliefs. But if for the moment we bracket this epistemic problem, it seems that other things being equal, retaining something like our racial identities is prudentially valuable.

Finally, consider some moral imperatives. Some of these should be evident by now, such as ensuring children's equal education, which at times might require repairing racial disparities in resource allocation. Another important moral duty that is relevant here, however, is simply that we should treat people as they want to be treated, and this means that we should identify people as they want to be identified, other things being equal. Of course, this cannot always be done: we should not identify a convicted perpetrator of corporate fraud as a law-abiding citizen simply because he sincerely claims to identify as a law-abiding citizen. However, when this can be done, that is, when all other things are equal, we should identify people as they wish to be identified. To refuse to do so without some important overriding obligation, without other things being *un*equal, seems morally problematic. Now, as indicated by the pretend law-abider, one overriding factor might be when one's identity is based on a relevantly false belief. A similar obligation overrider might, then, be when racial identities are based on the false belief that race is real. Again, I will return to this epistemic concern shortly.

Initially, though, it seems that there are several significant political, prudential, and moral imperatives that require something like racial discourse, which is a point in favor of conservationism. At the same time, this justification for using racial discourse has been qualified by a *ceteris paribus* clause. Many think that racial discourse incurs serious costs, which present the possibility that other things are far from equal. In the remainder of this section we will see that three of four such costs do not in the end motivate eliminativism. The fourth cost—the epistemic cost—will complicate things a little.

First, Appiah (1996, 97–105) worries that identities can "go imperial": some identities—racial identities in particular—are "tyrannical" enough to generate "scripts" for proper ways of acting that dominate other identities (cf. Stubblefield 1995, 360–361). This potential for racial identities to keep a vice-like grip on individual complexity and freedom is one reason why Appiah recommends eventually abandoning them. Second, Blum (2002, 102–103) suggests that "racial thinking implies a moral distance among those of different races" that is irrevocably divisive and, in what is the flip side of that coin, imposes a "false commonality" on members of each race that results in them being stereotyped. Finally, insofar as racial thinking is as "inherentist" as Blum thinks it is, it brings with it a false perception of "racial fate" and hierarchies of value, and so the retention of racial discourse may facilitate various racist beliefs and attitudes (Blum 2002, 103–105).

It might appear, then, that we face the tough negotiation of having to balance these costs against the aforementioned benefits of racial discourse. However, the costs can arguably be mitigated or avoided entirely. First, as Taylor (2000, 126–127) notes, the possible threat of identity-imperialism underdetermines the elimination question. Risk-taking is warranted when the threat is low enough or unlikely and the potential benefit high enough or likely. Accordingly, we must mitigate against the threat of imperialism by guarding against racial identities dominating our individual complexities, but this threat does not necessitate abandoning racial identities. Second, while social separation based on race might warrant expending extra effort to reach across social boundaries, it does not entail that we should get rid of racial discourse altogether. As an alternative, we could try our best to promote what Outlaw (1996a, 22) calls "the formulation of a cogent and viable concept of race that will be of service to the non-invidious conservation of racial and ethnic groups—a formulation, and the politics it facilitates, that also avoids the quagmire of chauvinism" (cf. Moody-Adams 1999, 420–421). Finally, while of course racial discourse *might* facilitate racism and stereotyping, it need not—and to be sure it frequently *does* not.[3] Below, I will articulate the view that we need to reconstruct racial discourse. For the purposes of engaging the race debate, the main goal of this reconstruction will be to eliminate the biological pretensions of that discourse, but it should go without saying that another important goal is to eliminate any remaining racist pretensions.

The main task in this section is to get a fix on whether the balance of normative considerations supports eliminativism or conservationism. So far we have seen several significant imperatives that require something like racial discourse, and while we have seen some potential costs of racial discourse, these costs can be mitigated. Of course, this has merely been an initial enumeration of some of the more pressing benefits and

---

3  Blum is very pessimistic about the proposition that we have left behind old, deeply racist conceptions of race. As is hopefully now clear, I don't share the view that merely using racial discourse traps us in this way, as evidenced not only by the sort of armchair reflections made in Chapter 2 but also the empirical research considered in Chapter 4. In a frame of mind similar to Blum's, Appiah (1996, 32) holds that "if we are to move beyond racism we shall have ... to move beyond current racial identities." For a direct response to this claim, see Taylor (2000, 127; cf. 2004, 125–127). For more replies to the broader assertion that using racial discourse is sufficient for being racist, see Arthur (2007, 52–58); Benedict (1999); Hardimon (2003, 454–455); Lauer (1996); Mosley (1997).

costs, one that is manageable but no doubt too simplistic. Nevertheless, if we take this range of impacts as probative, then on balance the benefits seem to outweigh the costs so long as we do in fact mitigate those costs. The discourse we need appears to have two other core requirements as well: it must allow both for something like racial identities (to satisfy the moral and prudential imperatives) and for something like racial groups (to satisfy the political imperatives). I will call discourse that fulfills all three requirements an *adequate* discourse. Thus the moral, political, and prudential imperatives generate a normative constraint that suggests the strongest rationale for conservationism, the **morality, politics, and prudence constraint** (MMPC).

**MPPC:** Theories of race should attempt to supply or preserve an adequate discourse that facilitates compliance with the political, prudential, and moral imperatives discussed here. Those theories that can do so are, *ceteris paribus*, preferable to those that cannot.

MPPC exposes what is so dissatisfying about eliminativism: it seems forced to discard morality, prudence, and justice with erroneous racial discourse. Now some eliminativists, such as Appiah (1996, 74–82) and Zack (2007, 104), acknowledge that even if race is an illusion, social use of racial terms can still have a real impact on real people's lives. On Appiah's particular story, our practice of using racial labels has both social and psychological effects that shape identification, "the process through which an individual intentionally shapes her projects—including her plans for her own life and her conception of the good—by reference to available labels, available identities" (Appiah 1996, 78). On this complex account, racial identities are formed by the subject's own identification with the racial identity, by others ascribing the racial identity to the subject, and by the norms for that identity guiding the subject's treatment (Appiah 1996, 80–82; 2007). So, since Appiah's austere account of racial identity acknowledges that real racial labeling results from practices that lean on an illusory concept, it allows that we have racial identities even if we have no races.

However, acknowledging the effects of racial discourse is not enough to fully satisfy MPPC. Some of MPPC's imperatives are complied with by adopting practices that seem to target racial groups, such as programs that specifically focus on non-white youth, and eliminativism denies the existence of those groups even if it countenances racial identities. Furthermore, while Appiah does think that some good comes from racial identities, in the end these too, at least in recognizable forms, must be done away with according to him, because of their imperialistic tendencies. Thus when we look at the race debate from a normative, rather than ontological, perspective, even the most normatively sensitive eliminativism seems weaker than conservationism.

However, I have postponed consideration of a fourth reason for eliminating racial discourse: we simply should not encourage false beliefs, and if anti-realism is true, then racial discourse runs afoul of this rule. Thus whatever political, prudential, and moral imperatives racial discourse might serve, if race is an illusion, then racial discourse causes epistemic harm by encouraging false beliefs. So granting anti-realism, conservationists must confront a second normative principle, which I will call the **epistemic constraint** (EC).

> **EC:** Theories of race must either demonstrate that the benefits of racial discourse override the obligation to not encourage false beliefs, or, alternatively, secure these benefits without encouraging false belief in race.

On the one hand, then, the use of racial discourse seems justified by its role in the satisfaction of certain moral, political, and prudential imperatives. On the other hand, if race is an illusion, then there is epistemic reason to avoid using racial discourse. Realists, of course, make an attempt to finesse this dilemma: they can advocate continued racial discourse, in line with MPPC, and claim that their view consistently satisfies EC, since, on their theory, racial discourse does not encourage false beliefs. However, I have argued that realism fails. At the same time, though, EC seems to tether anti-realism to eliminativism, which means giving up the benefits of racial discourse, in violation of MPPC. This dilemma appears to be the most basic problem in the race debate: justice, well-being, and morality seem to require that we presuppose the existence of racial categories and identities, but how can we justifiably believe in racial categories and identities if there are no races?

## 7.2  Reconstructionism Articulated

I used to think we really could have it both ways, on the thought that we could *change* racial thinking to characterize race as a *thoroughly* social kind, in which case race will be real and race-thinking will be epistemically sound (Glasgow 2006).[4] I now believe that this view, which I called 'racial reconstructionism,' is untenable. For, briefly, if 'race' is supposed to have at least a partly biological referent, then that reconstructed wholly social discourse won't be talking about *race* at all. It will be talking about something else, something like shmace. That is, we cannot make *race*, in the relevant sense, a wholly social reality, because it is conceptually non-negotiable that 'race' purports to refer to a set of biological kinds demarcated by visible traits.[5]

Thankfully, though, all is not lost. There is a nearby substitutionist position, which (at the risk of obfuscating) I will also call 'racial reconstructionism,' that is much more tenable. As understood here, reconstructionism is a substitutionist view, not an eliminativist view, and according to substitutionism we should replace racial discourse with a nearby discourse, with attendant proximate concepts and conceptions. According to my particular reconstructionist brand of substitutionism, that replacement should go as follows.

First, we should keep the word 'race' and cognate and related terms. It might be less misleading if we used some other terms, like 'shmace,' but the best part of conservationism cautions us against making less than maximally efficient modifications to our language. Second, we should, at least for the time being, keep the exact racial groupings we have now, and if we have good reason perhaps eventually move to some other (possibly more coherent) set of groupings. So we will still talk about things we call 'races,' and we'll have groups whose members we call 'black people,' 'white people,' 'Asian people,' and so on. Third, however, there will be one key difference that separates current racial discourse from post-reconstruction discourse: by 'race' we will, post-reconstruction, intend only to refer to social kinds, and we will get rid of any conceptual implication that there are even partially biological races. That is racial reconstructionism (recall its place in Figure 2 (page 9)).

4    If I follow them correctly, Tommy Lott (1999, ch. 4) and Stephen Prothero (1995) attribute something in the neighborhood of this position to Du Bois: in contrast to the standard interpretation where Du Bois held that race *is* a social kind (in a word, that Du Bois was a constructivist), he should be read as saying that race should be *reconceived* as something social (along with a reconception towards an anti-racist notion of race). In her more recent work, Zack has suggested, in a somewhat similar vein, that the "best option" is to revise racial discourse to eliminate its biological pretensions (Zack 2002, 7; cf. 111–116).

5    It took me a while to come around to this objection, and I am grateful for having had various conversations with Jan Dowell, David Sobel, Steve Wall, and Ryan Wasserman, as well as a series of conversations with Stuart Brock, where I was pressed on questions that ultimately led me to my current views. Without these discussions this book may very well have tragically contained one more falsehood than it already does.

## 7.3 An Initial Defense

So much for stating the view.[6] Let me begin its defense by introducing a convention that will allow me to keep my head on straight. I will keep using the word 'race' and cognate and associated terms to represent *current* folk racial discourse. I will use 'race\*' and cognate and associated terms when using the *post-reconstruction* discourse that is being recommended for adoption. More will be said about this below, but the main point of distinction, again, is that racial discourse presupposes that races are biological kinds, while racial\* discourse only presupposes that races\* are social kinds.

For racial reconstructionism to be defensible, we need adequate semantic, ontological, and normative accounts of how this reconstruction will work. The normative task is of course to satisfy our two main normative constraints, MPPC and EC. The basic satisfaction strategy is pretty straightforward. MPPC means that we should, other things being equal, try to make room for a discourse that can facilitate the satisfaction of the moral, political, and prudential imperatives discussed above. Of course, EC reminds us that other things are not equal: racial discourse encourages false beliefs. But reconstructionism proposes that by replacing race-talk with race\*-talk, we can make race\* real and therefore swap an epistemically harmful discourse for one that is epistemologically kosher. And, as I will explain below, race\*-talk seems capable of doing all the moral, political, and prudential work that race-talk can do; to the extent that we need to use something like the language of 'racial groups' and 'racial identities,' we can just as well talk about racial\* groups and racial\* identities. So reconstructionism satisfies both normative constraints.

Turn next to the ontological task. The proposal on the table is that, while race is not real, race\* can be made real. If we continue with our supposition that social kinds are ontologically respectable, we should focus on what is unique to them. One of their distinctive properties is what we might call their 'social existential malleability.' The existence of ballplayers, professors, Supreme Court Justices, or citizens is socially contingent. Obviously, it would now take quite a lot of work to wean these identities out of existence, but it is in principle possible. More to the point, it was very possible to *create* these social identities. Given

---

6   In Figure 1.2 I classify substitutionism as a kind of *anti*-eliminativism. This might be misleading, since substitutionists do say that we should get rid of racial discourse. But since we also recommend replacing racial discourse with some other, proximate discourse, we aren't outright eliminativists in the strict sense (which is to say: the sense we can happily stipulate), who just recommend that we get rid of racial discourse, *punkt*.

various goods, such as knowledge, productivity, stability, and recreation, we were able to justify creating new identities of being a professor or a Supreme Court Justice. Thus we can bring social kinds into existence, and, sometimes perhaps, we can eliminate their existence, all through 'mere' convention. Biological kinds do not appear to offer the same kind of existential malleability.[7] So, *if* races* can be made relevantly similar to judges, professors, or ballplayers, then we can go ahead and create them. That is, while at present race is not real, we can in principle add a social item to our ontological suitcase: since we can create social kinds, we can create races*.[8]

A crucial step in creating races* is to supply a general justification for having races* and racial* identities. Again, this work is done in the normative argument: certain important imperatives can only be fulfilled by certain discourses, including those that allow for either races and racial identities or races* and racial* identities. It is important that this justificatory framework is adequate. A proposal to create biologically real races by forcibly isolating various people and embarking on a state-run eugenics program would be morally inadequate. Since reconstructionism justifies the creation of real races* by MPPC, it should not face any moral problems.[9]

Finally, in order to forestall the objections constructivism faced, OSC must be satisfied—reconstructionism must be semantically kosher. OSC requires that, in the context of our present aims, theories of race must reflect the biosocial complexity of racial discourse, and more specifically the constraint that race non-negotiably purports to be biological. To comply with this constraint we can simply *start* by

---

7   That is, they would have to be created through biological manipulation and eliminated via extermination. To say that these are different *kinds* of creation and elimination is not to say that eliminating or creating biological kinds is *harder* than eliminating or creating social kinds; in some cases, in fact, it seems that the reverse is true.

8   Additionally, we can borrow the influential Duboisian point that we do not need *strict* criteria for identifying the morphological 'badge' of race*. Rather, it is sufficient that folk usage contains a working method of identification, allowing for epistemically borderline cases (Hardimon 2003, 445).

9   I am, of course, only presenting a general theoretical model for reconstructionism. Details about which particular identities we want and what particular justifications we can offer for those particular identities would have to be provided to complete the picture. These tasks are currently being tackled by some of those working on more concrete issues of identity. It is important that, as others have discussed in more detail than I will here, racial identities are 'two-dimensional.' That is, to recall Appiah's language, our identities are formed by both the subject's identification with the identity and ascription of the identity by others. In some contexts one dimension alone may be sufficient for identity construction, such as with infants or immigrants who have not (yet) identified with any identity but who are nonetheless racially identified by

acknowledging these facts. So, if we continue to hold that there are no biological races, OSC commits us to saying that race is not real. Reconstructionism, then, begins with racial anti-realism. A way to nevertheless refrain from encouraging false beliefs is to simultaneously recognize a need for a discourse that can adequately speak to social life. Thus the suggestion is that while we currently do not do this, we should neither simply eliminate nor conserve, but instead reconstruct, our discourse to treat races* as groups thoroughly structured by social forces.

It might be objected here that, for some combination of semantic, practical, or psychological reasons, it is impossible to replace racial discourse with racial* discourse (Zack 1995, 307). But I think this would be too cynical. First, the reconstructed definitions are, by hypothesis, stipulated as the ideal definitions, and if we're stipulating, there should no *semantic* problem in thinking that we can change our discourse (Haslanger 2000, 34). (Note also that, though stipulated, these definitions are not arbitrary, since the reconstruction is motivated by our imperatives.) Furthermore, reconstruction does not appear to be a *practical* impossibility with respect to race. Race, as we have seen, has been a volatile subject, repeatedly changing in meaning. One of the more obvious examples of this is that the once widespread belief in a natural or even metaphysical racial hierarchy is disappearing (even if some invidious remnants remain).[10] Such change is the result of, among other things, intellectual debate, social activism, racial conflict, and a resultant improved science. So history indicates that it is not practically impossible to treat racial discourse as open to change or improvement or substitution. According to reconstructionism, the next step in this evolution is to give up the belief that there are biological races. Indeed, the history of the meaning of 'race' and the data we have on current racial discourse suggest that the socially directed process of discursive

---

other-ascription. So saying that races* will be composed of people with similar racial* identities is not to suggest that both subject-based identification and other-directed ascription are always necessary for the identity to take root. One dimension may be sufficient. In his recent work, Appiah (2007) curiously denies that there can be social identities with which no one identifies. In addition to Appiah on two-dimensionality, see also Blum (2002, 148–149); Corlett (2003, 130); Gooding-Williams (1998); Haslanger (2003, 309–315); Mills (1998, ch. 3); Root (2005); Sundstrom (2001, 295). I am grateful to Sally Haslanger for comments on this point and these examples.

10 As the literature on the evolution of racial discourse makes clear, our linguistic history is rife with examples of how the concept of race seems to have changed. Jennifer L. Hochschild (2005, 71) notes, for instance, that it was once "common and uncontested" to use phrases such as 'the Yankee race,' which we don't hear too often anymore.

reconstruction has been going on for some time now.[11] To be sure, a significant amount of difficult social agitation will be required in order to effect these changes, but as to the question of mere practical possibility, we can take encouragement from the hardier revolutions waged in previous generations.

Finally, regarding the objection that eliminating race-thinking is psychologically impossible, recent empirical evidence from Robert Kurzban and colleagues (2001; see also Cosmides et al. 2003) suggests that race-thinking might, indeed, be psychologically eliminable, in the sense that we can stop racial encoding, at least in social contexts with signs of non-racial coalitional alliances, on the hypothesis that we encode race because it is a proxy for coalitional alliances. Indeed, something of a movement is emerging which holds that racial thinking is a by-product of otherwise non-racial evolutionarily based psychological processes, perhaps under the influence of social forces (for an overview and helpful discussion, see Machery & Faucher 2005a, 2005b), and if we can alter the conditions which enable that by-product to be formed, perhaps we can alter our representations of race. Note here that alteration is much less psychologically demanding than simple elimination (Alcoff 2006, 245). If we are cognitively cursed to represent humanity in something like racial ways, then eliminativism is dead on arrival, but reconstructionism remains a viable alternative, since it asks us not to entirely do away with racial thinking, but to replace it with racial* thinking.[12] The only way this would be psychologically impossible is if our putatively evolutionarily determined ways of representing race* were ineliminably tied to representing it as a biological kind. But it is doubtful that this specific representation is evolutionarily determined, given that we now have substantial data showing that we already in *some* respects see race as a function of non-biological, social factors.[13]

11  For historical analyses concluding that race has evolved from a scientific concept to a social one, see Goldberg (1993, 61–74); Omi & Winant (1994, 63–65); Taylor (2000, 2004, 38–48, 73–80). For the claim that social kinds' reality comes in degrees, depending on the level of influence had by the practices that create such kinds, see Sundstrom 2001, 2002a. Again, however, one of the central claims of this volume is that this conceptual and ontological evolution is at best incomplete, and its completion is required by OSC for 'race' to be considered the name for a social kind.

12  For further debate about replacement strategies, see Blum (2004); Levinson (2003). Needless to say, I find Blum's defense of the psychological possibility of replacing racial discourse with a nearby discourse compelling. One reason to at worst take an agnostic stance on this question is that it has been pretty difficult to do studies on the psychology of those who live in societies without race but with race*.

13  As Kelly, Machery, and Mallon (n-d) note, even if race-thinking is a by-product of evolution, it is still likely that developmental and environmental factors are required

Reconstructionism can thus retain something close to the Duboisian pragmatist intuitions with which Taylor (2000) sympathizes. It does not require new institutions, such as new language; rather, it requires attaching new meanings to existing words and practices so that they function properly. Similarly, while I've talked of creating races*, the proposal is not to literally create new material objects, either. Rather, reconstructionism is a project that requires fine-tuning our *conceptual* resources, to reconceive the nature of the categories into which people fall, so that those categories end up representing a (socially) real kind of thing. This proposal, then, does not seem to shoot for the impossible. It merely rejects the exclusivity of the conservation-or-elimination dichotomy and asks us to tweak our racial discourse and thought.

Again, none of this is to say that it won't be difficult. If for the purposes of the question, 'What should we do with popular racial discourse?' folk usage has some semantic authority, then reconstructionism requires actual social change—that same folk usage will have to go racial*. We will have to recognize the fact of continuity, rather than thinking that there are biologically principled boundaries between the races. We will have to look at the counterexamples to constructivism presented in the previous chapter and not see them as counterexamples:

---

to, we might say, 'activate' it. (The basic point is intuitive enough: if you were raised in a closed village of 200 people who looked more or less like you and who never talked about race, you would probably have no idea of race. The less basic point is that incredibly subtle social and even neurological mechanisms might affect how, and whether, we think in racial terms.) This, though, is not to say that manipulation or elimination of those factors is always an easy task, and as Kelly et al. observe, the costs of the required social reforms may be substantial, depending on the exact details of whatever ends up being the true evolutionary story. Just to keep the record straight, I should call attention to two places at which it might (incorrectly) seem that the reconstruction I am recommending and the facts reported by Kelly and colleagues are incompatible. First, they discuss literature showing that essentialism may be a crucial part of race-thinking; I hope (in Chapter 4) to have shown ways in which it is not so crucial (a possibility that Kelly et al. accept). Second, Kelly and collaborators direct us to fascinating, though troubling, research showing that people can avoid harboring explicit racist beliefs while still associating some races with good concepts and others with bad concepts (as measured on the widely discussed Implicit Association Tests, an indirect measurement of racial attitudes). Preliminary studies have shown that even these implicit associations are manipulable, rather easily sometimes (but definitely not all the time—it should be a truism by now that eliminating racism is, at least, hard work that must stretch across generations). Obviously, I am not recommending any particular *methods* for reconstructing racial discourse or for reducing society's frequency and kinds of racism; racial reconstructionism only implies that it is psychologically and pragmatically possible. In the absence of such possibilities, reconstructionism—and of much greater concern, hope—are doomed to the theoretical rubbish bin.

when imagining a racially\* egalitarian society—or a population entirely composed of racially unidentified babies, or one without sight, or whatever particular social factor we construct to be essential to race\*—we will have to be able to sincerely say that the people in such a society *have no races\**, perhaps even just for one hour. That is just to say that we would need to recognize that we attach our racial categories to biological properties, so that those categories are demarcated in socially dependent, biologically arbitrary ways. Such recognition—if it truly permeates the complex panoply of our representations, including explicit thoughts, behavioral reactions, visual identifications, and so on—is tantamount to replacing racial thinking with racial\* thinking.

Briefly, then, in contrast to constructivism's contention that race is actually a social kind, the conceptual facts seem to require the more austere position that racial discourse is laden with too much biological baggage to accurately call race a social kind. However, because the shift from biological to social connotation must be completed for race\* to be real, because EC requires that ordinary discourse match the facts in order to forestall epistemic harm, and because MPPC suggests that we need to satisfy various moral, political, and prudential imperatives that require something in the neighborhood of racial discourse, reconstructionism urges us to pursue this shift in meaning. Thus, reconstructionism is anti-conservationist in that it does not incorrectly presuppose that racial discourse is already epistemologically legitimate, and it is anti-eliminativist in that the conclusion is not to simply eliminate racial discourse, but, rather, to more usefully replace it with something nearby, namely racial\* discourse.

Perhaps it is worth emphasizing here that racial reconstructionism is not an anthropological, psychological, historical, or sociological *description* of how racial discourse has operated in the U.S., such as we find in Omi and Winant's theory of racial formation.[14] While it shares certain affinities with some such views, reconstructionism is a *normative* program for designing a coherent conceptual architecture that will bring about the reality of races\* and racial\* identities in order to satisfy both MPPC and EC. So reconstructionism's main point is not that racial discourse has been revised, nor that it can be revised in the future, nor even that it should be revised to be rid of any racist pretensions (Mosley 1997, 109; Outlaw 1996a, 22), though all of these points are important subsidiary steps in the reconstructionist project. Rather, the main point is that certain kinds of revision to our discourse and thought are

---

14  Racial formation is "the sociohistorical process by which racial categories are created, inhabited, transformed, and destroyed." This theory is intended to explain how "the concept of race continues to play a fundamental role in structuring and representing the social world" (Omi & Winant 1994, 55).

required if that discourse and thought are to be both epistemologically legitimate and available to us for the satisfaction of MPCC's political, prudential, and moral imperatives.

It is not claimed here that mere linguistic reconstruction is *sufficient* for making race* socially real. As Alcoff urges, race is a function not only of how we use racial terms but also our "perceptual habits" and how we interpret what we see, and Blum is surely right to say that race "is not just a 'discourse.' It is a way of thinking about, experiencing, perceiving, and relating to people" (Alcoff 2006, chs 7–8, 10; Blum 2002, 102). To be sure, then, the whole package will need to change if we are going to change how we think about race, and it might even be that, say, perception needs to be cultivated in new directions before we can alter the way we reflexively think in everyday contexts. So talk about the reconstruction of racial 'discourse' is at its most plausible when it is shorthand for talk about the reconstruction of racial discourse, thought, perception, and practice. On a similar note, we would be foolish to ignore the warning that getting rid of the concept of race is not tantamount to undoing the harm done in its name, a distinct problem that requires its own solution (Kitcher 2007, 311; Mosley 1997, 102).

A final potential objection to reconstructionism is that it incorrectly puts the normative cart before the onto-semantic horse. This complaint is based on a sensible view of language, reality, and normativity. The usual way of thinking about the intersection of these domains is that terms mean what they mean and reality is what it is. Accordingly, political, prudential, and ethical considerations must conform to language and reality, not the other way around. Racial reconstructionism might seem to violate this piece of common sense by recommending ontological and semantic changes on the basis of normative considerations.

The commonsense ordering is intuitive, and I won't suggest that the practical is primary to the descriptive or that normative considerations by themselves actually make things real. Instead, the claim is that normative considerations give us reason to make changes to our discourse, in a manner that comports with independently fixed ontological and semantic constraints. When it comes to social kinds, the normative is often the motivation for creating new social facts. Think, for instance, of relatively benign social kinds, such as those involved in basketball. The meanings of 'ballplayer' and associated terms (e.g., 'basketball,' 'point,' 'referee,' 'foul') are what they are precisely because they serve practical purposes. If a foul made for a worse rather than a better game, we would either eliminate the word from basketball discourse, and thereby eliminate the thing we call a 'foul,' or revise its meaning to improve the game. Or, we might even add some new contents to our conceptual suitcase (as was done with the three-point basket). Thus making ontological and semantic changes to our social world based on normative considerations can be normatively, ontologically, and semantically kosher. It does not put the cart before the horse.

So I take the fundamental principles of reconstructionism to be well-founded, indeed to constitute the architecture of the best overall theory of race. But within its substitutionist family there are some rival views that can agree on the fundamental principles while disagreeing with some crucial specific policy outputs. I want to wrap things up by considering these alternative proposals.

## 7.4 Family Rivalries: Alternative Substitutionist Theories

According to substitutionism, although racial discourse should be eliminated, we should at the same time replace it with some other, proximate discourse. Reconstructionism is one form of substitutionism: it counsels us to replace racial discourse with racial* discourse. Because it keeps our current terminology, and only requires us to make one, not insignificant, systematic conceptual change to racial discourse, namely to stop trying to talk about a biological reality, reconstructionism's replacement discourse is among the *most* proximate alternatives. But there are other, less proximate discourses that we might substitute for racial discourse. For instance, the proposal to replace race-talk with ethnicity-talk has received widespread attention. I'm sympathetic with many of the critiques of ethnicity-oriented substitutionism that others have thoughtfully developed, such as the critique that it would require us to abandon either whole racial groups, like black and white people, which are composed of several distinct ethnic groups, or whole ethnic groups, like *Haitian-American*, if racial groups like *Black* becomes all-encompassing ethnic categories. So I will not pursue that discussion here.[15]

But other forms of substitutionism, and in fact other forms of reconstructionism, can claim to compete more directly with the kind of racial reconstructionism I have been advocating.[16] According to Blum's substitutionism, roughly, in order to satisfy the demands of something like MPPC, we should replace our race-talk with talk about *racialized*

---

15 For just a few such critiques, see Alcoff (2006, ch. 10); Blum (2002, 167–169); Taylor (2004, 53–57; 2005). One recent ethnicity-oriented substitutionist is Corlett (2003).

16 There are, to be sure, many possible substitutionist proposals. Among other restrictions, here I am only considering *global* forms of substitutionism, which call for replacement of racial discourse in *every* domain. Some advocate for specifically *local* kinds of substitutionism, which target only one domain of racial discourse; for example, Helms, Jernigan, and Mascher (2005) propose that psychologists in particular should abandon racial categories in favor of related but non-racial categories, while Condit (2005) suggests that scientists should capture the quasi-continental clusters that some think are racial (discussed above in Chapter 5) by replacing the word 'race' with 'large diffuse geographically based populations.'

*groups*, since while 'race' purports to refer to a (biological, essentialist) kind that fails to exist, 'racialized group' is defined, as a term of art, as a social kind (Blum 2002, esp. chs 8–9). So the question arises as to whether reconstructionism or Blum's substitutionism is a better way of satisfying the constraints that concern us.[17]

The replacement of racial discourse with discourse about racialized groups, as contrasted with discourse about ethnicity, can directly secure many of the benefits that some say are reserved for racial discourse alone. Gracia (2005, 93, 97–99, 144), for example, holds that in order to make sense of racial identities and understand racial history and experience, we cannot treat race as a fiction; he, Hardimon (2003, 454), and Taylor (2004, 126) think that racial discourse is required to understand and combat racism; Kitcher (2007, 311) is concerned that the language of race might be required for affirmative action and for the formation of solidarity in response to racial injustice; and Sundstrom (2002b, 203) writes that the claim that race is an illusion is "disrespectful of our lived experiences and fail[s] to capture the presence and impact of social identities in our lives, their import in our lives and ... the ways our social worlds are organized." However, Blum's kind of substitutionism illustrates that while maintaining that race is not real we can consistently recognize that people unquestionably act *as if* race is real, and race-thinking and identification—and their social organization—can be understood, and racism can be fought, by recognizing that our behaviors seem to have created racialized groups. For instance, rather than target that Head Start program at a black community, we could target it at a community that has been (erroneously) racialized as black (cf. Blum 2002, 166–167; Shelby 2002, 263–264; 2005, 236–239). This kind of view thus shows us that it is not quite accurate to say that we need *racial* discourse to secure at least the vast majority of the benefits of racial discourse, including those covered in MPPC. What we need, instead, is some kind of *quasi*-racial discourse, a discourse that mimics racial discourse to a large enough extent that it can secure those same benefits without taking on the burdens of racial discourse, such as we find in discourse about racialized groups. Those discourses that are *closest* to racial discourse should do the best imitation job. So consider a spectrum of prescriptions about what to do with racial discourse (Figure 7.1).

So far, we have seen that neither outright eliminativism nor outright conservationism can simultaneously satisfy EC and MPPC (and I've sidelined ethnicity-oriented substitutionism and argued that Appiah's racial identities aren't enough to do all the work required by MPPC),

---

17  Blum presents only one of many accounts that use the language of racialized groups, but among these his is the most developed *substitutionist* proposal I have encountered.

| Outright eliminativism | Ethnicity-oriented substitutionism | Appiah's racial identities | Blum's substitutionism | Reconstructionism | Outright conservationism |
|---|---|---|---|---|---|
| | | Substitutionism | | | |

*Figure 7.1* What to do with racial discourse.

which leaves Blum's substitutionism and reconstructionism as the viable candidates among the policies displayed in Figure 7.1.[18] With respect to many of the concerns noted above—about racial solidarity, predicting experiences, Head Start or affirmative action projects, and so on—racialization discourse, racial* discourse, and racial discourse all seem *equally* useful. So for many of these concerns, by preserving quasi-racial discourse, Blum's substitutionism and reconstructionism are fully capable policy alternatives. However, these two views claim to have different strengths with respect to some other concerns.

For instance, Blum maintains that "[r]acialization does not, but race does, imply inherent characteristics, a virtually unbridgeable moral, experiential, and cognitive gulf among racial groups, and a hierarchy of worth" (Blum 2002, 162; cf. 160, 169–171, and ch. 5). So if race-talk is so wrapped up in old, problematic beliefs that we won't be able to strip it of its problems, we would do better to replace race-talk with racial-ized-group-talk than with race*-talk. However, I am less pessimistic than Blum about the extent to which our race-talk has already shed some of these outdated problems. His assessment seems to me to neglect the dynamic history of race-thinking in general and the ways in which its moralized and inherentist baggage has been significantly reduced in particular. Thus I believe that it is sensible and common to talk about race in non-'inherentist' terms, and I remain hopeful that we can adopt a discourse about race* that does not imply that each race* has a distinctive set of biologically inherent characteristics, a distinctive level of worth, or a hostile border.

18 Do we need the concept of race to have the concept of a racialized group (or of race*)? In one sense we do: racialized groups just are groups that have been constructed because they have been treated as if they were *races*. The right way to make sense of this seems to me to be to say that talking in terms of racialized groups (or races*) can be conducted without first-order uses of racial terms, but also that racial-ization-talk might need to employ the concept of race at the second order, as a way of talking about talk about race. In this way, substitutionism and eliminativism are most charitably construed as policies regarding what to do with specifically first-order racial discourse; they talk about talk about race all the time, so they must be consistent with the conservation of second-order race-talk.

If that is correct, there seems to be no reason to favor racialization discourse over racial* discourse. However, the latter appears to have the upper hand with regard to the prudential issue of identity integration. Here is how Blum (2002, 169) himself puts it: "Can there be racial identity without 'race?' Isn't the honoring and preserving of black identity a reason not to jettison race? I do not think so. If there are no races, then any racial solidarity presuming them is without foundation." So Blum's substitutionism would require that those who care about being, say, black have to stop thinking of themselves as members of a race, or even a race*, and instead conceive of themselves as members of erroneously racialized groups, so that their identities are, in some sense, fraudulent. By contrast, reconstructionism allows overall identities to stay relatively integrated by allowing for the preservation of legitimate racial* identities. Thus Blum's view seems to require a relatively greater disintegration of some people's identities, and unnecessarily so if reconstructionism is a viable alternative. Similarly, it unnecessarily requires us to not treat some people as they wish to be treated by identifying them as they wish to be identified. One way to avoid taking on these costs is to replace erroneous race-talk not with talk of racialized groups, but with ontologically proper race*-talk.

Now there are other versions of reconstructionism—other ways of running with race*-talk—besides the way I have proposed. On my particular brand of reconstructionism, races* are social kinds that we demarcate in terms of otherwise unimportant and continuous visible traits of the relevant sort, whose kind-hood *in and of itself* signifies nothing other than that we categorize people in that way. Some other views, which on my way of carving the theoretical space count as reconstructionist, add some content to this thinnish proposed concept of race*.

For instance, Stubblefield (1995, 362) has suggested that we "redefine the *meaning* of saying 'I'm black'" so that it means "'I am routinely labeled as [black],'" and so long as we can add to this that such attributions are devoid of racist content and that such attributions are keyed to socially partitioned visible traits, her view sounds fairly similar to mine. More recently, though, Stubblefield (2005) argues that we should understand 'race' as a certain kind of family. There are special obligations—the many products of *partiality*—that she thinks are part and parcel of family relations (pp. 166–167), and she is committed to reconceptualizing race so that we supplement a mere account of race with a political agenda (p. 156). So this is a much more robust kind of substitution than I have proposed here.

I believe that this thicker understanding of race has some drawbacks. First, insofar as we are trying to facilitate a transition that can speak to people's lives, we would do better to accommodate those who do not feel, and do not particularly want to feel, partial to those of their own race. I, for one, perceive no obligation to white people as white people, and I am quite content to think that this is a good thing. Stubblefield suggests that white folks have the familial obligation of helping each other do better, and, so far as that goes, of helping end white racism. While that is of course a laudable goal, I perceive no more obligation to help white people as such to do better than to help non-white people as such to do better. And to the extent that white folks have an *extra* obligation to end white privilege and domination, it is not, primarily at least, an obligation *to* other white people, but to the targets of racial exclusion, and such an obligation *stems* not from some relation to other white people, but from the unjustly gained benefits of white privilege, be that gain intended or unintended.

Second, insofar as substitutionists aim at a better world than the one in which we currently reside, obligation-oriented approaches seem burdened with a substantial limitation. Obligations spawned from constructed racial identities, like all obligations, in a certain sense constrain our freedom, as Appiah (1996, 97–99) so thoughtfully explores. We might have obligations related to race, but in shooting for a better world, why conceptualize race so that it *itself* constrains us in these ways? That is, there might be some race-related obligations that make sense, instrumentally, as ways of bringing racism to its knees, but that is to understand *justice*, rather than race, as the ultimate generator of race-related obligations in a non-ideal world. So in order to combat racial injustice, we don't need to define race in terms of family responsibilities, where such an understanding leaves us with a notion of race that is not, in the end, fully liberating. We can do better by simply having a definition of 'race*' that is consistent with, but does not by itself entail, behavior-constraining norms that independently flow from an adequate conception of justice.

Now consider a version of reconstructionism that takes the concern for justice in a different direction. In Chapter 6 I discussed the ways in which Haslanger has defended constructivism by recruiting the powerful mechanics of semantic externalism. In another strain of her work, she has run a parallel strategy of defending a kind of reconstructionism, where, whatever 'race' might mean in its ordinary sense, what it *should* mean, given various political and conceptual goals (not least of which is racial justice), is roughly race* plus one further element: social hierarchy (Haslanger 2000).[19] On this reconstructive analysis, our aims are such that we need to combat racial injustice, and the best way to do this

---

19 I will keep labeling Haslanger's view 'reconstructionist' just to keep things uniform, but it is my label, not hers. She, instead, calls it at various times a 'critical analytical' or an 'ameliorative' approach.

is to expose the ways in which racialized groups have been subordinated or privileged via racial discourse and practice, and the best way to do *this* is to build unjust social hierarchy into the definition of 'race*' itself, in which case certain races will be what they are in part because they are socially subordinated, while others will be what they are in part because they are socially privileged. After we end racial hierarchy, therefore, we will no longer have any races, in the prescriptive sense of 'race' recommended by Haslanger.[20]

I hope I share the sense of urgency with which Haslanger wants to address racial injustice. However, I also share with conservationists the pragmatic thesis that less revolution is, other things being equal, better than more. If there is a tool for exposing and combating racial injustice and the ways in which it has been fostered by racial discourse, which would at the same time allow us to replace racial discourse with a less drastic alternative, this would be better. I think we have such resources. A non-hierarchical racial* discourse would still call attention to the ways in which racial discourse has been socially constructed. It would also prohibit the inclusion of racism within the concept of race* itself. To the extent that racism is not embedded in the concept or in the language itself, I hope that we can expose it for what it is by calling it what it is, namely racism.[21] In this way, it does not seem unreasonable to hope that the oppression of people who might be categorized in certain value-neutral ways can end without also ending those value-neutral categorizations. If that is possible, then people can non-oppressively keep racial* identities that they (justifiably) find valuable, and we can revel in a newfound racial* equality. It remains possible, of course, that if we move from a racial and racist world to a racial* and post-racist one, nobody will value, or at least justifiably value, their racial* identities, and perhaps at that stage we can let even racial* discourse cease to work as a way of talking about our reality, keeping it only perhaps to make sense of an antiquated racialized history. But that strikes me as something best left to the people in that ideal society.[22]

---

20   Amy Gutmann (1996) has articulated a similar view. Unlike Haslanger, Gutmann seeks to replace 'race' consciousness with 'color' consciousness, but Gutmann's 'color,' like Haslanger's prescriptive sense of 'race,' focuses attention on the constructed nature of racial identities and builds oppression into the concept itself. (Haslanger alternatively uses 'color' to just refer to our visible physical traits that we take to distinguish races.) One other difference is that Gutmann focuses more locally on public policy, while Haslanger focuses on our discourse and practice considered generally.

21   For a similar response to Haslanger's reconstructionist account of gender, see Saul (2006, 136–137).

22   In one article, Haslanger (2003–2004) argues that losing the idea(l) of egalitarian race relations is no real loss, since no social goods are lost when we lose this idea(l). It

So while it is not hard to see the appeal of these thicker versions of reconstructionism, I think that thinned-out reconstructionism is the most tempting item on the substitutionist menu. But I have made one last presupposition that should be exposed and defended: why reconstruct to see races* as *social* kinds at all? Why not reconstruct our discourse in the direction of seeing races as ancestrally based breeding populations, of the kind proposed in the new biology of race (Arthur 2007, 82–84)? Why, in short, should we favor a constructivist-leaning rather than a populationist-leaning kind of reconstruction? Populationism faced serious trouble with the Arbitrariness Objection, but if we put that aside for current purposes, then once we agree that we are going to replace racial discourse with some new racial* discourse, why not go in a populationist direction, rather than in a social kind direction?

The only reason for preferring social-kind-based to biology-based reconstructionism is that social-kind-based reconstructionism is more likely to help us deal with our social ills and to preserve the identities that many find valuable. Recall that we do best if we have a way of talking about our ordinarily perceived racial groupings because these groupings have been central to the identity of so many people, because they need focused attention in order to resolve injustice, and because knowledge of one's position in a racialized world facilitates the prediction of experiences. Social-kind-based reconstruction can *exactly* keep our current groupings and identities and thereby directly serve all of those goals; it only asks us to thoroughly understand these groups as structured not by biology but by social forces. In order to match the biological facts, breeding-population-based reconstruction, by contrast, threatens more upheaval with respect to our ordinary identities and systems of classification. If we replaced racial discourse with discourse that was conceptually tethered to breeding populations, there is no guarantee (and, I suspect, little likelihood) that we will be able to address many of the moral, political, and prudential challenges that we want to face head-on. Reconstructionism as formulated here is intentionally geared to address those challenges.

Of course, we would be unwise to ignore the biological facts. So given the social concerns to which reconstructionism uniquely speaks,

---

does not count as a loss because there is no "reason for thinking that functional societies must acknowledge those physical differences that distinguish 'color'" (p. 10). I take the prudential arguments discussed above to show that there is at least one reason for thinking that it is a loss: people, at least in some cases justifiably, acknowledge those differences because they value them. (Haslanger considers an argument, inspired by Alcoff that is similar to this, but that argument relies on the claim that there must be some history and experience that will reinforce certain racial norms and thereby privilege some members of a race and exclude others. By going to a thin kind of reconstructionism, we can avoid this presupposition.)

and given that we simultaneously want to attend to the biological facts, it seems as though the thing to do is to have different terms for ancestral and socially relevant groupings, for the times when the two do not converge. I propose we keep 'race*' for the latter, for the groups we have thought were races. For the first, Ashley Montagu (1964a, 23) long ago suggested 'genogroup,' but maybe the best would be one of the more obvious choices, 'ancestry' (Lee et al. 2001, 57).

This kind of distinction has the virtue of allowing us to talk *both* in terms of a person as having this kind of ancestry and that kind of race* and racial* identity. And making the space for recognition of race* should allow us to confront the social issues that conservationists have rightly insisted we need to confront. Our race-conscious practices have structured our world and experiences in such a way that we would gravely err if we neglected them. The best way to attend to them, without staking any purchase in biological race-thinking, seems to be to pass the torch from race to race*.

# Afterword

This volume contains an account that all at once acknowledges that race is an apparition, attempts to adequately face the facts on the ground, retains some of the conceptual resources necessary for understanding, repairing, and ending our seemingly overwhelming legacy of racial injustice, recognizes the centrality of race to people's identities, and envisions a world with something very much like race but with neither racial injustice nor biological racial discourse. In these ways, it contains a view of race and race* that might be considered more optimistic than is typical of writings on this subject, and the fear, then, is that this might be asking for too much, for a utopia of sorts. Perhaps it is foolish or naïve to seek to accommodate hope, truth, and justice in one package.

So far as *that* goes, it is difficult to avoid being struck, repeatedly, by the fact that race is a delicate and confounding topic, a topic about which this book has said much less than needs saying. Those who are desperate for concrete policies that will end racial injustice, those who have felt their faces grow hot upon being made the targets of exclusion, those who would demand that their concrete differences be both acknowledged and appreciated in a world that sometimes seems to prize only conformity and the bare fact of difference itself, those who seek greater understanding of their own complicated identities, those who simply want a quiet space in which to live their lives under a light that overcomes the often consuming and oppressive shadow of race, and many others; such concerns are pressing, and for them this book, I know and regret, will be of limited use. But for those who confront a problem that all race-related concerns share at their deepest root—that our racial discourse is corrupt but seemingly too useful to do without—I have tried here to offer one solution, a theory of race whose shortcomings are hopefully contained by its strengths.

# References

Ahn, Woo-kyoung, Kalish, Charles, Gelman, Susan A., Medin, Douglas L., Luhmann, Christian, Atran, Scott, Coley, John D., & Shafto, Patrick. 2001. Why essences are essential in the psychology of concepts. *Cognition, 82,* 59–69.

Alcoff, Linda Martín. 1997. Philosophy and racial identity. *Philosophy Today, 41,* 67–76.

——. 2006. *Visible Identities: Race, Gender, and the Self* (Oxford: Oxford University Press).

Andreasen, Robin O. 1998. A new perspective on the race debate. *British Journal for the Philosophy of Science, 49,* 199–225.

——. 2000. Race: Biological reality or social construct? *Philosophy of Science, 67, Supplementary Volume,* S653–S666.

——. 2004. The cladistic race concept: A defense. *Biology and Philosophy, 19,* 425–442.

——. 2005. The meaning of 'race': Folk conceptions and the new biology of race. *The Journal of Philosophy, 102,* 94–106.

——. 2007. Biological conceptions of race. In Mohan Matthen & Christopher Stephens, eds., *Philosophy of Biology* (Amsterdam: Elsevier), 455–481.

Appiah, Kwame Anthony. 1985. The uncompleted argument: Du Bois and the illusion of race. In Henry Louis Gates, Jr., ed., *'Race,' Writing, and Difference* (Chicago, IL: University of Chicago Press), 21–37.

——. 1991. Social forces, 'natural' kinds. In Abebe Zegeye, Leonard Harris, & Julia Maxted, eds., *Exploitation and Exclusion: Race and Class in Contemporary US Society* (London: Hanz Zell Publishers), 1–13.

——. 1992. Illusions of Race. In K. Anthony Appiah, *In My Father's House: Africa in the Philosophy of Culture* (New York: Oxford University Press), 28–46.

——. 1996. Race, culture, identity: misunderstood connections. In K. Anthony Appiah and Amy Gutmann, *Color Conscious: The Political Morality of Race* (Princeton, NJ: Princeton University Press), 30–105.

——. 2007. Does truth matter to identity? In Jorge J. E. Gracia, ed., *Race or Ethnicity? On Black and Latino Identity* (Ithaca, NY: Cornell University Press), 19–44.

——. 2008a. Experimental philosophy. Presidential Address, Eastern Division American Philosophical Association December 2007. http://www.appiah.net/images/APA_Lecture_2007_for_Web.pdf. Accessed January 2008.

———. 2008b. *Experiments in Ethics.* Cambridge, MA: Harvard University Press.

Arax, Mark. 2002. The Black Okies, parts I and II. *Los Angeles Times,* August 25 and 26.

Arthur, John. 2007. *Race, Equality, and the Burdens of History* (Cambridge: Cambridge University Press).

Bamshad, Michael J., & Olson, Steve E. 2003. Does race exist? *Scientific American, 289,* 78–85.

Bamshad, Michael J., Wooding, Stephen, Salisbury, Benjamin A., & Stephens, J. Claiborne. 2004. Deconstructing the relationship between genetics and race. *Nature Reviews Genetics, 5,* 598–609.

Bamshad, Michael J., Wooding, Stephen, Watkins, W. Scott, Ostler, Christopher T., Batzer, Mark A., & Jorde, Lynn B. 2003. Human population genetic structure and inference of group membership. *American Journal of Human Genetics, 72,* 578–589.

Barbujani, Guido. 2005. Human races: Classifying people vs. understanding diversity. *Current Genomics, 6,* 215–226.

Barbujani, Guido, & Belle, Elise M.S. 2006. Genomic boundaries between human populations. *Human Heredity, 61,* 15–21.

Barbujani, Guido, Magagni, Arianna, Minch, Eric, & Cavalli-Sforza, L. Luca. 1997. An apportionment of human DNA diversity. *Proceedings of the National Academy of Sciences of the United States of America, 94,* 4516–4519.

Bastos-Rodrigues, Luciana, Pimenta, Juliana R., & Pena, Sergio D. J. 2006. The genetic structure of human populations studied through short insertion-deletion polymorphisms. *Annals of Human Genetics, 70,* 658–665.

Benedict, Ruth. 1999. Racism: The *ism* of the modern world. In Leonard Harris, ed., *Racism* (Amherst, NY: Humanity Books), 31–49.

Bernasconi, Robert. 2001. Who invented the concept of race? Kant's role in the Enlightenment construction of race. In Robert Bernasconi, ed., *Race* (Malden, MA: Blackwell), 11–36.

Blackburn, Daniel G. 2000. Why race is not a biological concept. In Berel Lang, ed., *Race and Racism in Theory and Practice* (Lanham, MD: Rowman & Littlefield), 3–26.

Blum, Lawrence. 2002. *"I'm not a racist, but..." The moral quandary of race* (Ithaca, NY: Cornell University Press).

———. 2004. Systemic and individual racism, racialization and antiracist education: A reply to Garcia, Silliman and Levinson. *Theory and Research in Education, 2,* 49–74.

Bowcock, A.M., Ruiz-Linares, A., Tomfohrde, J., Minch, E., Kidd, J.R., & Cavalli-Sforza, L.L. 1994. High resolution of human evolutionary trees with polymorphic microsatellites. *Nature, 368,* 455–457.

Boxill, Bernard. 2001. Introduction. In Bernard Boxill, ed., *Race and Racism* (Oxford: Oxford University Press), 1–42.

———. 2004. Why we should not think of ourselves as divided by race. In M.P. Levine & T. Pataki, eds., *Racism in Mind* (Ithaca, NY: Cornell University Press), 209–224.

Boyd, Richard. 1988. How to be a moral realist. In Geoffrey Sayre-McCord, ed., *Essays on Moral Realism* (Ithaca, NY: Cornell University Press), 181–228.

Brace, C. Loring. 2003. 'Race' is not a valid biological concept. In Yasuko Takezawa, ed., *Proceedings of the IRH International Symposium/IUAES 2002: Is Race a Universal Ideal? Colonialism, Nation-States, and a Myth Invented*, 61–83.

Brock, Stuart, & Mares, Edwin. 2007. *Realism and Anti-realism* (Stocksfield, UK: Acumen).

Brown, Lee M. 2004. Genetic reduction and its implications for theories of race. *The American Philosophical Association Newsletter on Philosophy and the Black Experience*, 3, 166–170.

Brown, Ryan A., & Armelagos, George J. 2001. Apportionment of racial diversity: A review. *Evolutionary Anthropology*, 10, 34–40.

Burchard, Esteban Gonzalez, Ziv, Elad, Coyle, Natasha, Gomez, Scarlett Lin, Tang, Hua, Karter, Andrew J., Mountain, Joanna L., Perez-Stable, Eliseo J., Sheppard, Dean, & Risch, Neil. 2003. The importance of race and ethnic background in biomedical research and clinical practice. *The New England Journal of Medicine*, 348, 1170–1175.

Burge, Tyler. 1993. Concepts, definitions, and meaning. *Metaphilosophy*, 24, 309–325.

Cantave, Cassandra, & Harrison, Roderick. 2001. Marriage and African-Americans. Joint Center for Political and Economic Studies Data Bank. http://www.jointcenter.org/DB/factsheet/marital.htm. Accessed December 17, 2007.

Cavalli-Sforza, L.L., Menozzi, P., & Piazza, A. 1994. *History and Geography of Human Genes* (Princeton, NJ: Princeton University Press).

Condit, Celeste M. 2005. 'Race' is not a scientific concept: Alternative directions. *L'Observatoire de la génétique*, 24.

Condit, Celeste M., Templeton, Alan, Bates, Benjamin R., Bevan, Jennifer L., & Harris, Tina M. 2003. Attitudinal barriers to delivery of race-targeted pharmacogenomics among informed lay persons. *Genetics in Medicine*, 5, 385–392.

Condit, Celeste M., Parrott, Roxanne L., Harris, Tina M., Lynch, John, & Dubriwny, Tasha. 2004. The role of "genetics" in popular understandings of race in the United States. *Public Understanding of Science*, 13, 249–272.

Cooper, Richard S., Kaufman, Jay S., & Ward, Ryk. 2003. Race and genomics. *The New England Journal of Medicine*, 348, 1166–1170.

Corlett, J. Angelo. 2003. *Race, Racism, and Reparations* (Ithaca, NY: Cornell University Press).

———. 2007. Race, ethnicity, and public policy. In Jorge J.E. Gracia, ed., *Race or Ethnicity? On Black and Latino Identity* (Ithaca, NY: Cornell University Press), 225–247.

Cosmides, Leda, Tooby, John, & Kurzban, Robert. 2003. Perceptions of race. *Trends in Cognitive Sciences*, 7, 173–179.

Dao, James. 2003. Report cites persistent bias among cabbies in Washington. *New York Times*, October 8, A24.

Diamond, Jared. 1994. Race without color. *Discover*, 15, 82–89.

Du Bois, W.E.B. 1984 [1940]. *Dusk of Dawn* (New Brunswick, NJ: Transaction).

———. 1997 [1897]. The conservation of races. Reprinted in David W. Blight & Robert Gooding-Willams, eds., *The Souls of Black Folk* (Boston, MA: Bedford Books), 228–238.

Dubriwny, Tasha N., Bates, Benjamin R., & Bevan, Jennifer L. 2004. Lay understandings of race: Cultural and genetic definitions. *Community Genetics, 7*, 185–195.

Dupré, John. 1981. Natural kinds and biological taxa. *The Philosophical Review, 90*, 66–90.

——. 1999. Are whales fish? In Douglas L. Medin and Scott Atran, eds., *Folkbiology* (Cambridge, MA: MIT Press), 461–476.

Ereshefsky, Marc. 2001. *The Poverty of the Linnaean Hierarchy: A Philosophical Study of Biological Taxonomy* (Cambridge: Cambridge University Press).

Feldman, Marcus W., Lewontin, Richard C., & King, Mary-Claire. 2003. Race: A genetic melting pot. *Nature, 424*, 374.

Fish, Jefferson M. 2002. The myth of race. In Jefferson M. Fish, ed., *Race and Intelligence: Separating Science from Myth* (Mahwah, NJ: Laurence Erlbaum Associates), 113–141.

Foster, Morris W., & Sharp, Richard R. 2002. Race, ethnicity, and genomics: Social classifications as proxies of biological heterogeneity. *Genome Research, 12*, 844–850.

Frye, Marilyn. 2001. White woman feminist 1983–1992. In Bernard Boxill, ed., *Race and Racism* (Oxford: Oxford University Press), 83–100.

Gannett, Lisa. 2004. The biological reification of race. *The British Journal for the Philosophy of Science, 55*, 323–345.

Gelman, Susan A., & Wellman, Henry M. 1991. Insides and essences: Early understandings of the non-obvious. *Cognition, 38*, 213–244.

Gil-White, Francisco J. 2001a. Are ethnic groups biological "species" to the human brain? Essentialism in our cognition of some social categories. *Current Anthropology, 42*, 515–554.

——. 2001b. Sorting is not categorization: A critique of the claim that Brazilians have fuzzy racial categories. *Journal of Cognition and Culture, 1*, 219–249.

Glasgow, Joshua. 2003. On the new biology of race. *The Journal of Philosophy, 100*, 456–474.

——. 2006. A third way in the race debate. *The Journal of Political Philosophy, 14*, 163–185.

——. 2007. Three things realist constructionism about race—or anything else— can do. *Journal of Social Philosophy, 38*, 554–568.

Glasgow, Joshua, Shulman, Julie L., & Covarrubias, Enrique. In press. The ordinary conception of race in the United States and its relation to racial attitudes: A new approach. *Journal of Cognition and Culture*, forthcoming.

Goldberg, David Theo. 1993. *Racist Culture: Philosophy and the Politics of Meaning* (Cambridge, MA: Blackwell).

Goldstein, Joshua R. 1999. Kinship networks that cross racial lines: The exception or the rule? *Demography, 36*, 399–407.

Gooding-Williams, Robert. 1998. Race, multiculturalism, and democracy. *Constellations, 5*, 18–41.

Gracia, Jorge J.E. 2000. *Hispanic/Latino Identity: A Philosophical Perspective* (Malden, MA: Blackwell).

——. 2005. *Surviving Race, Ethnicity, and Nationality: A Challenge for the Twenty-first Century* (Lanham, MD: Rowman & Littlefield).

——. 2007a. Individuation of racial and ethnic groups: The problems of circularity and demarcation. In Jorge J.E. Gracia, ed., *Race or Ethnicity? On Black and Latino Identity* (Ithaca, NY: Cornell University Press), 78–100.

——. 2007b. Race or ethnicity? An introduction. In Jorge J.E. Gracia, ed., *Race or Ethnicity? On Black and Latino Identity* (Ithaca, NY: Cornell University Press), 1–16.

Graham, George, & Horgan, Terry. 1994. Southern fundamentalism and the end of philosophy. *Philosophical Issues 5: Truth and Rationality*, 219–245.

Graves, Joseph L., Jr. 2001. *The Emperor's New Clothes: Biological Theories of Race at the Millennium* (New Brunswick, NJ: Rutgers University Press).

Griffiths, Paul E. 2004. Emotions as natural and normative kinds. *Philosophy of Science, 71*, 901–911.

Gutmann, Amy. 1996. Responding to racial injustice. In K. Anthony Appiah and Amy Gutmann, *Color Consciousness: The Political Morality of Race* (Princeton, NJ: Princeton University Press), 106–178.

Hacking, Ian. 2005. Why race still matters. *Dædalus, 134*, 102–116.

Handley, Lori J. Lawson, Manica, Andrea, Goudet, Jérôme, & Balloux, François. 2007. Going the distance: Human population genetics in a clinal world. *Trends in Genetics, 23*, 432–439.

Haney López, Ian. 1995. The social construction of race. In Richard Delgado, ed., *Critical Race Theory: The Cutting Edge* (Philadelphia, PA: Temple University Press), 191–203.

——. 2005. Race on the 2010 census: Hispanics and the shrinking white majority. *Dædalus, 134*, 42–52.

Hardimon, Michael O. 2003. The ordinary concept of race. *The Journal of Philosophy, 100*, 437–455.

Haslam, Nick O. 1998. Natural kinds, human kinds, and essentialism. *Social Research, 65*, 291–314.

Haslam, Nick O., Rothschild, Louis, & Ernst, Donald. 2000. Essentialist beliefs about social categories. *British Journal of Social Psychology, 39*, 113–127.

——. 2002. Are essentialist beliefs associated with prejudice? *British Journal of Social Psychology, 41*, 87–100.

Haslanger, Sally. 1995. Ontology and social construction. *Philosophical Topics, 23*, 95–125.

——. 2000. Gender and race: (What) are they? (What) do we want them to be? *Noûs, 34*, 31–55.

——. 2003. Social construction: The 'debunking' project. In Frederick F. Schmitt, ed., *Socializing Metaphysics: The Nature of Social Reality* (Lanham, MD: Rowman & Littlefield), 301–325.

——. 2003–2004. Future genders? Future races? *Philosophic Exchange, 34*, 4–27.

——. 2005. What are we talking about? The semantics and politics of social kinds. *Hypatia, 20*, 10–26.

——. 2006. Philosophical analysis and social kinds: What good are our intuitions? *Proceedings of the Aristotelian Society Supplementary Volume, 80*, 89–118.

Helms, Janet E., Jernigan, Maryam, & Mascher, Jackquelyn. 2005. The meaning of race in psychology and how to change it: A methodological perspective. *American Psychologist, 60*, 27–36.

Hirschfeld, Lawrence A. 1996. *Race in the Making: Cognition, Culture, and the Child's Construction of Human Kinds* (Cambridge, MA: MIT Press).

——. 1998. Natural assumptions: Race, essence, and taxonomies of human kinds. *Social Research, 65,* 331–349.

Hochschild, Jennifer L. 2005. Looking ahead: Racial trends in the United States. *Dædalus, 134,* 70–81.

Hoffman, Paul. 1994. The science of race. *Discover, 15,* 4.

Horgan, Terry & Timmons, Mark. 1991. New wave moral realism meets Moral Twin Earth. *Journal of Philosophical Research, 16,* 447–465.

——. 1992a. Troubles for new wave moral semantics: The 'open question argument' revived. *Philosophical Papers, 21/3,* 153–175.

——. 1992b. Troubles on Moral Twin Earth: Moral queerness revived. *Synthese, 92,* 221–260.

——. 1996a. From moral realism to moral relativism in one easy step. *Crítica, 28,* 3–39.

——. 1996b. Troubles for Michael Smith's metaethical rationalism. *Philosophical Papers, 25,* 203–231.

——. 2000. Copping out on Moral Twin Earth. *Synthese, 124,* 139–152.

——. n-d. Analytical moral functionalism meets Moral Twin Earth. In I. Ravenscroft ed., *Minds, Ethics, and Conditionals: Themes from the Philosophy of Frank Jackson* (Oxford: Oxford University Press), forthcoming.

Hull, David L. 1998. Species, subspecies, and races. *Social Research, 65,* 351–367.

Jackson, Frank. 1998a. *From Metaphysics to Ethics: A Defence of Conceptual Analysis* (Oxford: Oxford University Press).

——. 1998b. Reference and description revisited. *Philosophical Perspectives, 12, Language, Mind, and Ontology,* 201–218.

——. 2001. Responses. *Philosophy and Phenomenological Research, 62,* 653–664.

Jorde, Lynn B., & Wooding, Stephen P. 2004. Genetic variation, classification and "race." *Nature Genetics, 36, Supplement,* S28–S33.

Joyce, Richard. 2001. *The Myth of Morality* (Cambridge: Cambridge University Press).

Keita, S.O.Y., & Kittles, Rick A. 1997. The persistence of racial thinking and the myth of racial divergence. *American Anthropologist, 99,* 534–544.

Keita, S.O.Y., Kittles, R.A., Royal, C.D.M., Bonney, G.E., Furbert-Harris, P., Dunston, G.M., & Rotimi, C.N. 2004. Conceptualizing human variation. *Nature Genetics, 36, Supplement,* S17–S20.

Kelly, Daniel, Machery, Edouard, & Mallon, Ron. n-d. Racial cognition and normative racial theory. http://www.pitt.edu/~machery/papers/Race%20 Kelly%20Machery%20Mallon.pdf.

King, Mary-Claire, & Motulsky, Arno G. 2002. Mapping human history. *Science, 298,* 2342–2343.

Kitcher, Philip. 1999. Race, ethnicity, biology, culture. In Leonard Harris, ed., *Racism* (Amherst, NY: Humanity Books), 87–117.

——. 2007. Does 'race' have a future? *Philosophy & Public Affairs, 35,* 293–317.

Kripke, Saul. 1972. *Naming and Necessity* (Cambridge, MA.: Harvard University Press).

Kurzban, Robert, Tooby, John, & Cosmides, Leda. 2001. Can race be erased? Coalitional computation and social categorization. *Proceedings of the*

*National Academy of Sciences of the United States of America, 98,* 15387–15392.

Lao, Oscar, van Duijn, Kate, Kersbergen, Paula, de Knijff, Peter, & Kayser, Manfred. 2006. Proportioning whole-genome single-nucleotide-polymorphism diversity for the identification of geographic population structure and genetic ancestry. *The American Journal of Human Genetics, 78,* 680–690.

Lauer, Henle. 1996. Treating race as a social construction. *The Journal of Value Inquiry, 30,* 445–451.

Lee, Sandra Soo-Jin, Mountain, Joanna, & Koenig, Barbara A. 2001. The meanings of "race" in the new genomics: Implications for health disparities research. *Yale Journal of Health Policy, Law, and Ethics, 33,* 33–75.

Leroi, Armand Marie. 2005. A family tree in every gene. *New York Times,* March 14, A21.

Levinson, Meira. 2003. The language of race. *Theory and Research in Education, 1,* 267–281.

Lewontin, Richard D. 1972. The apportionment of human diversity. *Evolutionary Biology, 6,* 381–398.

Livingstone, Frank B. 1964. On the nonexistence of human races. In Ashley Montagu, ed., *The Concept of Race* (New York: The Free Press), 46–60.

Loeb, Don. 2001. Review of Grethe B. Peterson, ed., *The Tanner Lectures on Human Values, 17* (Salt Lake City: University of Utah Press, 1996). *Ethics, 112,* 172–175.

Long, Jeffrey C., & Kittles, Rick A. 2003. Human genetic diversity and the nonexistence of biological races. *Human Biology, 75,* 449–471.

Lott, Tommy L. 1999. *The Invention of Race: Black Culture and the Politics of Representation* (Malden, MA: Blackwell).

Machery, Edouard. 2005. Concepts are not a natural kind. *Philosophy of Science, 72,* 444–467.

Machery, Edouard, & Faucher, Luc. 2005a. Social construction and the concept of race. *Philosophy of Science, 72,* 1208–1219.

——. 2005b. Why do we think racially? Culture, evolution, and cognition. In H. Cohen & C. Lefebvre, eds., *Handbook of Categorization in Cognitive Science* (Amsterdam: Elsevier), 1009–1033.

——. n-d. Concepts of races are biological: A cross-cultural study. Unpublished Ms.

Machery, Edouard, Mallon, Ron, Nichols, Shaun, & Stich, Stephen P. 2004. Semantics, cross-cultural style. *Cognition, 92,* B1–B12.

Mallon, Ron. 2004. Passing, traveling and reality: Social constructionism and the metaphysics of race. *Noûs, 38,* 644–673.

——. 2006. 'Race': Normative, not metaphysical or semantic. *Ethics, 116,* 525–551.

Mayr, Ernst. 2002. The biology of race and the concept of equality. *Dædalus, 131,* 89–94.

Mayr, Ernst, & Ashlock, Peter D. 1991. *Principles of Systematic Zoology* (2nd edn) (New York: McGraw-Hill).

Michaels, Walter Benn. 1994. The no-drop rule. *Critical Inquiry, 20,* 758–769.

Mills, Charles. 1998. *Blackness Visible: Essays on Philosophy and Race* (Ithaca, NY: Cornell University Press).

Montagu, Ashley. 1964a. The concept of race. In Ashley Montagu, ed., *The Concept of Race* (New York: The Free Press), 12–28.

——. 1964b. The concept of race in the human species in the light of genetics. In Ashley Montagu, ed., *The Concept of Race* (New York: The Free Press), 1–11.

Moody-Adams, Michele M. 1999. A commentary on *Color Conscious: The Political Morality of Race*. *Ethics*, *109*, 408–423.

Mosley, Albert. 1997. Are racial categories racist? *Research in African Literatures*, *28*, 101–111.

Mountain, Joanna L., & Risch, Neil. 2004. Assessing genetic contributions to phenotypic differences among 'racial' and 'ethnic' groups. *Nature Genetics*, *36*, *Supplement*, S48–S53.

Navarro, Mireya. 2003. Going beyond black and white: Hispanics in census choose 'other.' *New York Times*, November 9, p. 1.

Nisbett, Richard E., Peng, Kaiping, Choi, Incheol, & Norenzayan, Ara. 2001. Culture and systems of thought: Holistic versus analytic cognition. *Psychological Review*, *108*, 291–310.

Nuccetelli, Susana. 2001. 'Latinos,' 'Hispanics,' and 'Iberoamericans': Naming or describing? *The Philosophical Forum*, *32*, 175–188.

——. 2004. Reference and ethnic-group terms. *Inquiry*, *47*, 528–544.

——. 2007. What is an ethnic group? Against social functionalism. In Jorge J.E. Gracia, ed., *Race or Ethnicity? On Black and Latino Identity* (Ithaca, NY: Cornell University Press), 137–151.

Omi, Michael, and Winant, Howard. 1994. *Racial Formation in the United States: From the 1960s to the 1990s* (2nd edn) (New York: Routledge).

Outlaw, Lucius. 1996a. 'Conserve' races? In defense of W.E.B. Du Bois. In Bernard Bell, Emily Grosholz, and James Stewart, eds., *W.E.B. Du Bois on Race and Culture* (New York: Routledge), 15–37.

——. 1996b. *On Race and Philosophy* (New York: Routledge).

——. 2001. Toward a critical theory of 'race.' In Bernard Boxill, ed., *Race and Racism* (Oxford, Oxford University Press), 58–82.

Pääbo, Svante. 2001. The human genome and our view of ourselves. *Science*, *291*, 1219–1220.

Parra, Flavia C., Amado, Roberto C., Lambertucci, José R., Rocha, Jorge, Antunes, Carlos M., & Pena, Sérgio D.J. 2003. Color and genomic ancestry in Brazilians. *Proceedings of the National Academy of Sciences of the United States of America*, *100*, 177–182.

Pigliucci, Massimo & Kaplan, Jonathan. 2003. On the concept of biological race and its applicability to humans. *Philosophy of Science*, *70*, 1161–1172.

Prothero, Stephen. 1995. Conjuring race. In Linda A. Bell & David Blumenfeld, eds., *Overcoming Racism and Sexism* (Lanham, MD: Rowman & Littlefield), 103–112.

Putnam, Hilary. 1962. It ain't necessarily so. *The Journal of Philosophy*, *59*, 658–671.

——. 1975a. Is semantics possible? In Hilary Putnam, *Mind, Language and Reality: Philosophical Papers, Volume 2* (Cambridge: Cambridge University Press), 139–152.

——. 1975b. The meaning of 'meaning.' In Hilary Putnam, *Mind, Language and Reality: Philosophical Papers, Volume 2* (Cambridge: Cambridge University Press), 215–271.

Race, Ethnicity, and Genetics Working Group. 2005. The use of racial, ethnic, and ancestral categories in human genetics research. *American Journal of Human Genetics, 77,* 519–532.

Ramachandran, Sohini, Deshpande, Omkar, Roseman, Charles C., Rosenberg, Noah A., Feldman, Marcus W., & Cavalli-Sforza, L. Luca. 2005. Support from the relationship of genetic and geographic distance in human populations for a serial founder effect originating in Africa. *Proceedings of the National Academy of Sciences of the United States of America, 102,* 15942–15947.

Rawls, John. 1999. *A Theory of Justice, Revised Edition* (Cambridge, MA: The Belknap Press of Harvard University Press).

Risch, Neil, Burchard, Esteban, Ziv, Elad, & Tang, Hua. 2002. Categorization of humans in biomedical research: Genes, race, and disease. *Genome Biology, 3,* 1–12.

Romualdi, Chiara, Balding, David, Nasidze, Ivane S., Risch, Gregory, Robichaux, Myles, Sherry, Stephen T., Stoneking, Mark, Batzer, Mark A., & Barbujani, Guido. 2002. Patterns of human diversity, within and among continents, inferred from biallelic DNA polymorphisms. *Genome Research, 12,* 602–612.

Root, Michael. 2000. How we divide the world. *Philosophy of Science, 67, Proceedings,* S628–S639.

———. 2001. The problem of race in medicine. *Philosophy of the Social Sciences, 31,* 20–39.

———. 2005. The number of black widows in the National Academy of Sciences. *Philosophy of Science, 72,* 1197–1207.

Rosenberg, Noah A., Pritchard, Jonathan K., Weber, James L., Cann, Howard M., Kidd, Kenneth K., Zhivotovsky, Lev A., & Feldman, Marcus W. 2002. Genetic structure of human populations. *Science, 298,* 2381–2385.

Rosenberg, Noah A., Mahajan, Saurabh, Ramachandran, Sohini, Zhao, Chengfeng, Pritchard, Jonathan K., & Feldman, Marcus W. 2005. Clines, clusters, and the effect of study design on the inference of human population structure. *PLoS Genetics, 1,* 660–671.

Sarich, Vincent & Miele, Frank. 2004. *Race: The Reality of Human Differences* (Boulder, CO: Westview Press).

Saul, Jennifer. 2006. Philosophical analysis and social kinds: Gender and race. *Proceedings of the Aristotelian Society Supplementary Volume, 80,* 119–143.

Schwartz, Robert S. 2001. Racial profiling in medical research. *The New England Journal of Medicine, 344,* 1392–1393.

Serre, David, & Pääbo, Svante. 2004. Evidence for gradients of human genetic diversity within and among continents. *Genome Research, 14,* 1679–1685.

Shelby, Tommie. 2002. Foundations of Black Solidarity: Collective identity or common oppression? *Ethics, 112,* 231–266.

———. 2005. *We Who Are Dark: The Philosophical Foundations of Black Solidarity* (Cambridge, MA: Harvard University Press).

Shreeve, James. 1994. Terms of estrangement. *Discover, 15,* 56–63.

Shriver, Mark D., Parra, Esteban J., Dios, Sonia, Bonilla, Carolina, Norton, Heather, Jovel, Celina, Pfaff, Carrie, Jones, Cecily, Massac, Aisha, Cameron, Neil, Baron, Archie, Jackson, Tabitha, Argyropoulos, George, Jin, Li, Hoggart, Clive J., McKeigue, Paul M., & Kittles, Rick A. 2003. Skin pigmen-

References 165

tation, biogeographical ancestry and admixture mapping. *Human Genetics, 112*, 387–399.

Shriver, Mark D., Kennedy, Giulia C., Parra, Esteban J., Lawson, Heather A., Sonpar, Vibhor, Huang, Jing, Akey, Joshua M., & Jones, Keith W. 2004. The genomic distribution of population substructure in four population using 8,525 autosomal SNPs. *Human Genomics, 1*, 274–286.

Shulman, Julie L. & Glasgow, Joshua. In press. Is race-thinking biological or social, and does it matter for racism? *Journal of Social Philosophy*, forthcoming.

Sinnott-Armstrong, Walter. 2006. *Moral Skepticisms* (Oxford: Oxford University Press).

Smedley, Audrey & Smedley, Brian D. 2005. Race as biology is fiction, racism as a social problem is real: Anthropological and historical perspectives on the social construction of race. *American Psychologist, 60*, 16–26.

Sober, Elliot. 1993. *Philosophy of Biology* (Boulder, CO: Westview Press).

Sterelny, Kim, & Griffiths, Paul E. 1999. *Sex and Death: An Introduction to Philosophy of Biology* (Chicago, IL: The University of Chicago Press).

Stich, Stephen, & Weinberg, Jonathan M. 2001. Jackson's empirical assumptions. *Philosophy and Phenomenological Research, 62*, 637–643.

Strevens, Michael. 2000. The essentialist aspect of naïve theories. *Cognition, 74*, 149–175.

———. 2001. Only causation matters: Reply to Ahn et al. *Cognition, 82*, 71–76.

Stubblefield, Anna. 1995. Racial identity and non-essentialism about race. *Social Theory and Practice, 21*, 341–368.

———. 2005. *Ethics Along the Color Line* (Ithaca, NY: Cornell University Press).

Sundstrom, Ronald R. 2001. Being and being mixed race. *Social Theory and Practice, 27*, 285–307.

———. 2002a. Race as a human kind. *Philosophy and Social Criticism, 28*, 91–115.

———. 2002b. "Racial" nominalism. *Journal of Social Philosophy, 33*, 193–210.

———. In press. *The Browning of America and the Evasion of Social Justice* (New York: SUNY Press), forthcoming.

Tang, Hua, Quertermous, Tom, Rodriguez, Beatriz, Kardia, Sharon L.R., Zhu, Xiaofeng, Brown, Andrew, Pankow, James S., Province, Michael A., Hunt, Steven C., Boerwinkle, Eric, Schork, Nicholas J., & Risch, Neil J. 2005. Genetic structure, self-identified race/ethnicity, and confounding in case-control association studies. *American Journal of Human Genetics, 76*, 268–275.

Taylor, Paul C. 2000. Appiah's uncompleted argument: W.E.B. Du Bois and the reality of race. *Social Theory and Practice, 26*, 103–128.

———. 2004. *Race: A Philosophical Introduction* (Cambridge: Polity Press).

———. 2005. Three questions about *Race, Racism, and Reparations. Journal of Social Philosophy, 36*, 559–567.

Tishkoff, Sarah A., & Kidd, Kenneth K. 2004. Implications of biogeography of human populations for 'race' and medicine. *Nature Genetics, 36*, Supplement, S21–S27.

Voltaire, François-Marie. 2000. Of the different races of men. In Robert Bernasconi and Tommy L. Lott, eds., *The Idea of Race* (Indianapolis: Hackett), 5–7.

Wade, Nicholas. 2006. *Before the Dawn: Recovering the Lost History of our Ancestors* (New York: The Penguin Press).

Weinberg, Jonathan, Nichols, Shaun, & Stich, Stephen. 2001. Normativity and epistemic intuitions. *Philosophical Topics, 29*, 429–460.

Will, George. 2003. It's time to remove the race [*sic*] from census form. *Chicago Sun-Times*, May 4, p. 35.

Wilson, James F., Weale, Michael E., Smith, Alice C., Gratrix, Fiona, Fletcher, Benjamin, Thomas, Mark G., Bradman, Neil, & Goldstein, David B. 2001. Population genetic structure of variable drug response. *Nature Genetics, 29*, 265–269.

Witherspoon, D.J., Wooding, S., Rogers, A.R., Marchani, E.E., Watkins, W.S., Batzer, M.A., & Jorde, L.B. 2007. Genetic similarities within and between human populations. *Genetics, 176*, 351–359.

Yu, Ning, Chen, Feng-Chi, Ota, Satoshi, Jorde, Lynn B., Pamilo, Pekka, Patthy, Laszlo, Ramsay, Michele, Jenkins, Trefor, Shyue, Song-Kun, & Li, Wen-Hsiung. 2002. Larger genetic differences within Africans than between Africans and Eurasians. *Genetics, 161*, 269–274.

Yzerbyt, Vincent, Rocher, Steve, & Schadron, Georges. 1997. Stereotypes as explanations: A subjective essentialistic view of group perception. In Russell Spears, Penelope J. Oakes, Naomi Ellemers, & S. Alexander Haslam, eds., *The Social Psychology of Stereotyping and Group Life* (Oxford: Blackwell), 20–50.

Zack, Naomi. 1993. *Race and Mixed Race* (Philadelphia, PA: Temple University Press).

——. 1995. Life after race. In Naomi Zack, ed., *American Mixed Race: The Culture of Microdiversity* (Lanham, MD: Rowman & Littlefield), 297–307.

——. 1997. Race and philosophic meaning. In Naomi Zack, ed., *Race/Sex: Their Sameness, Difference, and Interplay* (New York: Routledge), 29–43.

——. 2002. *Philosophy of Science and Race* (New York: Routledge).

——. 2007. Ethnicity, race, and the importance of gender. In Jorge J.E. Gracia, ed., *Race or Ethnicity? On Black and Latino Identity* (Ithaca, NY: Cornell University Press), 101–122.

# Index

Related titles from Routledge

# Philosophy of Science and Race

## Naomi Zack

In this concisely argued book, well-known philosopher Naomi Zack explores the scientific and philosophical problems in applying a biological conception of race to human beings. Through the systematic analysis of up-to-date data and conclusions in population genetics, transmission genetics, and biological anthropology, Zack provides a comprehensive conceptual account of how "race" in the ordinary sense has no basis in science. Her book combats our everyday understanding of race as a scientifically supported taxonomy of human beings, and in conclusion challenges us to be clear about what we mean by "race" and what it would require to remedy racism.

Hb: 978-0-415-94163-1
Pb: 978-0-415-94164-8

Available at all good bookstores.
For ordering and further information, please visit:
www.routledge.com

# Look, a Negro!:
# Philosophical Essays on Race, Culture, and Politics

### Robert Gooding-Williams

In *Look, a Negro!*, political theorist Robert Gooding-Williams imaginatively and impressively unpacks fundamental questions around race and racism. Inspired by Frantz Fanon's famous description of the profound effect of being singled out by a white child with the words "Look, a Negro!," his book is an insightful, rich and unusually wide-ranging work of social criticism.

These essays engage themes that have dominated debates on race and racial identity in recent years: the workings of racial ideology (including the interplay of gender and sexuality in the articulation of racial ideology), the viability of social constructionist theories of race, the significance of Afrocentrism and multiculturalism for democracy, the place of black identity in the imagination and articulation of America's inheritance of philosophy, and the conceptualization of African-American politics in post-segregation America.

*Look, a Negro!* will be of interest to philosophers, political theorists, critical race theorists, students of cultural studies and film, and readers concerned with the continuing importance of race-consciousness to democratic culture in the United States.

Hb: 978-0-415-97415-8
Pb: 978-0-415-97416-5

Related titles from Routledge

# Keeping Faith:
# Philosophy and Race in America

## Cornel West

*Keeping Faith* is a rich account of the work of Cornel West, one of today's leading African-American intellectuals. This powerful collection of essays ranges widely across politics and philosophy in America, the role of the black intellectual, legal theory and the future of liberal thought, and the fate of African Americans. In West's hands, issues of race and freedom are inextricably tied to questions of philosophy and, above all, to a belief in the power of the human spirit.

West situates the current position of African Americans, tracing the genealogy of the "Afro-American Rebellion" from Martin Luther King to the rise of black revolutionary leftists. He explains both the opportunities and limitations of liberalism and nationalism, and offers fresh strategies for a new generation of African Americans.

West insists that African-American oppression be understood within the larger crises of North Atlantic civilization. While maintaining the specificity of black identity and resistance, he provocatively suggests alliances with other intellectual and communal forms of American radicalism. Writing on "the new cultural politics of difference," the critical legal studies movement, American pragmatism, or race and social theory, West sustains the difficult balance between a subtly argued critique of the past and present, and a broadly conceived, daring vision of the future.

Hb: 978-0-415-90486-5
Pb: 978-0-415-96481-4

Available at all good bookstores.
For ordering and further information, please visit:
www.routledge.com